BACK TO BLACK

AMY WINEHOUSE'S ONLY MASTERPIECE

DONALD BRACKETT

Backbeat Books
AN IMPRINT OF HAL LEONARD LLC

Published in 2016 by Backbeat Books
An Imprint of Hal Leonard LLC
7777 West Bluemound Road
Milwaukee, WI 53213

Trade Book Division Editorial Offices
33 Plymouth St., Montclair, NJ 07042

Printed in the United States of America

Book design by John J. Flannery

Library of Congress Cataloging-in-Publication Data is available upon request.

ISBN 978-1-61713-629-0

www.backbeatbooks.com

To
musical torchbearers through history
and
to Mimi Gellman, my extraordinary partner,
and to Kevin Courrier, music-lover extraordinaire

"I sell the shadow in order to support the substance."
—Sojourner Truth

CONTENTS

FOREWORD

Imitation of Life

Donald Brackett asks highly pertinent questions about the importance of pop music in our contemporary culture in this incisive and fascinating study of Amy Winehouse's second and last album, *Back to Black*. They are key questions that open the door not only to the full experience of this great record—which Brackett correctly dubs "existential entertainment"—but which also explore the seductive hook that pop artists always quest for. At the core of pop artistry is indeed an unquenchable search for a seductive sound that touches a nerve, something that strikes a pleasurable chord in the listener. The best pop unifies the incompatible world around it, and even answers a deep subliminal calling.

In general, pop music is about the celebration and sharing of good times—and then creating a promise to stay true to those aims. When the Ronettes sang "Be My Baby," you definitely shared the intense joy in their voices. It was overwhelming to immerse yourself in such pleasure and still not lose yourself. You could melt into their sound and still be set apart from the herd. But not *all* pop music happily sets you free. In Amy Winehouse's case, the bluesy pleasure found in *Back to Black* also takes you to the root of a dilemma that even pop can't ever really deliver you from.

After doing full justice to her jazz and gospel antecedents, like Sarah Vaughan and Mahalia Jackson, on her stunning 2003 debut, *Frank*, Amy Winehouse reached back to the girl group sound of the 1960s for *Back to Black*. Her choice, as

Brackett reminds us in his book, wasn't an arbitrary one. "The girl group sound was borne equally from knowingness and naiveté," critic Vivian Mackay once explained in *Uncut* magazine. "Like teenage life, it was violently honest, it lived faster and more vividly than anyone over twenty-five can remember." Make that twenty-seven and it fits even better.

For an artist whose personal life became the melodrama that her songs both depicted and tried to transcend, Amy Winehouse put the knowingness and naiveté of that pining sound of the Shangri-Las, the Chiffons, and the Ronettes to the test on *Back to Black*. Borrowing Sharon Jones's veteran R&B band the Dap-Kings, Winehouse traced the long umbilical cord connecting the source of pop salvation to the dramatic realism of everyday life. Throughout the record, you can hear Winehouse and the Dap-Kings drawing on familiar echoes of pop hooks that instantly invoke nostalgic connections to the past.

Whether it's the opening notes of the Supremes' "Baby Love" that decorate the dark shadows of the song "Back to Black" itself, or the triumphant melody of Marvin Gaye and Tammi Terrell's "Ain't No Mountain High Enough," which provides a comfortable bed for the discomforting "Tears Dry on Their Own," *Back to Black* doesn't just pay a deferential debt to the past. Just like Jack White, who continually strips down the branches of popular music to draw from its muscular trunk, Amy Winehouse (with significant help from producers Mark Ronson and Salaam Remi) used the deep longing of girl group pop to fuel the torch-song sound she perfected earlier on *Frank*.

The most haunting corners of *Back to Black* are found, for me, on "Wake Up Alone" and "Some Unholy War." Amy Winehouse perfumes those songs with the heartache of the Shangri-Las. In an age when girl groups ruled in their own pop kingdom, the Shangri-Las were shimmering alchemists who took the melodrama of the teen angst genre in heartbreakers like "Leader of the Pack" and "(Remember) Walkin' in the Sand" and turned them into biting psychodramas. Formed in Queens, New York, this group could make you hurt and yet simultaneously make you glad that you indeed *could* be wounded in the first place. They were national anthems of the hurting heart.

"I Can Never Go Home Anymore," their song about a young woman who leaves home for a boy and then has too much pride to reconcile with her mother, is cutting enough to draw blood. Lines such as "she grew so lonely in the end, the angels picked her for a friend," or the part when Mary Weiss lets out her primal cry of "Mama!," immediately invoke the conclusion of Douglas Sirk's 1959 film *Imitation of Life*, when Susan Kohner, a young black woman trying to pass for white, comes back to the funeral of the mother she's rejected and dissolves in grief before our eyes. An ironic parallel perhaps with Winehouse herself, and what some critics mistakenly claimed was a white musician trying to pass for black.

It's lead singer Mary Weiss's sense of unrequited loss and its painful residue that makes the song so irresistible to the listener. "I had enough pain in me to pull off anything," Weiss would say in a recent interview for the A&E documentary series *The Songmakers Collection* about a song she recorded when she was all of sixteen. Another knowing declaration that also seems ironically applicable to Winehouse once again.

There's something of that same residue of dissipated romanticism in her "Wake Up Alone" as if, to paraphrase Norman Mailer, Amy Winehouse sets out to cash the check that the Shangri-Las wrote back in the '60s. She knows, though, that the heartsick yearning in the Shangri-Las, which kept us wondering whether the heroine of "Leader of the Pack" would survive the loss of her biker boyfriend or ever recover from the memories of "(Remember) Walkin' in the Sand," is one that remains unfulfilled because the true pop song is built on an endless quest of confronting unhappiness head on.

"If everyone was happy," Harry Nilsson once sang in his country song parody "Joy," "there'd never be a love song." In "Some Unholy War," Amy Winehouse also borrows from the prideful sentiments of the Temptations' "My Girl" and the mysteries of summer romance uncorked on the Drifters' "Under the Boardwalk" to create an unwavering portrait of obstinate self-immolation that's done with the same aching artful touches she brought to the low self-esteem in songs like "Love Is a Losing Game" and "Wake Up Alone."

The daily chronicling of Amy Winehouse's road to perdition in the media often distracted us from the naked beauty in her gorgeous songs. The ongoing press coverage was also far different from the self-destruction of other earlier pop heroes. Janis Joplin's neurosis getting transformed into devastating art might have been gleaned best from her powerful reading of Big Mama Thornton's "Ball and Chain" at the Monterey Pop Festival in 1967.

But what if we also had daily video, YouTube, and cellphone updates of Janis falling over due to her large consumption of Southern Comfort onstage? How would her powerful work and legacy have measured up against that?

The legendary performers of the past could still have some semblance of personal privacy in their lives while their music alone gave us windows into their troubled souls. For some artists, Brackett reminds us, sharing such rawness of emotion is all that seems to matter. His astute assertion is perched right on the cusp of the continued fascination we've had for her in the subsequent ten years since her record was released.

But it's the superb production and songs that make up *Back to Black* that go far beyond our potentially prurient fascination with her early demise five years ago and instead bring vibrantly to life the pop majesty that not only faces the blues straight on but also reminds us that maybe it's always knocking at our doors. That was one of her rare gifts: making poetry and music out of something apparently so inevitable. Facing the bluesy brilliance of *Back to Black* is just as important and inevitable, and this book invites us all to do just that. Face the music.

—Kevin Courrier

■ ■ ■

Kevin Courrier, a well-known Canadian music journalist and former CBC Radio producer, is the author of *Dangerous Kitchen: The Subversive World of Frank Zappa,* Trout Mask Replica (33 1/3 series)*, Artificial Paradise: The Dark Side of the Beatles' Utopian Dream,* and *Randy Newman's American Dreams.*

INTRODUCTION

Welcome to My World

"When I'm singing, I'm happy. I'm doing what I can do, and this is my contribution to life. . . ."
—Anita O'Day, *The Life of a Jazz Singer*

This is a book about Amy Winehouse's music and the music that inspired it; it's not about her problems or the flaws that caused them. You won't read the names of her boyfriends, ex-husband, family, or enablers in these pages, but you will read the many names of singer/songwriters, musicians, and producers who helped make her pop music masterpiece happen, as well as the diverse musical history that preceded and inspired them all.

In fact, her compelling songwriting narrative was so pronounced that it was often easy for people to overlook the brilliant singer, musician, and production collaborator who was declaring it so intimately. But in these pages it's solely her music that fascinates us, specifically the album *Back to Black* itself, which has proven to be so influential in its exotic fusion of styles, genres, formats, and delivery that it melted together. Blues, rock, ska, R&B, funk, jazz, hip hop, calypso, rap, folk, reggae, skiffle, soul, and finally pop music, all steamed into a dream soup that's quite rare in today's niche-driven marketing machine of contemporary music production, sales, and listening.

It might also have been something almost impossible other than in the early digital twenty-first century, when traditional listening borders were being bent out of shape in a way not seen since the days of those four fabulous Liverpudlians. The perplexing beauty of her genre-bending style is evidence that

Back to Black is absolutely all of those roots stirred together but none of them separately in practice, except for the last one. It transcends all the styles and sensibilities it stirred together to become what I would call quintessential pop music—music for global ears belonging to a drastically eclectic and multi-generational listening audience. Pop music is music that sells.

Winehouse clearly invented a hybrid form of her own imagining: one that heated up the varied inspirations she inherited along her own hyper-accelerated creative passage. It will be the central thesis of this book, and my main contention, that far from being a frivolous or transitory expression of passing trends, pop music is a deeply serious revelation about where we are as human beings at a given time and in a given place. Pop needs to be taken as seriously as it deserves to be.

Especially since the Beatles, but certainly since long before then, a perfectly crafted pop song is a work of art capable of reaching a mass audience with an intimate and nearly universal message. The first pop star, in our sense of the word, was probably Bing Crosby, followed by Frank Sinatra, followed by Elvis Presley, and finally, most artfully of all, by the Beatles.

What interests us here is that rare and special kind of album of pop songs. *Rubber Soul, Pet Sounds, Revolver,* and *Highway 61 Revisited* are a few shining examples: records that take giant steps forward by absorbing everything that came before them. They turn all earlier ingredients on their heads and carve feelings that are apparently totally new out of the oldest sentiments lodged in the human heart. By doing so, such albums alter the sonic landscape and push both recording and performing to startling new limits that had never been conceived before. Some albums, such as Amy Winehouse's only masterpiece, even go far beyond those limits and into a new self-invented territory that they alone can occupy.

In the process, of course, they demonstrate that in pop music there are no limits, and *Back to Black* is quite possibly the most emblematic example of a perfectly conceived, crafted, delivered, and performed pop record, because it fulfills all the essential creative requirements of a superlative pop gem. So, defining what makes great pop music is the logical place to begin.

Was Amy Winehouse a pop genius? Probably, but not of the garden-variety kind we're most familiar with; more the primitive kind exuded by the late John Lennon. I'm not comparing their music—that would be folly—but I am comparing the rough, untutored, alien brilliance of how they did what they did without even themselves knowing how to do it. Driven to do it, despite their shyness, their neuroses, their complexes, their fears, their insecurities; driven to do it the way a wild animal tries to escape from a trap that it stepped into of its own volition. A trap they even designed themselves, laid for themselves, sprung by themselves, and struggled desperately to free themselves from while we all watched, screaming in big gladiatorial arenas created exclusively for the purpose of witnessing the valiant victims in their heroic pop throes.

Like her heroes Tony Bennett, Ray Charles, and Donny Hathaway, and her heroines Billie Holiday, Dinah Washington, and Ronnie Spector, Winehouse created a new musical instrument with her astonishingly fluid voice, built upon the structure of her dreams, fears, desires, and disappointments, and on the very special relationship she had with the microphone. That magical instrument of emotional alchemy, the microphone—the invention that allowed singers to confide in a whisper rather than bellowing in a scream, and to use the intimacy of a new amplified technology to share deep and secret desires quietly while still being heard from a distance, and which was then followed by perhaps the ultimate transmission device for love songs, the car radio—was her real lover. And her exquisite microphone voice was perfectly suited to mobile pop radio itself.

Winehouse, a naturally untutored and consummate movie star by instinct and intuition if not by temperament, would also use the '80s art form of the music video as an amazingly fertile device to seduce and satisfy the audience. We all simply adored watching her strut as only she could, whether onstage in performance or on video in recordings.

It wasn't a wild strut like that used by Tina Turner when she asked what love had to do with it; it was more the strut of an exotic bird somehow confusing confidence with fear and at the same time short-circuiting our expectations through a combination of subtle raunch and permanently delayed gratification: the ultimate pop weapon. A weapon that would be loaded with heartbreaking ammunition and aimed at an unsuspecting musical world in an audaciously brave yet vulnerable way in *Back to Black*.

By definition, then, pop music is probably something without a precise definition, since we never quite know just who or what is going to strike a huge public chord, but we can certainly identify a range of ingredients that inform its style: rapid technological development, rapid economic growth, rapid turnover, rapid mass production, almost instantly rapid obsolescence, the rapid spread of American culture across the planet, the ultra-democracy of consumer society and its voracious appetites, and the rapid postwar nuclear attitude that made every moment precious. In short, great pop music is rapid in every way, which is why even the Beatles' earliest records still seem incredibly bright and shiny, fast and furious, and *loud*, no matter what volume you choose.

The breed of singer/songwriters who arose in the early '60s—the artists who inspired Winehouse's own later millennial style and who put the songwriter-for-hire out of business by insisting on singing their own original material in their own distinctive (and often almost alien) voices—insisted on demonstrating, if not proving, how basically "real" they were. The singer/songwriters who most inspired *Back to Black* may have had different styles of delivery, but they shared a single obsession with being honest. Eschewing artifice, and often poetry, in favor of raw truth on its own terms, they frequently created a whole new kind of poetry altogether. Certainly Winehouse studied them often and well, and though she may have been a disruptive student, she did her homework carefully.

This new kind of poetry, so clearly delineated in *Back to Black*, seems to thrive best in a climate of tortured romanticism associated most often with the torch-song tradition, and both her albums are about betrayal, breakups, and the compulsion for getting back together again at all costs. The critic Lionel Trilling (in his 1972 book *Sincerity and Authenticity*) even traces this intensely emotional romanticist lineage all the way back to certain eighteenth and nineteenth century denigrations of conventional beauty in search of the energy and power of what used to be called the *sublime*, an awesome power that leaves us trembling in its overwhelming wake. I can quite comfortably assert that *Back to Black* is sublime, and that it certainly left me, and many others, trembling in its shadows. It still does so a decade later.

If the pop song evolved into the personal and public soundtrack for the last century, as it so clearly seems to have done, what does that tell us about the emotional existential movie we all live in? In addition to her own personal testaments on her 2006 album *Back to Black*, Amy Winehouse gave us all a clue to the secret basement of our popular culture in her intimate and yearning cover interpretation of Al Kooper's soul song "I Love You More Than You'll Ever Know," which she made all her own in a haunting live rendition.

"We're still alive," she said at the end of her performance of the song at the Carling Academy in Liverpool in 2007. "We're still alive, we're still standing." Even then she sounded surprised, and she hadn't even started her final descent yet. When it comes to making your life into your material and your theme into a breathing emblem of your living sorrows,

Winehouse seems to have achieved a new high-water mark for such rare creative transformations. In essence, her torch songs soon became home movies. Before she left us, though, we were given the gift of her remarkable music in a personal way seldom seen or heard before.

When I say she made that great Blood, Sweat and Tears song, written by a male artist forty years earlier, all her own, I mean that she actually colonized the song with such grandeur that she occupied it, channeled it, rewrote it, and owned it. At least during that one stellar performance—before the later concerts when she started forgetting herself and her gift—she embodied the essence of ideal pop music as only a sublimely skilled and innately inspired artist can do. It was a gift that, luckily for the rest of us, sitting comfortably at home safely away from her talented but troubled fray, just keeps on giving, a swift decade later.

Winehouse was a Dusty Springfield drenched in darkness. She was a Petula Clark from hell, who instead of taking us all downtown took us all down there, *la bas*, where she seemed to spend so much of her short talented life. She also makes me think of the sentiments in the early Rolling Stones song "Paint It Black": of "no more colors," everything fading away to black. Suddenly and spookily, that Richards/Jagger song could have been written for her, or about her, or even by her.

■ ■ ■

Born September 14, 1983, died July 23, 2011. That's her biography, plain and simple. This book won't delve overly into Winehouse's personal biography (except where it informs the technical purposes of elucidating her album), since there are of plenty of biographies out there, littering the media landscape. Her own autobiography, however, is mostly embedded in the two fine records she released while still alive and strutting, and that musical memoir is considerably more complicated than her personal history.

The genesis of the second album in the seeds of the first will be explored, as will the conditions, circumstances, and vital collaborations that made it possible, because the second album was an utter rejection and repudiation of her first. In order to escape a mythical image she deplored, she embraced an epic alternative that endangered her survival.

It's always important to dismantle a mythology to see what lies at the bottom of it, assuming the figure being mythologized stands at the top. One of the best ways to do this is to try and focus as much as possible on the artworks the artist actually accomplished, and that's the critical intention of this book. Along the way however, it must be acknowledged that in some special cases, the life lived and the art produced were so synonymous that they need to be examined in tandem in order to even remotely succeed in the task of fully appreciating and assessing them.

It's difficult, for instance, to assess the paintings of Jackson Pollock or Francis Bacon without allowing some awareness of the sheer amount of alcohol mixed with their paint, or of William Faulkner or F. Scott Fitzgerald's words not being equally saturated. In the case of musicians, it's obviously difficult to divorce Charlie Parker or Kurt Cobain from their poor choice in vitamin supplements. But in all cases the effort must be made to tread gently on such personal flaws and rush quickly toward the paintings, the books, and the music; to look, read, and listen carefully, so as to be transported to another dimension in a manner equal to their talents, and not only be distracted or absorbed by their torments.

For instance, the parallels with the notorious Sid Vicious and Nancy Spungen sideshow in 1978 are so obvious we don't even need to go there (with the roles of musician and groupie being reversed, in this case), but we can still be surprised that, in Winehouse's condition, she managed to record an album at all. But of course, as we'll see, she didn't exactly record the album: much to her own good fortune, she sang her sublimely suffering songs on the album her producer, Mark Ronson, recorded for her.

So it goes with the mercurial soul sample known as *Back to Black*, and to paraphrase the hippie novelist Richard Brautigan, unloading that mercury with a pitchfork is quite a challenge. She tends to slip right through the fingers of even the most earnest of interpreters.

One of the side effects of her legend is the inherent difficulty in ever getting a firm grasp on her fluid and sometimes mythic status. She's not alone in this respect. As a case in point, the *Globe and Mail* journalist Alexandra Molotkow recently assessed the 2015 documentary on Winehouse's fellow musical genius and soulful sufferer Kurt Cobain, a film that reveals him to be a far more complex and multi-layered human being than his customary mythology would usually allow. Brett Morgen, the producer of *Montage of Heck*, decided from the beginning to try to deconstruct not only the artist but also the myth, to avoid romanticism, to "peel off the legend," and to focus as much as possible on the music itself.

Molotkow's observations on Cobain are salient and the same strategic approach should apply to the living music of the late Amy Winehouse: "It's true that dead artists never get old. Dying for your art is the ultimate endorsement for it, and suffering adds value. Tragedy makes the artist forever interesting and adds pathos to the work. Of course, romanticizing dead artists involves taking pleasure in their pain. At the same time, a romantic through line turns bad pain into good pain, and sometimes it's necessary even for those who were there."

Most strikingly perhaps, Cobain's daughter observes in the film that her father "got to the point where he had to sacrifice every bit of who he was to his art . . . because the world demanded it of him." And Cobain himself is quoted as saying, "I feel like people want me to die, because it would be the classic rock and roll story." Poor Cobain's mother, perhaps most astutely of all and more compassionately than any fan or journalist could ever hope to be, reportedly commented shortly after his death, "I told him not to join that stupid club!" Winehouse also seemed too eager to join a club without benefits.

While it's sometimes true that we have difficulty separating the source of an artist's torments from the origins of his or her creativity, the effort is required for the sake of the work itself if it's important enough, and Amy Winehouse's work certainly is that important. So we have to attempt to find the obscure borderline between personal pain and musical brilliance, to go deeply into one without getting lost in the other.

After all, surely we all feel somewhat guilty when a gifted singer such as Winehouse writes a song like "Rehab," the opening salvo from *Back to Black*, and we chime in chorus along with her, *no, no, no*, instead of what we might've been saying: *go, go, go*. Though clearly it was her family, ex-lovers, managers, and agents who should've been intervening, not us, since we're only the lucky beneficiaries of her inspired bedlam. We were all perhaps understandably distracted by her high-spirited defiance.

Maybe most telling, as also observed by Molotkow, the painful thing about such artists and performers is that they often demonstrate an awareness that they simultaneously share with us—the fact that they're actually capable of fulfillment—and, even more, they seem to know their own inherent or innate capacity for fulfillment, as well as how badly they're screwing it all up. "The idea of the suffering demigod," Molotkow writes, "torn apart by the demands of fame, is much more palatable than that of a vulnerable person on the brink of a terrible mistake."

This applies in a very spooky way especially to Winehouse, whose final performances often make it impossible not to think of Judy Garland's late Carnegie Hall appearances, and also the late duets Judy did with Barbra Streisand, which so eerily echo Amy's own later duets with the great Tony Bennett. This is especially so in the case of their simultaneous singing of two different songs that tragically captured some of Judy's own upcoming demise: Barbra sings "Happy Days Are Here Again" while Judy croons "Come On Get Happy" at the same time. They don't, as they say, make 'em like that anymore.

Amy Winehouse had in her soul a little bit of both Streisand and Garland: she was that gifted, and yet also she was just as doomed as Judy was, mostly because the ever solipsistic Amy created and lived in her own private Oz. In a strange way, Amy herself was a combination of both the innocence of early Streisand and the demolition derby of late Garland. Surely that's one of the features that made her so special.

There's also a seemingly antique epigram that applies ironically to Winehouse. It's from an "Epistle to a Lady," written by the British poet Alexander Pope in 1735 as a piece of feminine moral advice. Pope's admonition on the overarching ambition of passion defeating reason could also serve as the ideal emblem for the short, sad, gifted life of one of the most inspired and inspiring jazz-blues-soul singers to come along since . . . fill in the blanks, if you can:

Wise wretch, with pleasures too refined to please,
With too much spirit to ever be at ease . . .
You purchase pain with all that joy can give,
And die of nothing but a rage to live.

Turns out it isn't so antique after all, in fact it's timeless and terribly true.

Both Billie Holiday and Nina Simone, whose styles Winehouse merged in a manner that poured Marianne Faithfull through a sieve made of similar white British angst, and also the gifted white American jazz singer Anita O'Day, each suffered from the identical rage to live that took Winehouse away from us. Like all of them, she was a wise fool, an emotional medium who spent her life at the threshold of the unnamable. But unlike their prolific output, hers was only two albums. The second and last was her one true masterpiece—and it influenced nearly every female pop and R&B singer who came after her. It was a candid tale of idealists and libertines, sung by a young woman of fierce strength and tenderness, despite her obvious weaknesses and flaws. It was also Bessie, Billie, Dinah, Anita, Nina, Diana, Janis, Joni, and Marianne writ large, larger than life itself, with music and words and a magic voice that powerfully shared her singular rage to live.

To call it deeply personal would be an understatement. Amy Winehouse's music was often more of a documentary work of self-analysis than one aimed at conventional entertainment, though somehow it still managed to do that too remarkably well. As such it was already an idiosyncratic kind of *cinéma vérité* art form, and requires a particular kind of critical appreciation and assessment.

She was always documenting her feelings in a manner commensurate with the best musical storytellers, and my way of finding a backdoor entry into *Back to Black* is to claim for it a special conceptual brand of creativity first proposed by (of all people) the avant-garde American composer Frank Zappa to describe his own music. He called music a movie for your ears. The movie Winehouse sang so passionately to us was all the more amazing in that it was basically her own private diary.

Back to Black is a movie for our ears because it paints moving pictures of hyper-personal feelings and life experiences in a manner so image-evocative that the songs are virtually perfect for the video medium that was used very effectively to promote them. The excellent video for the song "Rehab," for example, or the even more stellar video for the album's riveting title song, for another, both work so well because the songs themselves are already movies for our ears.

So perhaps Alexander Pope's clever moral epigram might even be an eternal verity. Winehouse *was* a wise wretch. Her pleasures *were* too refined to please. She had too much spirit to ever be at ease. She had too much quickness to ever be taught. She did too much thinking to have a common, shared thought. She obviously purchased pain with all that joy can give. And, alas, she clearly did die of nothing but a rage to live. Suddenly, the classical social commentator Pope becomes just as pertinent, prescient, and visionary a plumber of the human heart as Nina Simone or Joni Mitchell. Who, as they say, would have thunk it?

Incredibly enough, it's been ten years since she released *Back to Black*; even more startlingly, it's been another half a decade since she passed away. Like the ratio of dog years to human years, in the shimmering world of pop music a decade feels like an eternity. Now is perhaps an ideal time to listen again, probably to cry again, and, most importantly, to remember just how huge a creative shadow her brief presence has cast across our popular culture.

Why is the *Back to Black* album from 2006 so important? Why does it deserve to be cherished and called her only masterpiece? So far, there are more than twenty million reasons worldwide. Each one represents a human being from a diverse culture who owns a copy, and for whom it has a special meaning. It therefore has over twenty million embodied meanings, each one being the true and correct reading of its message. In the ten years since it was dropped like a seed by a strange and exotic bird flying high overhead, it has come to symbolize a heartfelt insight about the human condition *in extremis*, composed especially for each listener.

It's a message that transcends cultural boundaries, and it's recognized as that rare work of art that is destined to withstand the test of time. In other words, it's a pop classic, albeit a very exotic one. She may well have been a savant; only time would have told, and time, as the jazz giant Artie Shaw once shrewdly remarked, is all we've got. But even if she was a freakish bolt of lightning, hitting us only once, the exotic light she shed and the exquisite darkness she illuminated are still well worth acclaiming.

Once something so personal transcends the private realm and breaks through to the universal realm, it gets to be regarded as a classic. A classic is any work of art, whether it's a painting, a book, a film or a musical composition, that instantly makes the viewer, reader, or listener feel that the work in question was painted, written, or composed for them. It also remains permanently situated in the present moment, no matter how much time passes since our initial encounter with it.

A classic piece of music is not necessarily one that's classical but rather one that transcends the time in which it was produced, influences a great deal of what follows it, and has a shared meaning long afterward. But in the end, the more compelling reasons for *Back to Black*'s privileged position in pop music history are these even more basic ones: how it was composed, how it was produced, how it was recorded, how it was performed live and on film, and, perhaps most importantly for us, how it sounds today.

Ten years later, it still sounds like a predestined blind date between life and death, a perfect marriage between heaven and hell, a combined technical production achievement and poetic musical accomplishment that remains aloof and untouchable. In a strangely alluring way, there's everyone else in pop music, and then there's her.

BACK TO BLACK
AMY WINEHOUSE'S ONLY MASTERPIECE

1
WHEN I PAINT MY MASTERPIECE
Amy the Storyteller

"Trouble is part of your life—if you don't share it, you don't give the people who love you a chance to love you enough."
—Dinah Washington,
in *Queen: The Life and Music of Dinah Washington*

Perhaps the secret key to understanding her music, or at least one of them, is to place her firmly in the context of the torch-song tradition. That way she doesn't rattle around quite so much in the historical wind, and she also appears far less alien and strange than at first glance and hearing.

Amy Winehouse didn't exactly come out of nowhere. She didn't just suddenly arrive like some alien on a spaceship. It only seemed that way. We owe it to Salaam Remi—a gifted recording artist and performer himself, as well as being the producer of her debut album, *Frank*—for bringing her to our collective attention. After sharing her early charms with us, he also laid the essential groundwork leading to *Back to Black* ten years ago.

Remi would go on to co-produce the album in question, combining his own vital funk-soul and hip-hop vibe with the bright and shiny white DJ-dance pop vibe of Mark Ronson in order to together craft her perfect sonic monument to melancholy. It was clearly a production collaboration made in heaven, to create a record about a love affair and marriage made in hell, though even that producer/artist collaboration also had its own challenging moments, like most of the best ones do.

Winehouse was just the latest model of a storytelling vehicle with a long and established history, even though she managed to mash together several idioms in a fresh and new way, elevating all of them while vastly extending their reach to a huge global pop audience. While the story-blues form she alchemized (along with jazz and soul) was an African American invention, there's a far older incarnation for songs lamenting loss dating back to the female slaves in the ancient Middle East. Called *giyan*, these female slave dirges formed the basis for courtly love and loss songs long before they were ever known by troubadours in Medieval Europe, right up until their music spread into Europe via North Africa during the Muslim conquest of Spain in the eighth century.

Despite the acres of words written about these historical troubadours themselves, these early romantic complaints were largely omitted from the singer/songwriter history books. But the key elemental ingredient that carries forward all the way from the *giyan* to Winehouse's fusion of forms is the public telling of private stories, sometimes harrowingly intimate and private stories, in a kind of empathic theater of the often broken heart.

Some singer/songwriters like having experiences and writing about them but hate making records out of them; some even compare the record industry to working in a coal mine. Winehouse hated having her experiences but seemingly loved making scintillating records out of them. She worked in that same artistic coal mine of stories where great songs are dredged up from the hubris of personal experience, but she only got the chance to go down there twice—though clearly with startling creative results both times.

People like Amy Winehouse and Joni Mitchell, Marianne Faithfull and Linda Thompson, like all the best singer/songwriters, are poetic chameleons who channel feelings and appear to assist us in coming to terms with and even explaining our own emotional experiences, our own love affairs, our own fears and hopes. That's what makes for perfect pop music, though few did it quite as exquisitely as Winehouse did at her youthful peak.

Ironically, though, in the speeded-up hybrid and hyperactive musical world of the twenty-first century, Winehouse was already feeling fed up with the music business even after her very first record release. Her second album clearly represented a fearful flight from one early personality into another later persona, its exact opposite in temperament, tone, intentions, and ambitions. The big surprise, especially for her, was just how popular her second album would prove to be. Few artists have been embraced so enthusiastically for their first recorded outing, or so worshipped for their second one.

Salaam Remi was the architect of the first building of songs by Winehouse, songs we could all dwell in for their short and snappy duration. His first name, Salaam, is an Arabic word literally meaning "the peace" and is also commonly used as a friendly greeting to strangers and friends alike. So maybe he was the perfect partner for *giyan* songs, though the time he spent with Winehouse on her superb debut in late 2002 must have been one of her briefest excursions into anything resembling peace of mind. It too would end with considerably disgruntled feelings when the merely twenty-year-old sudden starlet subsequently expressed her extreme displeasure with the final product. And she wasn't shy about voicing her distaste.

We'll never know what she may otherwise have had in mind for *Frank*'s production, song sequences, and mixes, but the end product still shimmered with a special glow reserved for very few artists who have only been alive for two decades. Her main complaint seemed to be centered on its marketing and promotion and her privileged location on the map of young new retro-jazz singers from England and elsewhere.

Other fast-breaking and rapidly rising musical stars have also had challenges to face with their early fame, of course, but few chose to literally spit in the face of their label, alienate their management, divorce themselves from their friends and family, switch agent-managers and lifestyles, and then pursue a whole new persona they felt liberated them from the heavy yoke of that early fame.

After soaking up the early '60s girl group vibe in the same way she had soaked up the early '40s jazz vibe, she would embark on an entirely new direction leading to the sheer grandeur of *Back to Black* with the ultimate "I'll show you who I really am and what I can really do" gesture. Even if they make a breakthrough while still very young, most vocal artists undertake a slow and gradual evolution, at least compared to young Winehouse's speedy shift angrily away from *Frank* and blithely toward *Back to Black*.

Lesley Gore was still a teenager when she broke big with her anthems of pre-adult angst and her landmark release "It's My Party" is practically a pre-*Black* premonition—one indeed that Amy would later sing live with Mark Ronson at a party in honor of producer giant Quincy Jones.

Gore was clearly one of Amy's artistic ancestors. Connie Francis is another performer who also had a far too youthful plunge into fame's rapids, one whose stylistic delivery would also be channeled perfectly through the profound Winehouse talent for filtering history, and whose searing torch songs achingly resonate with Winehouse's own later laments so precisely in their vein. Connie at her peak was the same age as Amy was when she made *Frank*, when *her* own father forced her to record "Who's Sorry Now?," and she was later only twenty-three (Amy's age at *Black to Black*) when she released "Don't Break the Heart That Loves You," another torchy tune that could practically have been written for or even by the forlorn voice of the brilliant but lost heroine of this narrative.

The names of many other famous singers will be mentioned as the momentum of the Winehouse story begins to pick up speed and depth. They all contributed to the veritable tsunami that she became. However, it's important—maybe even imperative—to appreciate the fact that in channeling so perfectly these equally talented prior singers, Winehouse would absorb through her own emotional antenna and the radio-like body of her impressive jukebox talents the parts that created her own unique whole. Though she was an ideal vessel for receiving and transmitting songs, she would paradoxically remain utterly singular as a writer and performer, just as she still is to this day, ten years later.

This could be because no matter how talented the many artists she channeled (and there were almost too many to count) and no matter how she literally grafted some of their singing styles and emotive material onto her own body of work, she was still *transcending* and not merely copying or imitating them. Artists like Winehouse don't imitate others, no matter how many historical references we journalists may cite as a means of helping ourselves comprehend her origins. She was so innately musically intelligent that she remained a consummate and perpetual original, even when her historical musical sources are transparently obvious. Naturally, her emotional intelligence was another matter altogether, but luckily that doesn't concern us here.

It's important to point out that I'm not saying she's better than *your* favorite singer/songwriter (Lorde, Sia, Julien Baker, and Grimes are all quite talented) or that she is the best singer/songwriter who ever lived (her own influences are among the historic titans). I'm only saying that she was and is unique. The word unique is a superlative, which means one can't be very unique, or extremely unique, and my point is that it's pointless to compare her to anyone else—not because she's superior but because comparison is a waste of time.

That's the whole point of this guided excursion. To emphasize the fact that she was a one-of-a-kind writer, performer, and recording artist, regardless of the diverting sideshow that often swirled around her and formed the basis for so much media acreage, and that she was still also the kind of musical genius who comes along only once, period. Or maybe twice, if we had been lucky. We'll never know, of course, since we have just *Back to Black* by which to judge her. But how do you go from *Frank's* bright pregnancy to *Black*'s dark delivery in only three short years? There lies both her and our conundrum.

■ ■ ■

Amy Winehouse's sparkling debut record, named after one of her vocal heroes (and her dog, as well as her bold attitude) was an effervescent banquet celebrating a young life devoted to the charms of up-tempo music of several genres bending together through a shiny new pop personality on the musical scene. There is, however, no easily quipped answer to that ominous question of transition. She remains today what she was back then: the kind of phenomenon that Winston Churchill characterized as a riddle, wrapped in a mystery, inside an enigma. But by giving birth to *Black* she also became both a musical emblem and a pop-culture brand, one that curiously mapped the future of nostalgia.

One potential response to her enigma is another musical one. Paul McCartney's second solo record after the Beatles disbanded contains a great song called "Too Many People," in which he tries to explain to his befuddled former songwriting partner the cause of Lennon's then current self-image dilemmas. "You took your lucky break and broke it in two."

This sentiment also applies to Amy Winehouse, whose first album was a great lucky break leading her up to the top of the pop mountain and preparing the way for her second effort, which, given the acclaim it would go on to garner, was an even bigger lucky break. But she too broke it in two, and what could be done for her? Very little, it turns out.

Winehouse was obviously unable to survive her blockbuster follow-up record and move forward into a mature, post-*Black* career. After all, courting songs should logically lead to torch songs and then hopefully lead to reconciliation songs, or perhaps to a whole new cycle of courting songs, or so at least we the audience imagined. But her torch would be extinguished after only one sequel.

Frank was released on October 20, 2003. It was laid down in multiple studios over a year's time: Creative Space in Miami, EMI Studios and Mayfair in London, the Headquarters in New Jersey, and Platinum Sound in New York. It was an undeniably perfect debut record on all levels. Released by Island Records, it mutated jazz, soul, reggae, and hip-hop into something utterly other, yet something totally Amy. And Salaam Remi's legendary hip-hop fingerprints are all over it.

At almost sixty minutes long, it is nearly twice as long as the follow-up would be, and it boasts a veritable army of producing talent, which may account for why there was such friction over its final format and mixing motifs. Salaam Remi, Commissioner Gordon, Jimmy Hogarth, Jony Rockstar, Matt Rowe, and Amy Winehouse herself are all listed as providing the production guidance. Only Remi, in concert with Mark Ronson, would remain on board the good ship Amy for her sequel blockbuster effort three years later. But, though it would take three years to arrive, its actual production would occur in a dizzying three months.

The distinction between the two records is simple, apart from the obvious evolution of her sound both technically and stylistically: *Frank* is a love song courting record celebrating a breakup; *Back to Black* would be a memorial breakup album, a torch-song record drenched in Wall of Sound longing and loss.

The art of melodies and words serve both wooing and

breaking up equally well, and as Ted Gioia points out in his recent book, *Love Songs: The Hidden History*, not only do crooning and courting have a storied past but sung melodies have been rooted in finding and losing romance since the very beginnings of music.

Juan Rodriguez wrote an appreciative essay on the subject of this history that reveals how valuable this book's insights might be for lovers of love songs. From my perspective, it also helps anyone hoping to understand Winehouse's rapid creative progression from chirpy *Frank* to *Black*, the apotheosis of all heartbreak albums.

Rodriguez commences his essay by referencing several of the greatest lovers' laments in musical history. "I can't stop loving you, it's useless to try," Ray Charles wails. "Love hurts" Roy Orbison moans. "Love stinks," the J. Geils Band concludes. To these I would add several songs by the greatest girl group in history (and one Amy both adored and learned from) Diana Ross and the Supremes, who clearly shared a love hangover in "Stop! In the Name of Love" and "Baby, Baby, Where Did Our Love Go?"

Every single one of these songs touches on the same subject as both of Winehouse's records, and several could have been sung to great effect in her own plaintive and pleading voice. She also actively borrowed their sounds, their very sonic identities, with long-lasting impact, and profitably deposited them into her own already growing artistic credit account.

Rodriguez goes on to remind us that singing and listening to love songs has been with us for at least 5,000 years, and that pop songs overlap the arbitrary borderlines of sacred and profane in the most entertaining manner, leaving us "hooked on a feeling" by B. J. Thomas, or "dazed and confused" by Led Zeppelin. Either way, the sentiment is the same, and as Led Zeppelin itself later loudly concluded, the song remains the same.

As Rodriguez writes, "Conflict and controversy mark the history of this ubiquitous popular art form"—one so ably explored in Gioia's book on its hidden history. The same author has also written extensively about jazz, delta blues, and the birth and death of cool, and has spent twenty years "researching the main narrative of our lives contained in the woefully underestimated genre of the love song." Gioia reports that people looked at him smugly when he said he was working on a history of love songs, even though he pointed out that at least 90 percent of all songs released are about this very subject. Music critics, he observes, usually write about the other 10 percent, perhaps wanting to be more *serious*.

"The ancient Romans thought no sane person would willingly fall in love, as it made you vulnerable and exposed," Gioia writes. "They tried to ridicule it. In many ways, we're doing the same things now, yet we can't get rid of love songs." Being vulnerable and exposed are clearly at the very core of the craft that Amy Winehouse practiced so very well, as demonstrated so vividly on *Back to Black*.

Incredibly, Gioia starts his love song exploration with Darwin's theory that "just as birds sing to attract the opposite sex, primeval man first used his voice in producing true musical cadences that were handy in courtship and expressed various emotions such as love, jealousy, and triumph, and which would have served as challenges to rivals." In the most basic of ways, it appears that virtually *all* songs were originally love songs. "It gradually occurred to me that love songs have been an agent for expanding a person's liberty and personal autonomy, coming from those who wanted more freedom over their love lives. The next thing that jumped out at me was that people who created innovations in love songs generally were marginalized individuals. They might be a slave, a woman, a bohemian, an outcast. It usually took the outsider to be daring enough to sing about things other people are afraid of." Naturally, few singer/songwriters could ever be considered more emotionally marginalized than the self-doubting Winehouse.

"I discovered that new ways of singing of love tended to threaten people—parents, priests, whoever," Gioia continues. "Again and again I asked myself, what comes first? Do we sing of love in a new way and then change how we romance each other, or are changes in courtship greatly spurred by the songs?" Perhaps not surprisingly, he discovers that the songs themselves change how we deal with love, and I also believe that Winehouse's method of self-revelation, her blurring together of blues, jazz, hip hop, and soul, was all about singing the truth as she saw it in a dazzling new way that has altered the entire sonic landscape of pop music itself to some degree.

Gioia then moves in a parallel direction, observing that the creation of the blues motif itself "marked the most important shift in songs about romance—and attitudes about romance—since the dawn of the troubadours. The blues expanded the love song vocabulary toward vivid images that made effete parlor songs obsolete. Thinly veiled sexual references abounded."

I have to concur by pointing out that there are few images in pop music, and in love song history, quite so vivid as Winehouse's earlier song "Fuck Me Pumps," or the subsequent sexually raw opening lines of the title song on *Back to Black* itself, or the indelibly vivid later image of letting "tears dry by themselves." Meanwhile, listening to her private confessions en masse, all of us in the enraptured audience were more than willing to help her wipe away her tears, if only she would let us.

■ ■ ■

Amy Winehouse was officially "discovered" by renowned impresario and manager extraordinaire Simon Fuller, who would give (or at least try to give) the precocious and already aggressively opinionated singer the musical guidance required to navigate the recording industry proper. Fuller was the force behind her first exposure to the world via his already daunting publicity and marketing skills (think Malcolm McLaren and his Sex Pistols, but focusing globally on snappy girl groups instead of punks). He would be the creative fuel and mentor she needed to capture her particularly slippery brand of lightning in the proverbial recording bottle.

Simon Fuller, a child of 1960 and the man behind the Spice Girls (and as such the template against which Winehouse would later rebel with *Black*), has always been candid about what he does best. He's a self-declared maestro at creating fame, profit, and celebrity, and he knows that he's one of the most gifted manufacturers of musical talent in the world—not always the best or greatest music but often definitely the most high profile.

Profile is his business. Selling is his passion. After working at the legendary British label Chrysalis, then in music publishing and A&R (artist and repertoire), where his key role was talent scouting and overseeing artistic development, as well as serving as the liaison between artists and their labels primarily up to the point of an album's production and release, he ambitiously branched out on his own at the relatively tender age of twenty-five.

In the 1980s, Fuller encountered the singer Paul Hardcastle and heard the early chimes of his own prescient cash-register psyche. After releasing a hit single (by Hardcastle) called "19," he immediately set up his own artist management company, logically also called 19 Management, followed by a subsidiary, Brilliant 19. Then, in rapid succession, he discovered Cathy Dennis and led her to a global string of hits in the 1990s. He even "rediscovered" the legendary post-Eurythmics Annie Lennox and helped her become an even bigger success as a solo artist.

But his true claim to publicity infamy would be taking over the management of the Spice Girls in 1996 and shooting them into the stratosphere, after which, ever the commercial visionary, he made the lateral move over to television just as *Pop Idol* and *American Idol* were staking their claim to being global launch pads for new talent. He then moved into image management, his true forte, eventually taking ownership of the rights, the name, and the *images* of both Muhammad Ali and Elvis Presley's Graceland. He clearly knows and understands the esoteric nature of product, or at least he knows how to point it in the direction it already seems to be heading, which is still no mean feat on any day.

Once under the wing of Fuller's Brilliant 19, and while still a shaky if sultry teenager barely out of the BRIT Performing Arts and Technology School in Croydon, south London, Amy Winehouse was signed and represented by Fuller protégé Nick Godwyn, whose role was to nurture and polish the raw talent unearthed by his boss. Turning the lump of coal into a diamond, so to speak—something he did with obvious aplomb, having learned from the master how to successfully market the dizzying Spice Girl phenomenon.

The hip-hop DJ known as Major, who had worked with Soul II Soul, was the first producer to bring Amy to the attention of the nineteen-year-old *wunderkind* Nick Shymansky, who along with Godwyn would form a kind of tandem team to strategize her way to what Lennon once called "the toppermost of the poppermost."

I've tried to resist calling her the Space Girl counterpart, but it's so appropriate that I've given in. I'm also tempted to say that she was like a multiphrenic combination of all four of those Spice Girl personalities and temperaments rolled into one package: good, bad, cute, and nasty at the same time, and I won't resist that either.

Upon mentioning that he was searching for the next young exponent of retro-jazz, Godwyn's sidekick from the Spice Girls universe would accidentally learn from a close young Winehouse friend named Tyler James (who knew her from her student days at the Sylvia Young Academy) about this fresh young "jazz singer" he knew very well personally. Both creative and commercial ignition resulted almost immediately.

It would be these players who mutually introduced Salaam Remi, already a well known young hip-hop artist and producer, to the fledgling singer/songwriter in late 2002. Even then she was, in Godwyn's words, "frustratingly frank"—a phrase that may define her first album's perspective almost as much as the Sinatra evocation.

If this rattling conveyor-belt movement toward fame seems supercharged, it was exactly that. It's also worth remembering that the "product" in question here was still largely a naïve, if precocious and willful, young girl, albeit someone who already sent chills up and down the spine of those who heard her warble even back then. She, Fuller, and Godwyn would eventually and inevitably part company, once they had fulfilled their function, at which point she began to be represented by the far hipper Raye Cosbert. This would later be problematic, though, since he was also her record promoter—a clear conflict of interest in the long run. Such was her sudden girlish incarnation as a global superstar.

Soon enough—even faster than soon—she had signed her first record deal with Universal/Island Records (on December 22, 2002). One of her audition performances for the suits was "There Is No Greater Love," a 1936 jazz standard composed by Isham Jones and Marty Symes, most famously delivered by the great Billie Holiday (in 1947), the amazing Dinah Washington (1954), the sizzling Aretha Franklin (1965), and the chilling Etta James (2001). Now it was young Amy's turn. She aced it.

Even back then as a teenager she had industrial strength charisma and a maximalist approach to music making. Though we were already in a post-rock and fluidly hybrid pop-music world that had embraced rap and hip hop in the mainstream markets, her jazzy renditions apparently knocked the suits out of their chairs enough for them to start declaring that *they* had discovered the next Billie, the next Dinah, the next this, the next that.

Strangely enough, though, they were right: she really was the next big thing. Of course, she was just being spooky Amy, massaging the past through her gifted pipes into a future no one in the music business had quite imagined yet. Naturally, no one ever quite sees or hears the future of music, but suddenly the sound of the future had come crashing into that boardroom, and it would soon echo out into the streets, the place where music really matters.

■ ■ ■

Music is everything to Salaam Remi. A talented artist-producer when he first met Winehouse, he would progress far beyond that role: in 2012 he was named executive vice-president of A&R for Sony, and in 2013 he launched his own independent imprint, Louder Than Life, through Sony Entertainment. On the basis of his grassroots association with musical artists such as the Fugees, Black Sheep, Fergie, Estelle, Nas, Lemar, Nellie Furtado, Jazmine Sullivan, Kurtis Blow, and many others, he's become a production powerhouse. This in addition to a long list of highly listenable releases as an artist in his own right. But of course it was as the main creative production credit on the platinum debut record by a young north London jazz-soul singer named Amy Winehouse that he would have a rightful claim to his own page in the music history books.

Remi has what's been called a reggae-tinged approach to production, something often referred to as the "broken bottle" style, but it was undoubtedly his own roots as a singer/songwriter, performer, and recording artist that allowed him to both help mentor Winehouse's early promise and gently collide and creatively clash with her prematurely demanding ways in the studio right from the beginning.

Remi was accustomed to strong personalities in the studio, having worked with Ms. Dynamite, Toni Braxton, and Lauryn Hill, whose own debut record was often cited by Winehouse as having had a giant influence on her when she first heard it as a youngster (ironic, since she still was one when she said it). He grew up in a musical family where jazz giant Elvin Jones would come by for a visit and listen to a six-year-old Salaam drumming with such proficiency that Jones crafted a miniature cocktail percussion set of drums to encourage young Remi to continue on with his music.

But nothing could have prepared him for the firestorm of making the Winehouse debut album itself, the post-production problems with the artist, or the press storm that ensued when she all but disowned it, claiming to hate it and to literally despise performing its songs. She never was much of a diplomat when expressing her displeasure, regardless of the fact that she and Remi had become musical siblings while making it together. By that time, she was already moving rapidly toward what would be *Back to Black*—a creative vortex into which Remi would willingly be pulled.

To be more accurate, Winehouse said she didn't mind performing a *few* of the *Frank* songs in concert, but she refused to listen to the album itself. Soon enough, she wouldn't even be able to perform them. Either way, it was a combination of his own gifts and skills that allowed Remi to navigate her rough personal and professional waters, especially his two most salient features: a humble and quiet presence behind the scenes blended with a phenomenal talent for mixing and matching sounds, mashing genres and bending their borderlines way beyond recognition. This gifted man is creatively flexible and passionately devoted to great music first and to limited musical territories second, if at all.

Salaam Remi's own music has what listeners have come to identify as his signature invitingly gentle approach to rap and hip hop spiced with a considerable dose of heavy funk. This is most evident on his album *One in the Chamber* from 2013, but it had started to emerge as far back as his participation in the first of a horde of singles over the years, among them "Young Girl Bluez" with Biz Markie in 1993, "Here Comes the Hotstepper" with Ini Kamoze in 1994, "Skettle Combo" with Ricky General in 1995, and "Fu-Gee-La" with the Fugees in 1996. In 2002, he was actively engaged creatively with the rapper Nas (Nasir Jones, later referenced by Winehouse in "Me and Mr. Jones") on stellar tracks such as "Made You Look," "I Can," and "Get Down."

The recognizable Remi vibe is also spread all over *The Score* by the Fugees, Toni Braxton's "You're Makin' Me High," and Ms. Dynamite's *A Little Deeper,* while in 2006 he contributed tracks to Jurassic 5's *Feedback* and Nas's *Hip Hop Is Dead*. He's also been actively associated with Lemar, Noel Gourdin, Julian Perretta, Leona Lewis, Corinne Bailey Rae, Tamia, Alicia Keyes, Mack Wilds, and Craig David, in addition to venturing into music produced for both television and films. His production and in some cases his song co-authorship with Amy Winehouse alone have guaranteed his entry into the pantheon of highly regarded producing giants: "You Sent Me Flying / Cherry," "I Heard Love Is Blind," "In My Bed," "Just Friends," "Me and Mr. Jones," "Moody's Mood for Love," "Mr. Magic," "Some Unholy War," "Stronger Than Me," and "Tears Dry on Their Own" (my own favorite Winehouse song from *Back to Black*), and as co-writer of one of her most provocative early songs, "Fuck Me Pumps."

As a producer and mentor, it was his ability to move from one artist to the next, utilizing drastically different styles and formats, often at the same time and without any creative strain, that he believed held him in good stead for both making *Frank* a success and laying the groundwork for *Back to Black*. This stylistic versatility is one of the reasons Winehouse's debut album has so many different flavors: one spirit, perhaps, but many sonic shades, much to the consternation of some, including maybe Winehouse herself. Given the hybrid nature of the album and its merging of jazz with hip hop and some reggae flavors, it seems logical that Remi would share some of the executive producing mantle with another key collaborator, Gordon Williams, also known as Commissioner Gordon. They each took on half of the mentor and producer functions for her debut record—an arrangement that worked so well that Island Records decided to follow a similar course of dual-producer collaborators when bringing Mark Ronson on board for the follow-up effort.

Recording together in his home studio in Miami, which Remi calls his Instrument Zoo, he and Winehouse made a schizoid courtship record with a dark secret heart. In his cozy zoo he had many talented, trained, and performing animals at his disposal. It was not quite a circus but certainly not the kind of rigidly confined corporate studio that more commonly crafts great, big, shiny pop records. Swirling around the artist and producer were an eclectic mix of creative figures: guitarists Binky Griptite and Thomas Brenneck, drummers Troy Auxilly-Wilson and Homer Steinweiss, saxophonists Andy Mackintosh, Chris Davies, Jamie Talbot, Mike Smith, and Neil Sugarman, and the pianist John Adams. Handclapping (a device first championed by the Beatles) would be contributed by Vaughn Merrick, Mark Ronson, and Victor Axelrod, with special sound effects created by the rapper and producer RZA. Even back then, several members of the superb Dap-Kings band were already present and accounted for, and, as we'll soon see, they would play a pivotal role in Winehouse's future career.

Salaam Remi is a behemoth, almost a mythological creature in the hip-hop domain, and something of a one-man juggernaut. He's a self-designed vessel for the transport of hip hop's various deities, including this new skinny white kid who *seemed* to come out of nowhere and blend everything that preceded her into a near-perfect sonic dream soup.

Like the rappers she aspired to emulate, such as Mos Def or Nas—both of whom she got to know through her association with Remi—Winehouse wanted to tell lifelike stories through her music, but in a new format, one that would merge the gritty street immediacy of rap with the smooth sophistication of electric blues, jazz, and soul. She admired the way a rapper like Nas could make the listener feel like he or she was standing in the same room and sharing the same sensations as the performer.

After her warm-up record, that same approach would of course achieve its full impact on *Back to Black* itself, which the *Sunday Mirror* called "impossibly smooth and ridiculously good"; the *Financial Times* would reference the "sort of brilliantly florid lament that Ennio Morricone used to write for spaghetti westerns." However, that florid feeling is only the record's emotional temperature; musically, it harkens back more to songs like "Jimmy Mack" or the superb "Baby Love" by Martha Reeves and the Vandellas.

Early on, Winehouse would occasionally be taken to task for channeling the black vibes of jazz and blues, and she would later would be criticized for borrowing the black vibes of rap and soul. In response, she bluntly said she just wanted to tell *her* stories in the deepest and most effective way possible, regardless of the color of their traditions.

Even back in April 2004, she was already downplaying any blackness in her music to *Blues and Soul* magazine, though it would become even more evident as it shifted from jazz/blues flavors to R&B/hip hop. She was also already acknowledging the huge power of the producer as artist in her creative process: "I wrote my songs on guitar; I went to a producer, and he *did* them for me. I just sing and write reflecting everything I've ever heard. The minute I even start to think about what I'm doing I just lose it. I have to just shut my eyes and flow." Later on, of course, Winehouse would petulantly take Mark Ronson to task for his identical explanation of how he transformed her simple guitar riffs into the formal band arrangements and opulent orchestrations on *Back to Black*.

In telling her highly personal stories so artfully on *Frank* with Remi, Winehouse created the ideal context within which she eventually could paint her second masterpiece with Ronson. Back then, whether or not that work would be "smooth like a rhapsody," as Dylan puts it in "When I Paint My Masterpiece," remained to be seen and heard. All she had to do was live through it first.

■ ■ ■

I can't help thinking that the Winehouse phenomenon is an ideal situation to explain using the Rashomon effect, named after a famous Kurosawa film from 1950 and referring to seemingly contradictory interpretations of the same event by different people. Depending on which witness you encounter to clarify what happened in the clearing in the pop forest she burned down, you'll get a slightly different angle and perspective on the same occurrence. So we're circling around that clearing and finding a multi-faceted chronicle with several different and almost recursively overlapping angles. These differing views of the same musical event are quite varied, but all are equally true.

Mark Ronson, however, could definitely see the forest for the trees, *and* the startling musical event that occurred there. Yet as important as Ronson was to manifesting *Back to Black*, luckily he's still smart enough to have often declared, "I didn't make her career, she made mine!" Let's agree that they made each other's.

A snapshot of the broader musical world that Winehouse exploded into might be a useful way of situating both her and Ronson in the proper pop context. Speaking to Q-Tip, the rapper/producer and co-founder of the band A Tribe Called Quest, for *Interview Magazine* in 2015, Ronson recalled the music business back at the time of Winehouse's ascent and remarked that it had been a *weird time* for music: "The industry is bottoming out, now there's CDJs [CD players that emulate vinyl control of music] and people are not bringing vinyl around to DJ anymore, the gate is starting to open with all these different types of talent coming through, music is changing."

For Ronson, it was definitely a time of upheaval, but meeting EMI's Guy Moot made him feel "relevant" again, more grounded and somewhat more able to take advantage of the hybrid phase music was going through at that time. It was Moot, of course, who first introduced Ronson to Winehouse's music, just at the time when Ronson was feeling burned out by the whole music industry scene. He was even, he has since readily admitted, about to chuck it all in.

The musical environment into which the Ronson–Remi–Winehouse collaboration would be plunged was being ruled at the time by several concurrent streams of retro-styled artists. In 2004, Winehouse's fellow young British singer/songwriter James Blunt released his ironically titled album *Back to Bedlam*, which was promoted almost concurrently with her *Frank*. The August 2006 release of Christina Aguilera's ironically titled *Back to Basics* (ironic mostly because she cleverly changed styles with each release of her five records up to that point) signaled an overall shift in public taste slightly away from rock traditions toward a more nostalgic mode. *Back to Basics*, while not nearly as interesting musically, did reflect this trend in its R&B-flavored jazz-soul vibe, and it cleared some ground for the blockbuster arrival of *Back to Black* itself in October that same year. The public appetite was becoming ever more tantalized by the potential for fewer hard techno-driven tsunamis and more gently sincere song waves to tell basic human stories.

Sometimes it seems like the music industry and the listening audience alike were just waiting for someone like Amy Winehouse to come along. The time was ripe, and the merging stylistic context was ready for her rapid ascent. After her critically and commercially successful concert tours in support of *Frank* ended in 2004, her busy schedule allowed her to take some much needed time off to rest, recuperate, and contemplate her next creative moves. She did this, of course, by carefully surveying the music scene, both present and past, and digesting them together with her first producer.

Remi's self-effacing "I'm not the star here" producer's style is evident in his comments in Chas Newkey-Burden's early, rapid Amy bio. "I didn't want to be seen as a public figure," he recalled. "An industry person, that's cool—all the presidents and senior VPs I've crossed path with because I've been around that long—but I'm not really a public figure. I like to be known by industry people and people I work with, but I like the fact that I can walk around." He especially liked to walk around in Miami instead of New York (from which he fled after 9/11) or London, Amy's principal haunts; and he made it creatively possible for her to visit him down south as much as he could manage in order to extend a hiatus from her non-musical temptations. It certainly worked wonders with Winehouse.

He described his strategic approach as follows: "I'm concerned with songs that are going to stick, and that takes a vehicle, great lyrics that are going to stick, that's when you're going to get a classic album overall. I really get in there and work with people and work on a lot of music if I have my choice, and even if someone only wants to do one song, I'm like—let's do four and you can pick the best one off it." The only downside to that approach, of course, comes after an artist is gone and their record label wants to release *all* their demos, alternate versions, and outtakes to cash in on them as if they were finished works, as per her posthumous *Lioness* album of so-called "hidden treasures," for instance.

Winehouse enthusiastically extolled the virtues of Remi's approach to *Blues and Soul*. "I'd never met anyone who can tap into an artist like he can; which to me is the mark of a great producer. With Salaam I feel that musically anything can be done—and I've never felt like that working in England, where they don't wanna listen to a girl who thinks she knows what she's talking about. Basically all they care about is listening to the record company." True enough, but still surprisingly astute, coming from so youthful a performer still caught up in her own personal meteor shower.

The word meteoric is used a little too often in the world of pop music, but this is one case where it really does apply. We can't emphasize enough how supersonic the Winehouse trajectory was and how swiftly both her rise and fall came. Way back in February 1999, the sixteen-year-old Amy sang "Moon River" to her young friend Nick Shymansky more passionately than most seasoned veterans could have managed and caused him to suggest she might try to make records (she assured him that music was never a career choice for her but would eventually relent and make a few demos with him). All of those demos were what she called "personal story" songs, and one of them, another gem, "There Is No Greater Love," would click for Guy Moot of EMI Music and lead to her signing with Nick Gatfield of Island Records in February 2003. By October of the same year she would be on a promotional tour for her first record, appearing at the North Sea Jazz Festival to sing about how she would "demonstrate her Freudian state" and how her "destructive side had grown a mile wide." All of this definitely does, I believe, qualify as meteoric. And, as we now know, the best and worst were still to come.

After winning an Ivor Novello Award for her Remi-co-write "Stronger Than Me" in 2004, Winehouse was already at a point most artists take quite a few years of struggle to reach and was declaring to TV Host Tim Kash that she didn't understand what all the hoopla was about: all she's good for is "making tunes," and she just wanted to be left alone so she can make some more.

By January 2005 she was adrift in Camden and dealing with her writer's block by taking up residence in the Trash nightclub run by Phil Meynell, where she would eventually meet the love of her life and the bane of her existence. Everything changed in her life at this stage. After six months of creative inactivity, she was growing rusty; after appearing at the B-Live Festival in London she received a scary warning from her record label's chief executive, Lucian Grainge: "That was *Frank*, this is now, we need another record, and soon!"

Just as with any highly acclaimed young artist, and just like every outlandishly gifted pop star before her, the record label she "worked for" was also equally anxious for more product. That, after all, is what they do; they're the conduits that bring us these remarkable talents, one after the other, and Island Records was no different. So the label's own angle of vision was bound to be somewhat skewed.

And, just as with many other pop artists before her, the interstitial zone between sales bonanzas during her brief Christmas break prior to and during 2005 was seen by ambitious manager/promoter Raye Cosbert and label rep Darcus Beese (her versions of Brian Epstein), as well as the business executive team at Island Records, to be a time for corporate consolidation—a brief working lull in which their new discovery was expected to buckle down and be the twenty-three-year-old genius she was supposed to be.

She was expected to get creatively busy and get down to business, without much of a chance to experiment with new music or even to live the new experiences she was supposed to write about so intimately. For the new goldmine's landowners, not surprisingly it was just business as usual: onward and upward, and upward, and upward. It was equally important to do so as quickly as possible, before the bubble burst—as they knew it had to, sooner or later. Which was cynical of them, perhaps, but still accurate.

Commenting on the transformation from jazz-girl to torch-woman in a 2007 interview with *Music Week*, Cosbert said, "She's an incredible live performer now." In response to *Black*'s success and how many copies it might be expected to sell, he added, "How long is a piece of string? Let me put it this way, all the predictions we had originally are now out the window because of the success of the record. We all had different views of what we thought the album would achieve commercially and we've exceeded them all." Naturally I tend to question his liberal use of the word "we."

In a similar strategy to the one deployed for her first album, where Remi and Gordon each mixed their parts of the record in their own hometown studios in Miami and New Jersey, for the second one, Remi and Ronson would do the same separate balancing act from Miami and New York. The shift in managers, which alters your relationship to your label, would be almost as transformative for the singer/songwriter as her shift in producers, which obviously always alters your relationship to your own music.

O'Shea accurately observes that the business side of a creative industry has a profound impact on the creativity at the heart of the finished product: "Island Records weren't overly concerned whose hand was on the tiller of Amy's ship as long as it remained anchored in their harbor." However, Guy Moot was particularly delighted at hearing the news of Winehouse's management change, telling *Music Week* that Cosbert coming into the mix put a real period of stability into the whole creative and commercial campaign. "He is incredibly calm and by remaining calm, he focuses on what the goals are and at the same time harnesses the more erratic artistic moments that Amy has."

As we've all seen time and time again in the music business, no matter how successful an artist's debut album may be, the corporate heads want more of the same. In the case of Winehouse, this meant having no opportunity for a well-earned Christmas break between 2004 and 2005, and instead being expected to dig deep into some fresh heartaches in order to fill the bill. She did her best to oblige.

It turns out that her new and improved heartache, and her next ex-lover, would fatefully materialize in the Georgian-styled Hawley Arms on Castlehaven Road, just off Camden High Street, in February of 2005, where her perspective changed forever. "People change when they are in love," her earlier manager Godwyn demurred in a *Sunday Times* interview. "There's a different priority in life, I accepted that, but then other things started to change. Her behavior became more erratic. She wasn't doing anything, not going away, not going to the studio. We arranged a trip for her to go to New York to meet producer Mark Ronson and she wouldn't go." Obviously she liked saying no.

It was, of course, an infamously volatile and brief but intense romantic relationship, which ended with her ominous beau going back to his old girlfriend and with Winehouse going back to . . . the Hawley Arms. But now, at least, she had something to write about. And that was the first time that emphatic *no!* really entered her emotional lexicon with such force that it would follow her all the way to the streets of New York. Apparently the pop charts were ready for a dose of dark defiance.

As if perfectly conspiring both for and against her, her new love affair was over, and she'd acquired all the research and raw material she needed for her next record. Meanwhile, her young friend Shymansky was desperately trying to intervene and shake her off her troubled path, but to no avail. Her label now even threatened to drop her completely from its roster. All of this before *Back to Black* was even a glimmer in her dark eye.

Douglas Wolk, looking back from the vantage point of 2010 at this transitional phase of Amy Winehouse's career for *Pitchfork,* felt that *Frank* "came off as the first chapter in a romantic myth of a poet who feels too deeply and ends up killing herself for her audience's entertainment." Even he probably didn't entirely suspect that her mythical romantic story would have only two slim chapters. Future historians may have to assess the true nature of Winehouse's legacy, but at least we have her second chapter to, dare I say it, entertain us.

She would do so in a manner reminiscent of the great Traffic song, "Dear Mr. Fantasy" from 1967, altering only the gender of the song. The message was still prescient: "You are the one who can make us all laugh, but doing that you break out in tears."

2

ARRIVAL OF A DEMONIC DIVA

The Club You Don't Want to Join

"You know, you can only bite off so much, so you gotta know what you want to do."
—Lesley Gore, speaking on *In the Life*, 1991

Amy Winehouse was not only an unlikely debutante but also an unwilling one. In 2003 she'd been one of the most mesmerizing young talents in the music industry and had made her presence on the scene known in a big way. But debuts are strange things, and debutantes are often even stranger, especially when they come in as odd a package as the one that contained Winehouse's skillful gift for channeling. She was so disdainful of being labeled one of the new young crop of freshly minted jazz-pop singers (among them Jamie Cullum, Katie Melua, and Norah Jones) and so distressed by her roots as the "next big thing" discovered by infamous Spice Girl mogul Simon Fuller that she literally reinvented herself from the ground up.

She was busy conducting what amounted to a complete identity change in public, a high-stakes gamble that would yield the kind of tasty grist that both she and Island Records needed for its perpetually grinding mill. To *Entertainment Weekly* in 2007 she characterized it like this: "The songs I wrote for the album [*Back to Black*] were from times when I was messed up in the head. I had literally hit, not rock bottom, I hate to use such a phrase, since I'm sure I will sink lower at some point." Presumably in order to grind out her imaginary third album. "I was clinically depressed and I managed to get something I'm so proud of out of something so horrible," she continued. "I have to feel very strongly about something before I can write about it." And to the *Sunday Herald* she opined, "When I start, I'm on a roll. I am on a roll. This album, *Back to Black*, took me about six months to write. I guess someone reading this might think that that was really long, but fuck you, it took me four years to write my first album." She would still be trying to write her third album almost six years later.

She told *Beats Bar* in 2006 about the arrival of Mark Ronson in her life. "We met and we had a lot more in common music-wise than I thought. I had about three or four songs together, but I really wasn't ready, that wasn't enough to get started properly. I only got to that stage when I met Mark." Ronson himself was fully aware of the transformative nature of the encounter. "I've always been really candid about saying that Amy is the reason I am on the map," he told the BBC in 2010, "If it wasn't for the success of *Back to Black*, no one would have cared too much about my record *Version*."

Among the many things they shared in common was a healthy obsession for the Ronettes and other '60s girl groups, which we'll explore in some detail. "Once me and Mark started doing that stuff, I was ready to start work on a new album, and that's what we spent the first half of the year doing," she said, as reported in O'Shea's *Losing Game*.

While Ronson would be channeling the girl-group spirit of Phil Spector, Remi was channeling some of the magic of giants like Tom Dowd of Atlantic Records and Jim Gaines, a sound engineer at Stax Records, to reach back to an equally retro but different vibe for inspiration: the granular snap, crackle, and pop of vinyl. "The songs were twisted around that tempo," he told *Remix* magazine, "and were lyrically all the same. What pulls the album together is Amy's confidence and what she wanted to hear."

The head honchos at Island Records knew gold when they heard it in the early rough takes, and they all congratulated themselves for having paired the (on the surface) drastically different producers Ronson and Remi, each of whom brought not only their own styles and sensibilities into the mix but also a blend of their respective creative and musical partners into the venture as well. The boardroom family immediately heard something special in this cocktail, even apart from the music itself, which was gorgeous, sparkling, and hypnotic. They heard the sound of a loud cash register ringing in the sky, and the rest, as they say, is *herstory*.

But of course, to anyone listening closely enough, an echo of Bette Davis's cackled diva declaration in the 1950 film *All About Eve* could also easily have been heard loudly reverberating around young Amy: "Fasten your seatbelts everybody, it's going to be a *bumpy* night!" And, obviously, the "diva" label seemed to arrive very early in her brief career. As Helen Brown of the *Daily Telegraph* opined in 2006, "Her voice slithers from the soapy-sinuous sound of a woman who can wrap two lovers around her little finger, to the heartbroken throaty graze of one left crying on a kitchen floor. Living with raw conviction through the emotional experience of each song on *Back to Black*, Winehouse proves herself a true urban diva."

Beccy Lindon of the *Guardian* once called the early Winehouse voice as being "somewhere between Nina Simone and Erykah Badu, at once innocent and sleazy." That same quirky combination of paradoxical and seemingly opposite elements was clearly evident in her personality during an interview with the *Daily Telegraph*: "I'm probably already a diva, if that means you don't give a fuck about anyone else's opinions."

The amazing transition from reluctant debutante to the demonic diva of *Back to Black* in 2006 was not only a fully conscious choice and a deliberate act of stylistic and aesthetic transformation; it was also one of the swiftest and most startlingly defiant changes of artistic direction in pop music history. Suddenly it was anti-spice all the way.

One purpose of this narrative is to explore the reverse engineering of her second album as if it were a vehicle of transportation. Although Mark Ronson definitely wanted to produce a great pop record (something he had been cognizant of doing ever since he first encountered Winehouse's seductive vibe) making a pop record was the furthest thing from Amy Winehouse's melancholy mind. Pop music was something she had been running away from ever since the acclaim of her debut record, since from her somewhat skewed perspective to be popular meant something was wrong with you as an artist. This reverse engineering is made all the more compelling because *Back to Black* was a vehicle for the most profound, if sorrowful aspects of contemporary Internet society and its scary embodiment of private relationships lived out in public.

Given how disdainful she was of the personality of her first record, it might be surprising to some that Winehouse accepted Salaam Remi back as the co-producer on her follow up effort. But it's not really that surprising when we remember that firstly she didn't have a lot of choice in the matter (her label had waited patiently for three years to get a sequel), secondly that she and Remi had by then become close friends and collaborators, and thirdly that he himself was an accomplished musician and also the co-writer of some of her best *Black* songs, among them "Tears Dry on Their Own." In short, they shared their creative space very effectively, as would Remi and Ronson during the album's intense five-month incubation period, even though Winehouse was in London, Remi was in Miami, and Ronson was in New York.

With her label bosses breathing down her nervous neck, and Winehouse herself almost in danger of jeopardizing her career even before it really took off, Remi allowed a shaky post-breakup Amy to visit his home in Miami, where she regained some balance and spent peaceful days writing songs in his tranquil garden—songs he helped her with as musical midwife. She had four or five other raw songs that needed development but not yet the blockbusters that would later emerge from the still smoldering ashes of her extinct love affair. She knew she had to do something brilliant and do it fast.

What she did was meet Ronson. They caught fire famously and clicked enormously together. I believe he saved her life a second time, so it's not like she didn't have several chances. She had to quickly return to England, however, where among other things her beloved paternal grandmother Cynthia passed away in May, after which Amy's true downward spiral sped up considerably.

Despite all the emotion and commotion, three brief months later she was in Metropolis Studios in London, trying to finish what she'd started. *Back to Black* was rapidly birthed and took the world by storm in October. By then, of course, she'd renovated herself musically almost beyond recognition, shifting from jazzy-soul to big-production powerhouse pop and inventing a whole new genre along the way, one that she alone could occupy. Her new genre was called Winehouse, but it was Mark Ronson who helped invent it for her.

■ ■ ■

What we're trying to explore here is her second album's audio perfection, to grasp exactly what made it not just such a blockbuster but also a work of art that's worthy of ongoing appreciation a decade later. And, make no mistake, it will be studied by future music historians, not because of the troubled life it documented but because of the practically magical fusion between its writing, its singing, its recording, and its performance. This is what the art of recorded music can actually sound like on those rare occasions when all the proper ingredients are in position to generate a perfect storm; and, whatever else it may be, *Back to Black* was most certainly a perfect storm.

How to demonstrate that it wasn't blind luck, or a flash in the pan, or just good karma, or merely astute management, but *really* the result of their own superior gifts, their willpower, and their sheer stamina for withstanding the pressure? Only by listening to her sheer artistic audacity. Winehouse was nineteen when she made *Frank* and twenty-two when she made *Back to Black*. Such scintillating talent often arrives early, matures young, and flickers out too soon. In fact, almost all the best singer/songwriters in the modern tradition reached a dizzying peak of talent at around the age of twenty-four, among them Brian Wilson, Scott Walker, Lennon and McCartney, Richards and Jagger, and Simon and Garfunkel, to name but a few. What interests us here and now is not why she made her music but *how* she made it, and surely that story is equally compelling.

But talk about biting the hand that feeds you. Almost immediately upon *Frank*'s release, Winehouse had begun to purge herself of her recent jazzy past and to dive deep, almost with a demonic devotion, into the experiences that she wrote about in her dark 2006 sequel record. Through it all, though, the two men who helped her make that sequel so brilliant always maintained a fierce loyalty, an admiration, and a faith almost bordering on worship for the tremendous talent they saw teetering dangerously on those stiletto heels in front of them.

The insights the *New York Times* critic A. O. Scott offers while trying to explain this kind of precarious genius are most informative here. "The lives of musicians tend to follow a tried and true outline: a rise to fame is followed by a personal and professional crisis, often involving drugs, which is followed by a redemptive third act. What is often missing from the formula is any real insight into the reason why we might be interested in the first place, which is the music." Through the technical virtuosity of her musical alter egos, Remi and Ronson, Winehouse was able to create layers of bewitchment and enchantment in songs which, as Scott so aptly put it, "are at once exquisitely simple and astonishingly sophisticated."

Just as performers often conceal themselves behind their personas, producers often conceal themselves carefully behind the musical artists they produce. Remi and Ronson's personal insights into Winehouse's strange magic are therefore highly instructive. Speaking to Jeff Mao at the Red Bull Academy in 2010, Mark Ronson still sounded stunned by the whole experience: "Amy's voice always brought out the best in me as a producer and arranger. Her vocals and her material gave me license to create a sound that I never would have found without her. The spring day she came to my little studio on Mercer Street in Manhattan changed my life forever and I will probably never again be able to create something as singularly magical as the stuff we made on *Back to Black*."

Ronson has often remarked that there seemed to be an element of destiny involved in their brief collaborative venture together. He felt like the stars aligned and things happened above and beyond their control. For him, a large part of it was the background they both shared, a North London Jewish childhood, and a love for similar musical traditions. He still seems amazed that just by talking about music they literally dreamed up the chords of "Back to Black," and by walking down the street together they accidentally developed the seductive hook for "Rehab." But mostly it was her inspiring and free-spirited soul that seemed to stay with him. "I think to myself that if I can make music and live my life with a shard of the level of honesty and sincerity with which she lived hers, I will be a better man because of it," he told Mao.

■ ■ ■

At first, Winehouse's official website described her high profile debut as a "grand and suitably blunt-speaking breakup record, winning her a battalion of fans around the world, marking her out as one of the most distinctive new voices in pop; confessional, elemental, and with that rarest of combinations: humor and soul." But, as we've seen, she quickly and retroactively declared that she was only 80 percent behind the album in the first place. That was then, this is now.

"I can't even listen to *Frank* any more," she told the *Guardian* in 2004, "in fact I've never been able to. I like playing the tracks live because that's different, but listening to them is another story. Some things on this album make me go to a little place that's fucking bitter. I've not seen anyone from the record company since the album came out. And I know why. They're scared of me and they know I have no respect for them whatsoever."

Winehouse was seldom reluctant to express her low opinion of both the critics who lumped her together with other young retro-jazz peers such as Jamie Cullum and Katie Melua and also the artists themselves. She was often virulently disdainful of her musical peers, especially the many who did not write their own material. And not only did she claim to never to have *heard* the album from start to finish but also to not even own a copy of *Frank*. Her rancor was so deep she wouldn't be able to write another song for over a year and a half. After a little hiatus away from the limelight, nursing her first writer's block in the shadow of her unexpectedly big success and her wounds from the slings and arrows of outrageous fortune, Winehouse would return with a vengeance—quite literally. With a striking new beehive hairdo, a much thinner body, and more tattoos left and right, she was also partnered with a new, young, and gifted white, blue-eyed soul-loving producer and creative collaborator.

As usual, Amy Winehouse was characteristically resistant when her manager and label executive wanted her to go and meet Ronson in New York, possibly because that was her instinctual response to people advising her to do something, anything. She confided to friends that she thought he was a mere sound engineer at first and also, for some odd reason, expected him to be "an old Jewish man with a beard." (Note to reader: some of the greatest record producers on earth are old Jewish men with beards.) Instead, of course, Ronson was not only just a few years older than her but also a visionary producer who would invent her future by embracing the musical past they both loved.

■ ■ ■

There's still some mystery as to Winehouse's whereabouts and activities prior to the creation and release of *Back to Black*. Her own explanation for her mysterious absence was, as usual, fairly simple, blunt, and direct, like most of her intimate and professional declarations: "I started drinking and I fell in love."

In many ways, her new creative material was not exactly new, not just because we have a long and storied history of beautiful female torch songs whose stylistic fingerprints are all over *Back to Black* but also because she herself had already explored the themes of betrayal, infidelity, reunion, and heartache on her bright and shiny debut record. With *Back to Black*, however, she'd be revisiting heartbreak with a striking new image and an innovative style of technical delivery—one that obliterated all traces of the healthy, bouncy jazz girl who had captivated everyone in her debutante mode. Add to that impulsive desire for accelerated personal evolution the new presence of Mark Ronson, shaken not stirred with earlier mentor Salaam Remi and saturated in the early '60s Spector Wall of Sound motifs they both shared a fondness bordering on obsession for, and the chess pieces were quickly set up on a brand new board.

With one queen and two pawns each ready for a winning game of high stakes, the Ronson/Remi team was amply able to guide her dark majesty onward to chart supremacy, industry-award frenzy, and a pop celebrity status not seen in many years. The combination of two producers as gifted as Remi and Ronson to collaborate creatively with each other as well as with her was itself a rare form of synchronicity—a fancy term for the meaningful coincidence that results when two archetypes emerge and encounter each other in an overlapping situation, partially circumstantial and partially destiny. Chance is the fool's name for fate once again, in other words.

Ronson has often expressed how thunderstruck he was when, while visiting from England with her friends, Winehouse came to his studio. As he explained to *Billboard,* they casually hung out and talked about music in a very relaxed way. "She was so magnetic, and just her energy—I just instantly liked her and I wanted to impress her, basically," he said. "I wanted to have a piece of music that would make her be like, wow, I want to work with this guy."

Five months is not a long time to create such a memorable work of art, especially when you consider that someone like Scott Walker (singer of the very Winehouse-like "The Sun Ain't Gonna Shine Anymore" in 1966) takes as long as nine years between one album and another. On the other hand, one of the greatest pop/rock albums of all time, *Highway 61 Revisited* by Bob Dylan, was recorded in barely one week. But in the case of Winehouse, it's especially impressive when you consider the amazing fact that her and Ronson's actual work time in the studio together was shockingly minimal—also barely a week—and that the singer didn't even meet her amazing backup band until *after* the recorded product was finished. Ronson's was clearly the magic guiding hand in creating this amazing pop artifact, though he's always quick to share the glory with his collaborators. "The Dap-Kings are incredible musicians,"

Ronson told *Billboard*, "but Amy had actually never met them . . . because she had to go back to England."

As he explained to the *New Yorker*, his meeting with Winehouse was serendipity in its purest form: Ronson imagined a future hit pop song while hearing his young new friend's complaints about her family and friends wanting to help her. His description of the fateful encounter is further enhanced by his characterization of how speedily and organically their brief creative collaboration would unfold, and why. "No one's ever going to compare to Amy because of the talent she had and the unique bond we had, that rapport, that energy in the studio. For all the stuff I did on *Back to Black*, I think we only spent six days together in the studio. 'Valerie' was done in two hours. Her thing was so effortless . . . well, because she would just . . . it was just what came out—that's it. She would say that's it, that's what came out of me and I'm not changing anything. And every time is was obviously good enough."

Together, this unique talent matchup left us the map of a sparsely populated but huge sonic landscape—one that floats by at a minimalist pace for a mere thirty-five minutes of short, snappy, radio-friendly songs in a package that harks back to the brief length of vinyl albums from the '60s. Even though as an emblematic CD product of the twenty-first century it was possible for an album to run for a duration twice as long in the digital format, the fact that she didn't extend her songs beyond that skeletal ten short tunes makes us realize that she'd said everything she needed to say and saw no plausible reason to fill a larger timespan just because she could.

She was an emotional maximalist in terms of her lyrical delivery and Ronson's lush accompanying orchestrations, but she was all back to basics when it came to what really mattered to her in the end: the accidental crafting of a shining pop artifact in an almost beat Kerouac-like spontaneous manner. In actual fact, *Back to Black* is still pop art of the highest order.

As high art, though, it came about from fairly humble beginnings, as Ronson recognized early on.

"Her first record had come out, and I just remember really liking this one song off it called 'In My Bed,' and being a little bit enamored," he told NPR in 2015. "She's this young Jewish girl from North London—and I'm the same thing, from a Jewish family in North London. She has this incredible voice, so I said, 'Yeah, I'll meet her.' To be honest, it wasn't like I was some big shot; at that point I was meeting with anybody who might want to make music, because you never know where chemistry is going to come, or your break." As usual, the big break came from a big romantic breakup, and from having the blues.

There's a common element here—a haunting quality to all the best pop torch songs—and this core content is a shared sentiment, no matter what style they assume as a disguise. They don't need to be slow soul or blues songs. That's the whole essential point of the torch song in the first place, whether it's delivered by Peggy Lee, Eartha Kitt, Stevie Nicks, or Amy Winehouse: *lover come back, I love you more than you'll ever know, I cried a river over you*. Hers though are especially idiosyncratic insights into the shared human condition, odes of betrayal and abandonment, of loss and the hunger for reconciliation we might all feel sooner or later but which only she can rhapsodize about quite so powerfully.

At the core of the affection we have for these special kinds of sad love songs—and especially for the dark torch songs on *Back to Black*—is the simple fact that they do something no other art form can quite accomplish in as deep or immediate a way. A veteran of the craft, Julie Wilson, who died just last year at the ripe old age of ninety, defined what makes up a great torch song in the most straightforward and succinct manner possible when she quipped, "Truth, and it comes from the heart."

The unvarnished truth: that's what Winehouse gave to us on *Back to Black*. She gave us the truth, or at least her own truth, and man, no matter how bad it was, did it sound good when it was dropped on an unsuspecting listening world on October 27, 2006.

■ ■ ■

The first time the listening audiences of the world perked up to her newly discovered sound was on Mark Ronson's show for EastVillage Radio, an internet station supporting the free radio movement that used to broadcast from a studio storefront in Manhattan. Ronson premiered two new songs from Winehouse's *Frank* follow-up early in May 2006 in the form of demos which certainly must have startled listeners more familiar with her former jazzy dance tunes: "Rehab" and "I Told You I Was Trouble." Gone forever was the cute Amy of their dreams, and here for a short time was the raw Amy of their nightmares.

She didn't hesitate to share with the world that her second album was written in extremis: she had split up with another lover and gone back to "what she knew." In her case, what she knew included playing pool everyday, waking up drinking, listening to the Shangri-Las, and then starting all over again. Her survival mechanism was basically to turn her whole experience into songs, and by doing so she managed to get through it. Barely. And what songs! Upon her return to public life, she was suddenly the reincarnation of Ronnie Spector, she was Shirley Bassey without the Angels, she was all four of the Dixie Cups and all the Shirelles rolled into one skinny, quivering, tattoo-covered dame with acres of talent to burn—and burn it she did.

Considering how original a vocal stylist she was, she was impressively free of the need to appear to be artistically original. As with everything else in her personal life, she was quite forthright about the creative influences in her professional life and openly admitted that she was influenced by all the sounds she listened to, regularly emphasizing how everything from doo-wop to sixties soul, Motown, and girl groups had soaked deeply into her own style. Indeed, she was equally eager to evade the complex jazz idiom for which she first became famous and explore the basic simplicity of pop songs about both finding and losing love.

The results are among the most immediate, direct, raw, and visceral songs ever recorded since the immortal Dinah Washington, Billie Holiday, or Nina Simone. They were also delivered in an effortless nasal Dinah voice, mixed and matched perfectly with the borrowed rhythms from another more innocent age, all mentored and crafted by the dance sparkle of Mark Ronson and the funk depth of Salaam Remi.

While these songs were still consumed by human dynamics in their content, they evidenced a more mature and supportive attitude toward the lost lover (possibly even too supportive) compared with the defiant rage of her first album. Winehouse felt this demonstrated her graduation from teenage relationships to adult ones. She would even go so far as to admit that she was a lot less defensive on *Back to Black* and had tried to think about things before just blurting them out. Her brutal personal honesty still remained, but was now couched in a creative pride over her accomplishments on her second record and a satisfaction in letting that record do the talking for her.

Ronson himself has often expressed his own occasional guilt about listening to such personal and revealing confessions from a newfound friend but only managing to hear what they might be transformed into: pop magic. "We wrote 'Back to Black' and 'Rehab' while we were there in the studio," he told *Spin* magazine. "It just instantly sounded like a hook to me. I remember it so well. She was telling me this really deep story, and I'm kind of like, 'Is it gross? All I can hear is a big pop hook in there." Gross it may have been, but it was also glorious.

Shortly before Amy's demise, Mark Ronson was in New York, conducting press interviews for his album *Record Collection*, but in his exchanges with MTV's James Montgomery in July of 2011, he was unable to avoid commenting as well on his epochal collaboration with Winehouse, and on her much anticipated follow-up record. Like Ronson, many of us also hoped that the thesis of *Frank* merging with the antithesis of *Back to Black* would yield a resolution of sorts, a synthesis that would reconcile her outsized talents with her equally grandiose challenges. "Before [*Back to Black*] came out there was nothing else on the radio that sounded quite like it," he observed, by extension noting the seismic shift that had occurred in pop music in its wake.

Ronson's insights take on an automatically elegiac quality that has never quite gone away, since no matter how dramatic her personal life was, it is her music that will form the basis of any legacy attached to her now household name. "I am really proud of the sound of Amy's record," Ronson commented to Jeff Mao, at a Red Bull Academy event in August 2010. "It kind of influenced things and it became quite regular to hear something that sounded like that. But I don't think there's anything quite as good as it, or as raw as Amy's vocals and her songs." He also focused on her cover version of Lesley Gore's "It's My Party" as a possible shape of things to come on the much anticipated third album. As for his own record—the ostensible reason for a press tour—he usually explained that he would try to place a little distance between it and the raw retro motifs of *Back to Black* in order to continue to carve out a personal space for himself after her meteoric rise to pop stardom. As he humbly told James Montgomery, "Amy's record . . . forced me to change it up."

The accolades for this album were immediate and often identical. Across the board, critics and audiences alike embraced a pop classic that totally stood out from the bland uniformity of the pop music industry at the time. John Lewis in *Time Out* commented that the album was "brilliantly executed by producers Salaam Remi and Mark Ronson, recalling the soul pastiches of labels like Desco and Daptone, but crucially, Amy's lyrics, with a splendid assault on therapy culture, retains the contemporary man-baiting." Another useful comparison was made by the *Sunday Herald*: "Whereas the originals (Motown and the Ronettes) swayed, this one jitters, its urgent drums the perfect backing to the pleading, brash tones of Winehouse, with whom Ronson can seem to do no wrong."

He would never look back. Such is life in the fast lane. The demonic diva had arrived, made her presence felt and now proceeded to take us all on a rough but romantic ride. Mark Ronson was more than happy to go along for that ride, and he quickly saw that his days as a mere DJ were fading fast. Soon enough, he would never have to play records made by other people again. He would be far too busy making them himself.

3

THE ANXIETY OF INFLUENCE

Borrowing a Sound and Creating a Brand

"Remember: always walk in the light.
And if you feel like you're not in it, go find it. Love the light."
—Roberta Flack to William Price King, *Smorgasbord*, May 2, 2015

First of all, a disclaimer. There's nothing at all wrong with borrowing sounds and styles; the best pop artists do it all the time. Elvis Presley borrowed from "Big Mama" Thornton, the Beatles borrowed from Elvis, and everybody borrowed from the Beatles. Anyone who doubts that brilliance at the Beatles' level still borrows would be well advised to listen to a few of their most famous songs *after* listening to the tracks they borrowed from: "Revolution" after Pee Wee Crayton's 1954 "Do Unto Others"; "Come Together" after Chuck Berry's 1956 "You Can't Catch Me"; "I Feel Fine" after Bobby Parker's 1961 "Watch Your Step"; "I Saw Her Standing There" after Chuck Berry's 1961 "I'm Talking About You"; "Lady Madonna" after Humphrey Lyttelton's 1956 "Bad Penny Blues." Not to mention George Harrison's overt "borrowing" of the Chiffons' "He's So Fine" from 1963 for his 1970 solo hit "My Sweet Lord" and that same girl-group smash again inspiring Winehouse's own vibe on her "Some Unholy War."

Readers interested in a true archeology of Amy would also do well to search out the moving music of another young gifted white Jewish female singer from East London named Helen Shapiro. She hit it big only twenty years before Winehouse was born, singing exactly the same kind of sad but beautiful love ballads, tunes such as "Walking Back to Happiness," "Don't

Treat Me Like a Child," and "My Guy." She even had the early Beatles, who wrote a song called "Misery" especially for her, as *her* opening group act back in the day. She also had a spookily similar face and the same hairstyle as our melancholy mistress, once again demonstrating that music history is a prism reflecting many fractured images.

One of the most captivating aspects of the prismatic, multi-angled *Rashomon* effect is the fact that it reminds us that the actual path to exploring something as singular as Winehouse's music is not a straight line at all but a spiral. The spiral path returns over the same ground again but allows us to see and hear it afresh with newly added insights. One of the more compelling perspectives on the Winehouse phenomenon must therefore naturally be that of Sharon Jones, the front-line singer for the band that Ronson employed as his recording session musicians for *Back to Black*. As we now know, back during the Amy Winehouse firestorm she saw borrowing in a whole different light.

T. S. Eliot once said that talent imitates but genius steals. So it was that Remi and Ronson borrowed from Stax Records and Motown, from Phil Spector and the girl groups of the '60s, and from the Daptone records of today. Since Amy never even met her fantastic backup band until after *Back to Black* was already recorded and released, it obviously wasn't Winehouse, the artist as performer, who made the fateful connection to the Dap-Kings but rather Ronson, the producer as artist, who did so. He also forged a fellow producer's creative alliance with Daptone's great founder, Gabriel Roth, which paid huge dividends for all concerned.

In 2015, in a revealing conversation with Hilary Hughes of the *Village Voice*, Ronson made a casual remark that strikes me as totally salient when we try to explore Winehouse's music. "I remember when she called me when she first got the CD booklet with the credits and she said, 'You mean to tell me that the guy that played on my album is named Binky Griptite!?'" It seems inconceivable that she didn't know.

Among the most remarkable aspects of this record—apart from the sultry intensity of her songs, its superb production standards, and the glorious arrangements and instrumentation—is the fact that it's poised in a realm of pure luck, chance, and coincidence in equal measure. Having hinted at Ronson's pilgrimage to Daptone in search of the holy grail he'd been trying to duplicate digitally and instead deciding to invite them to participate in the flesh, it might be worthwhile to pause and recognize the old world ambient domain that Daptone and Sharon Jones had been engineering for over a decade already when he entered their Bushwick New York studio in the spring of 2006.

Jewly Hight captured some of the essence of their collaboration for *SF Weekly* once the Amy hit the fan. "Much has been made of British soul sensation Amy Winehouse employing Sharon Jones's soul-funk band the Dap-Kings to create the sound—and success—of her album *Back to Black*. But *rivalry* is really the wrong word to use for the two singers' relationship. *Ironic* is more like it. It is ironic that Winehouse—a skinny young white girl—inadvertently boosted Jones and the Dap-Kings beyond the modest following of retro soul enthusiasts they'd accumulated. 'It hit the mainstream thanks to Amy and her producer . . . they got the Dap-Kings out there,' Jones says."

Music has always been a strange mixture of art and science in which past traditions and precursors merge with present inheritors sprouting new branches. This has never been made more obvious than in the case of the triumphant creative conversation between Winehouse, Ronson, and Daptone. By borrowing Jones's superb band, Winehouse—or to be more accurate Ronson—created her own fresh new brand based on their already firmly established groove. And of course, by doing so, they also accidentally brought that Dap groove into a huge public spotlight they may never otherwise have entered. Jones and the Dap-Kings know that very well.

James Montgomery noted as much for MTV News in mid-2007 as he was watching the juggernaut start rolling across the globe following the release of *Back to Black*, noting how Jones and Winehouse were so dissimilar that "even the phrase 'tenuous ties' is probably a bit of a stretch" and that Jones was finding the increased exposure "a bit annoying," as she herself explained: "When I was left out of Winehouse's album, I thought, that's okay. But it was good—wasn't weird, it was great. The Dap-Kings were doing some stuff; it's great that there's a demand for them. But I was still thinking, 'Get your own band!' We started something and now there's other people doing it. They get some major people behind it and it's been seen and now people think they started it. Nah, *we* started it."

■ ■ ■

Sharon Jones is far more than a mere footnote in this Winehouse saga; in fact, she's the root of the very fuel she loaned out to the gifted young white upstart soul singer, and she's exactly where that whole Amy legend became solid, like a rock. Jones and the Dap-Kings were tighter than tight; the music they made together was already something like Amy Winehouse in James Brown overdrive.

Born in 1956, when Elvis was channeling Big Mama, she can accurately be described as the quintessential American soul and funk singer and has been a driving force in a lively soul revival with almost religious overtones and fervor, a true believer in the back-to-basics analog movement. In her case, the basics in question are the feeling and spirit of late '60s and mid-'70s soul music, and Jones's is the kind of overnight success that often takes decades to arrive.

The ultimate tough dame in that old-school sense, Jones struggled away on the fringes of the music world until she appeared as a backup singer on a chance 1995 session with Lee Fields organized by the now extinct Pure Records label run by Gabriel Roth (aka Bosco Mann) and Philip Lehman. She was the only one of four backup singers to show up for the recording session that day, so, as fate would have it, she completed all four backup parts by herself, impressing her handlers enough to be asked to record her own solo track, "Switchblade," by herself, as herself. She was instantly recognized as a hot performer in all respects, and her door was opening ever so slightly.

This song, along with another tune called "The Landlord," was featured on the Soul Providers' 1996 album *Soul Tequila*. Chance is the fool's name for fate, yet again. The Soul Providers would go on to form the bare bones of the Dap-Kings, the band she still fronts fabulously to this day, after she released several singles for another extinct label called Desco Records. "Soul Tequila" was re-released with the eminently Brown-like title "Gimme the Paw," along with some other gritty funk tunes like "I Got a Feeling," an actual J.B. song that she takes to pieces and puts back together again as only she can.

After releasing a string of other fine singles and a couple of albums, the Desco founders had the inevitable difference of creative and business opinion leading to the dissolution of their company, with Gabriel Roth going on to start up Daptone Records in 2000. He then partnered with the more personally compatible Neil Sugarman, lead saxophonist for the Sugarman 3 band, thus insuring the heavy horn bottom for all future records. Using the valuable experience of Desco as fertilizer, they grew Daptone Records into a going concern, with their first release being a full-length Sharon Jones album, now featuring her new backup band, one of the best in the business, the Dap-Kings.

The Dap-Kings were themselves the proverbial phoenix that rose out of the smoldering ashes of Desco Records, with remnants subsequently combining the fragments of the original Soul Providers group with the broken pieces of yet another defunct Desco label survivor, the Mighty Imperials. Once these particular pieces of the puzzle were in place, suddenly the pedal hit the floor and the Dap-Kings hit their stride. They weren't retro, they were revival, and time was on their side, because eventually the industry itself would inadvertently create an artistic and audience appetite for something more gritty, real, earthy, crackling, and human: the glory that was analog. Nostalgia just isn't what it used to be. Maybe it never was.

From the original Soul Providers came Roth as producer/arranger on bass, guitarist Binky Griptite, percussionist Fernando Velez, trumpet player Anda Szilagyi, and organist Earl Maxton; from the original Mighty Imperials came Leon Michels on saxophone, drummer Homer Steinweiss, and finally, added in for a double dose of steaming horns, Roth's close cohort Neil Sugarman. Suddenly we had the band that would become a huge part of the genuine roots feel and the essentially borrowed dark guts, grit, and soul glory for the skinny white girl from north London and her second album.

In 2002, the freshly minted Dap-Kings released their debut album, *Dap Dippin' with Sharon Jones and the Dap-Kings*, one year before three of their majesties, Griptite, Steinweiss, and Sugarman, would lift up Winehouse's *Frank* into a new groove that was then only gestating in her dark ether. Jones and the Kings garnered some much needed and well deserved attention for this initial salvo, which they followed with another bombshell, *Naturally*, in 2005, a year before the *Back to Black* juggernaut started to roll across the planet.

In 2003, while Amy was dropping *Frank*, Daptone Records had planned a double record release for Jones and the Dap-Kings but personal difficulties with Gabriel Roth caused them to delay and streamline the release process and concentrate on a single album instead. Awaiting the arrival of the demonic diva, on *Naturally* they checked into a permanent groove of their own and really got down to some seriously fine musical business, broadening styles and mixing genres a little more than they had with their first effort.

Roth's subsequent observations to *Tape Op* magazine capture some of the essence of just how rootsy they were hoping to be: "Somewhere between banging on logs and the invention of MIDI technology, we [the music industry] have made a terribly wrong turn. We must have ridden right past our stop. We should have stepped down off the train at that moment when rhythm and harmony and technology all culminated in a single Otis Redding whine. That moment of the truest, most genuine expression of what it means to be human." In other words, we shouldn't be relying so much on digital mastery and machine magic; instead, we should all be musically focused more on our insides.

Sharon Jones and the Dap-Kings went on the international road to perform *Naturally*; almost immediately after their relative success the band started to splinter apart, and fragments of it resurfaced in new but self-serving incarnations. Leon Michels would depart to form Truth and Soul Records, bringing with him an album, *Sounding Out the City*, originally slated for release by Daptone. Meanwhile, Phil Lehman closed down the Soul Fire brand and retired to the Bahamas, having apparently had enough of the music business entirely. The Soul Fire back catalogue would be absorbed by Truth and Soul, which would utilize many of the former's stalwarts, such as Fields, Steinweiss, and Brenneck, while Michels would be replaced in the Dap-Kings by the superfine sax player Ian Hendrickson-Smith.

At this stage in late 2005 and early 2006, the Dap-Kings would also find a drastically new role as freelance professional session musicians. It was this platform that would bring them to the attention of a global public when they were hired by, among others, a young Mark Ronson for a number of his evolving projects.

The creative powerhouse known as the Dap-Kings had done for Sharon Jones, and would soon do for Amy Winehouse, what the Wrecking Crew had done for so many other historically important artists: give them the utterly distinctive rhythmic flavor and sonic spirit without which we wouldn't be talking about them in quite the same hushed reverential tones.

■ ■ ■

Many music lovers still feel that this band's crucial creative role was drastically unrecognized, underappreciated, and under-acknowledged when the final product emerged into the glare of the planet's musical industry. Indeed, as with her other stylistic inheritance from the '60s girl groups, Amy Winehouse cashed the IOU check the Dap-Kings wrote way back when.

The Dap-Kings would also become the quintessential backing band for Winehouse's first US tour and later her global concerts in support of *Back to Black*. Audiences who saw them, or viewers who watched the songs' videos, can certainly attest to their astonishing prowess at elevating the artist in the front spotlight while laying down the actual musical ground on which the performer was standing (or more frequently shaking, in Jones's case). Especially in their unexcelled use of horns and percussion, the Kings often put me in mind of another of the great soul-funk backing bands, the J.B.'s, possibly the greatest supporting musicians in the soul genre, as they furiously cooked up the fierce stew that boiled around the majestic James Brown at his most frenzied peak in the mid-'60s.

Concurrent with their now famous studio session work, in late 2006 the Dap-Kings also released another breathtaking album with Jones, *100 Days, 100 Nights,* which should almost be listened to before and after any playing of *Back to Black* in order to firmly establish the crucial role played by this scintillating band and the soul-queen legacy of Sharon Jones. They were pivotal in the gorgeous genre mutation achieved by Ronson, Remi, Roth, and Winehouse (a great name for a new legal firm in heaven). Mutation, by the way, is not meant as a negative criticism; on the contrary, it's the way all artistic evolution actually occurs; in the end, all music history is just a genealogy of influences.

A still lively sixty years of age today, Sharon Jones is on record as having expressed a little bit of natural bitterness as she was forced to watch the incredible rise and incendiary fall of the skinny white British girl who so supersonically grabbed the Grammys and then ran aground, all while Jones herself plugged away the old-school way for decades to get where she was. But where was she?

Jones was perhaps understandably blunt when Ben Sisario brought up the subject of Winehouse when he interviewed Jones for a 2007 *New York Times* profile, which he introduced by reminding his readers there was "an elephant in the room . . . a skinny, British elephant with an enormous beehive hairdo and a knack for getting her picture in the tabloids."

"Oh, what's-her-name," Sharon Jones in response. This was clearly a dame with both anger and style in big doses.

Sisario went on to perfectly characterize the creative-dilemma at play here, describing Daptone Records as an underground label so devoted to its pursuit of verisimilitude in '60s-style soul and funk that it built a studio of vintage equipment and released far more vinyl 45s than CDs. In other words, old school writ large. At the time of his *New York Times* article, Jones was preparing for the release of *her own* old-school masterpiece, while also getting ready to appear at the Apollo Theatre, the mecca of funk and soul music in America.

She mused openly on Daptone's ambivalence about the mixed blessing the Winehouse association was proving to be. The true irony of her situation was that now that Amy was so big, audiences that were not aware of her own years of hard work with the Dap-Kings may come to the erroneous conclusion that *they* were jumping on *Amy's* bandwagon, when in reality, and historically, it was *their* bandwagon all along. It was just that Winehouse was now driving it with considerable determination toward her own rightfully deserved fistful of Grammys the following year.

"They jumped on *us*!" Jones declared, in a voice that echoed through the converted row house with microphones in the bathroom and reels of audiotape (remember those?) filling the kitchen cupboards in Daptone's decidedly old-fashioned digs. Tongue plunged firmly into cheek, she described Ronson—"what's-his-name"—coming to *them* "to get the sound they wanted . . . we were just sitting here minding our own business, doing our little 45s and albums, and all of a sudden they were, like, 'I want your sound.'" They got it, they took it, they ran with it. Though to be fair, they did also produce a new kind of pop classic from of it.

Unlike Winehouse, who was clearly a gifted retro-artist, the Dap-Kings were strictly an authentic revivalist band. As such, while they were obviously thrilled with the massive and welcome attention to their longtime mission, they were also a little puzzled by their new high-profile role as ironic competitors with a hugely famous young singer who had been lucky enough to borrow their sound.

At first, Jones has admitted, she was somewhat angry about it all, but she has also acknowledged that if it took Winehouse to get the Dap-Kings heard by a wider audience, then it was a good thing. "I say, it's great," she concluded. "Thank you." This is what used to be called being a gracious and generous professional. As Sisario also observed, the eight-piece Dap-

Kings had honed their delivery technique and considerable stage presence over many, many years of club gigs as well as on their intense records. On record and live onstage they carefully and with consummate craftsmanship revived and recreated that sweaty '60s Stax Records spirit of the hardest-working man in show business.

So, it's plain to see and hear that *Back to Black* was by no means a virgin birth. For Winehouse and Ronson, the Arthurian sword pulled from the stone moment was his chance hearing of a Sharon Jones song and his encounter with the analog grail of tape to tape. Together, their Camelot would be in Bushwick, New York, where he accidentally discovered both the history of tape and Amy's future history at the same time. He readily surrendered to that old-new sound when he first brought her roughly demoed songs to the Dap-Kings in their studio. "It just sounded a million times better," he told *Paste*'s Bud Scoppa.

In an almost uncanny manner, the Dap-Kings would become an integral part of the exceptional example of musical ventriloquism achieved by *Back to Black*. Meanwhile, Daptone's regal Roth would also coolly comment to Saki Knafo, author of a 2008 *New York Times* profile entitled "Soul Reviver," that the Winehouse project was just something they spent a few afternoons knocking out very quickly so they could pay some old-school bills in the real world they still inhabited. He has called it a good honest piece of work, but also qualified the stint by explaining that "their own Dap-Kings music" was something they had been developing as a family for a dozen years and was the hard-won result of "dedicated work, love, and shared creativity."

A good example of this communal and authentic old-fashioned approach to the music business is the fact that the aforementioned Sharon Jones and the Dap-Kings' album dropped into the dizzying Winehouse whirl of 2007, *100 Days,*

100 Nights, would have no remixes, no overdubs, no digital dazzle, not even one single selected to be played on pop radio. It was sheer guerilla warfare—a kind of insurgency against the still-rising tide of technologically manufactured music. "In almost every way," Sisario had pointed out, "It could have been made in 1966."

The Dap-Kings then followed up their own time-tested way after the perfect Amy storm had subsided with the possibly ironically titled *I Learned the Hard Way* (2010) and *Give the People What they Want* (2014), with which their long-awaited Grammy nod finally arrived. Listening to these albums is a vital living history lesson for anyone who loves the intensity of Winehouse's music.

■ ■ ■

Often, the term "old school" is misused and confused with mere stylistic nostalgia. It's not, however, just a question of how music like the Dap-Kings is technically produced or even how the soul presence of Sharon Jones inspired the later iterations of artists such as Amy Winehouse. It's actually more a question of motivation and intention at the outset. The old-school approach was embedded in making music first and foremost; music that communicated whatever was stirring in the hearts of musicians, rather than the desire to make hit records. If their records were popular, that was just a bonus, not a target.

As we'll see, Mark Ronson was captivated by the pop hooks in Winehouse's music, especially when he felt it viscerally grab him in the song "Rehab," which both he and the label executives instantly knew would be a huge hit single. They quite rightly saw the potential for that song and the album's title track to catapult the young singer into the realms of pop superstardom. There's nothing at all wrong with that reality, especially when the music machine encounters someone as special as their gifted but volatile protégé, as long as we're all living in a world of sales figures qualifying excellence and not in some distant utopia. Occasionally, though, a producer does stumble upon a singer whose gifts could realistically be described as utopian. This was just such a scenario.

For readers interested in some in-depth examination of what Joni Mitchell famously called "stoking the star-maker machinery behind the popular song," I can heartily recommend the works of Simon Frith, former rock critic and current cultural scholar. While slightly academic in tone, his several fine books explore the spooky parallels between the music business operating model and the mass production of the food industry, with especially insightful glimpses into the making of modern pop mythologies and the manufacturing of icons and idols. While it's hard for the rest of us to think of Amy Winehouse as a muffin on a baking tray, that tends to be exactly how she and other artists are perceived by their corporate zookeepers: as exotic pets and living investments.

As early as 1978, Frith was offering prescient analysis of the music industry in *The Sociology of Rock*, a theme he developed in three works published in 1987, *Music for Pleasure: Essays on the Sociology of Pop*, *Towards an Aesthetics of Popular Music*, and *The Industrialization of Popular Music*, and especially in 2007's *Taking Popular Music Seriously*. All provide highly entertaining if slightly scary revelations.

Ironically, Winehouse's British singer/songwriter peer and fellow *Bedlam* explorer, James Blunt, wrote his actual undergraduate thesis, *The Commodification of Image: The Production of a Pop Idol*, under the intellectual influence of Frith. But Winehouse's own undergraduate thesis of course would be on the Ronettes and the Shangri-Las, presented in the form of *Back to Black*.

You really don't have to be an academic to see where Frith's going (I'm certainly not one myself), and any astute reader will glean great insights into the industry pressures placed upon creative artists such as Winehouse by their business handlers and corporate masters. As the gatekeepers in between them and us, and between the music as cultural artifact and commercial product, they remind us that whether we like it or not, records are both at once.

Such an attitude offers a snapshot of precisely the vagaries and dangers that beset figures like Winehouse and other musicians who suddenly become the next big thing seemingly overnight, as opposed to the old-school Sharon Jones overnight sensation method, which took thirty years to happen.

Talented singer/songwriters such as Winehouse can often become mere grist for the mill of that star-maker machinery, even if it does reward them with a platinum plate of golden cookies with their names engraved on it.

■ ■ ■

Recycling great form and content in music is no more dishonorable than doing the same thing in painting, literature, or architecture; in fact, it's almost identical to the way great themes are regularly reexamined in every single other form of cultural expression.

In 2015, *Billboard*'s Elias Leight quite rightly pointed out that America had long been in the habit, especially during the first decade of the twenty-first century, of re-importing retro-style soul music from England, mostly since the advent of young Winehouse herself in 2003 and the legacy she left behind. This of course comes long after England first imported the foundational African American R&B/rock stylings from America in the '50s, with the pendulum swinging wildly back and forth ever since.

When we think of Amy Winehouse, Duffy, Adele, or even Sam Smith (of whom I personally try not to think at all), Leight observed, we're witnessing the phenomenon of a gigantic bonanza of success at *repackaging* musical motifs from the late '60s and early '70s, that historic period when Motown and Stax Records were the sole kings of the soul mountain. It's always been give-and-take on a grand cultural scale, with great gifts accruing on both sides of the Atlantic.

Leight also asked the obvious question quite forcefully in his piece: "Why doesn't America fully embrace its *own* soul singers first and foremost?" If you liked Adele's "Rumor Has It" or Winehouse's "You Know I'm No Good," you'd probably find plenty to enjoy about both the Daptone Record label in general, and especially Sharon Jones and the Dap-Kings' records in particular.

In January 2015, *Billboard* exclusively premiered a new song by this sparkling and gifted group who, he lamented, never get played on the radio and hardly ever receive the same frothy praise as that heaped on their young British reincarnations. Is it just a youth fetish, he wondered? With that new song, "Little Boys with Shiny Toys," Jones and the Kings delivered, as they always do, what Leight accurately identified as their key ingredients: "A balance of force and precision, featuring powerful vocals from Jones, a crisp beat, and a driving horn section." In other words, Winehouse music without either Amy or what Roth referred to as her angsty self-involvement; just perfectly polished contemporary soul music.

When Jones and her erstwhile band finally earned their first R&B Grammy nomination for *Give the People What They Want*—something they've been doing now for twenty years—Jones was as humble and gracious (and sarcastic) as ever, having seemingly long since given up on the wild idea of ever being fully recognized for who and what they are. "The guys were pushing to see if we got nominated [over the years] and this year it was like, 'Eh, who cares?' And then we got it. My manager didn't even know about it." Sharon Jones, giving waxing philosophical a whole new meaning.

Naturally, as a longtime lover of Jones and company, I concur totally with Leight's diagnosis for some of their former malaise: the stinging fact that such faithful and talented representations of vintage soul and funk were suddenly in high demand. "It's tough sitting year by year and watching other people get praised for the style that the Dap-Kings have been employing for so long," he wrote—especially, I would add, when it's in the original, down and dirty, gritty, analog-grooved, tape-inspired, non-computer, and anti-auto-tuned delivery format they have so long championed. It's always come, in the words of Little Richard, directly from their hearts to you.

"But the Dap-Kings didn't get the bump they hoped for from that collaboration [with Ronson and Winehouse]," Leight observed.

"We're just getting acknowledged in 2015," Jones noted, "and we've been out here since 1995." Had Daptone known what was about to happen with Amy Winehouse and *Back to Black*, she added, "they did they would have handled the business a little differently."

Yes, Daptone creator Gabriel Roth did win a Grammy Award as recording engineer on *Back to Black*, but he has yet to be awarded one for his overall production work for the label he helped start. For Sharon Jones, the reasons she and the Dap-Kings have been ignored are legion, but one of the key factors among them is apparently categorical. "Even right now, we're nominated for R&B!" she complained to *Billboard*. "Why is there no category for soul? That's my goal. Put me in the *right* category!" Amen. "There are no soul singers out there right now—or there are singers, but they're not being recognized. And if *we* are gonna bring people to realize what's out there, then we're making history." Hope springs eternal in the heart of Jones.

For Amy Winehouse, the four-letter synonym for love was

pain, whereas for Sharon Jones, the four-letter word is hope. In 2015, Sharon Jones and the Dap-Kings were back on the road as usual. The *New York Times* called them a spectacle to rival James Brown when they appeared at the Performing Arts Centre and crowned them the finest soul-funk revivalists in town (I would say in the world). Stacey Anderson pointed out that after undergoing treatment for pancreatic cancer, Ms. Jones has resumed blazing her way across stages to promote the group's recent album, *Holiday Soul Party*, which invokes both the Ronettes and Tina Turner in a supremely swinging way.

Another positive contribution to the Sharon Jones narrative, and to the celebrity-rehab of her band, was the release last year of a fine documentary film on her work with the Dap-Kings over the years. The film chronicles her health struggles, her successful treatment, the career challenges she and her amazing band have faced, and the triumphant release of their Grammy-nominated album. They're finally being recognized as themselves alone, and especially for giving the people what they want for so many soulful years.

As one viewer shared with me, instead of being all about the angst, like Asif Kapadia's Oscar-winning film *Amy*, this one is all about the music. When you see *Miss Sharon Jones!*, which was directed by another Academy Award–winning documentary filmmaker, Barbara Kopple, you'll understand why so many of us are saying: we want more Sharon Jones.

I was pleasantly surprised when Kapadia's creatively innovative, narration-less film won the Academy Award for best documentary, as I was half expecting the doc about one of Winehouse's heroines, Nina Simone, to win in that category. But even though I feel it focuses more on her personal troubles than on her music, it is still a well made, honest, respectful, and deeply moving chronicle. It tells her personal story the same way her songs tell her musical stories, and it does what every great documentary should do: it demonstrates how and why the artist resonated so powerfully with her audience. It's a film that reminds us of the dizzying heights and the dark depths to which emotionally inspiring soul music can rise and fall.

4

THE AURA AND ITS ECHO

Recreating the Wall of Sound

"When I hear applause onstage, it's like I'm having an orgasm."
—Ronnie Spector to Caroline Sullivan, the *Guardian*, 2014

While Amy Winehouse was always talented enough in her own right to be considered a true original, knowing the origins of her style still helps us get a more accurate picture of her allure. She was practically a do-it-yourself assembly kit of musical archetypes. She was clearly just the latest and most dynamic incarnation in a long line of female singer/songwriters who lived large and plucked on our heartstrings while doing so.

Cultural critic James Adams once pointed out that when it comes to artistic activities, origin stories, whether they're humble or mythic in stature, are usually fuzzy in the details. In fact, they often happen the same way weeds sprout. This is doubly true in the case of Winehouse's rapid climb to the top of pop's Olympus. No matter what percentage of her delivery and acclaim were due to a combination of chutzpah and hubris, they were still both contingent upon her amazing ability to emulate the soul power of girl groups active twenty years before she was born.

Barbara O'Dair, editor of *Trouble Girls* and another avid listener to and critic of the feminist rock-pop sensibility, writes of how her own musical growing-up was characterized by the cult-like group of damsels who were not in distress but could always cause it. These were the bold women who also cleared the path for Winehouse to creatively fuse literally everyone who preceded her into one shimmering pop package: Patti Smith, Lucinda Williams, Kim Gordon, Liz Phair, Sam Phillips, Debbie Harry, Joni Mitchell, Marianne Faithfull, Veruca Salt, Aimee Mann, Ani DiFranco, Chrissie Hynde, Joan Osborne, Sheryl Crow, and, of course, the mistress of gender mayhem herself, Madonna Ciccone. This diverse group of female artists is bracketed at either end by Courtney Love and Alanis Morissette, "each with her own ferocious take on female rage in the service of art and commerce, and each with her own perspective on success and stardom."

As O'Dair observes so accurately, ever since Elvis Presley pop music has been as much about style and attitude as it has been about music. The surge in "trouble girls" has continued to garner them more attention for varied reasons, some more valid than others, although as O'Dair notes, the current trends in gender-bending, troublemaking singer/songwriters are by no means a new thing at all. Amy, though, was a wild renaissance unto herself, and she seems to have been in a league of her own.

"The recent surge notwithstanding," O'Dair writes, "women have been engaged in making this history all along, ever since a woman laid down the tracks of the very first blues recording, Mamie Smith, 'Crazy Blues,' in 1920. And their stories, their lives and career paths, their work, often parallel larger social shifts and cultural movements. Their contributions have intersected with the culture in powerful ways, juxtaposing, refracting, or even representing a delayed reaction to changes in it."

If it's true, as O'Dair astutely puts it, that Courtney Love may be the logical by-product of what happens "when the myths of Madonna climax with the cult of Patti Smith," could it be equally true that Amy Winehouse was the logical conclusion of a three-way love affair between Anita O'Day, Ronnie Spector, and Sharon Jones? I'd like to think so. Just because it feels so damn right, and it's so easy to prove the creative and emotive provenance operating in the birth of *Back to Black*.

One of the best books to use as a resource for readers wanting to get an accurate creative snapshot of the musical world that welcomed Winehouse with open arms is *She Bop: The Definitive History of Women in Rock, Pop, and Soul* by Lucy O'Brien. It helps to contextualize a post-Madonna music industry willing to celebrate a female singer/songwriter who not only told us she was trouble but even openly declared that she had cheated herself (just as she knew she would).

In her excellent book, O'Brien, a journalist at the *New Musical Express* in the '80s, gives more coverage to the distaff side and is very good at exploring trends, themes, and genres. She helps to explain how the audience was just waiting for someone like Winehouse to walk in and capitalize on the five decades of hard work that had preceded her sudden rise and fall. Her forebears had negotiated their places in the music industry to such a degree that she was able to fully inherit all of their capital, and to successfully improvise on each of their testaments.

The question O'Brien asked in her interviews seems deceptively simple but is profoundly revealing: how do you express yourself? "From the sassiest soul singer to the most hardcore rocker," she writes, "all would blink, take a pause, and think. Some cried. And I realized how much women have been written about in terms of what Penelope Spheeris has dubbed 'The Marilyn Monroe Damage'—that is, primarily as men-pleasing angels, or as victims of problem personalities—rather than in terms of their actual body of work."

Of course, the original hybrid of cult and pop was the woman O'Brien baptized "the mother of lullaby," Billie Holiday, whose style is so saturated underneath the borrowed girl-group template in Winehouse that it forms a kind of basement foundation. But other bad girls after Lady Day had also poisoned the popular song in similar ways. The karma of the great '60s girl groups—especially the primal vibe of the Ronettes and Ronnie Spector's style, sensibility, and fashion influence—literally saturates *Back to Black* and soaks right through to the bones of the record, as does master-producer Phil Spector's haunting and haunted technical sonic influence on Mark Ronson and his own personal Lady Night.

■ ■ ■

As I've suggested, there are actually acres of historic fingerprints all over *Back to Black*, so she didn't do it entirely alone, and she obviously wasn't some exotic creature born from the head of the goddess Venus. As we will see, her brilliant producers, Salaam Remi and Mark Ronson, were channeling Barry Gordy Jr. and Phil Spector, respectively—something they're both smart enough to readily acknowledge. But it's now useful to consider Anita O'Day, Ronnie Spector, and especially the Shangri-Las as the prime nourishers of Winehouse's musical attitude and image.

O'Day and Spector were also hard-livers who produced some of the most gorgeous grief sounds the human ear has ever heard. Like Winehouse, they were geniuses in spite of themselves, or perhaps even *to* spite themselves, and their slippery vocal style gave Amy further permission, if indeed she needed any more than she already gave herself, to let her languid voice pour out instead of pushing it out like so many less gifted vocalists do.

Winehouse magnificently transformed and transcended the whole heavenly court of female torch singers that preceded her. This mediating continuum is in no way meant to diminish the considerable gifts of the young white female soul singer from north London. Quite the contrary: my view is that her amazing skills are all the more magical and hence even more mythical from the retrospective vantage point of the swift decade since her record. Her deceptively easygoing skills are therefore now even more worthy of the word "legacy."

In the case of the Winehouse continuum—and apart from her obvious vocal and stylistic similarities between Billie Holiday, Dinah Washington, and Nina Simone—the legacy link starts with Josephine Baker and Edith Piaf, passes through Anita O'Day and Ronnie Spector, courses into Etta James and Gladys Knight, folds in Dionne Warwick and Diana Ross, and charges ahead with Minnie Riperton and Tina Turner. The historical arc moves into Carole King and Roberta Flack, then picks up steam with Laura Nyro and plunges headlong into Madonna Ciccone, and even the far less talented Mariah Carey and Whitney Houston are part its torchy lava flow. Eventually the Amy arc achieves a kind of crescendo, a musical flood of sorts, as it then absorbs Aretha Franklin and Sharon Jones along the way before crashing into the skinny open arms of Amy Winehouse. From her very beginnings she was a genuine lover of the entire shared historical vibe she inherited.

You can easily see and hear how we get from Josephine Baker to Amy Winehouse in what feels like the blink of an eye, or in this case an ear. One can only imagine how the next great singer/songwriter in this vein will feel, sound, and look in performance once we get up even higher into the musical Fibonacci sequence, up there among the yet-to-be-born Amy inheritors. The mind reels. But the map of her music is easy to read for the history buffs among us.

As Winehouse was returning to the circus of recording and performing in 2006—quite a few pounds lighter and wearing her new persona, teetering in her figure-hugging mini and tottering under her architecturally splendid beehive hairdo and Kohl's-black Cleopatra makeup—the listening audience was suddenly also a rapt viewing audience, eyes agog at her haunting likeness to the great Ronnie Spector. Now she really *was* a psychic medium, for real.

The aura and style shadow was so pronounced that New York's *Village Voice* reported at the time, "Ronnie Spector, who it could be argued, all but invented Winehouse's style in the first place when she took to the stage with her fellow Ronettes at the Brooklyn Fox Theatre more than forty years ago—was so taken aback at a picture of Winehouse in the *New York Post* that she exclaimed, 'I don't know her, I've never met her, and when I looked at that picture I thought, that's me! But then I found out, no it's Amy! I didn't have my glasses on.'" In some strange magical way, it wasn't her, and yet it really *was* her.

Ronnie Spector has since recorded *Back to Black*'s title song herself in what must be considered one of the most endearing examples of reverse homage in music history, and she delivered it with the same Ronnie verve that inspired Amy in the first place during her pre-*Black* research vacation. Fortunately, Winehouse was there to see this song performed live by one of her musical idols, and the result was a great deal of tear-stained mascara all around, to be sure. For Winehouse, this was too good to be true.

Almost immediately, two things were instantly apparent upon the return of the renovated Amy: her music had undergone a radical transformation, and her personal life was being used even more deeply as the raw material and creative impetus for her songwriting. At the time, she expressed it to the *Daily Telegraph* this way: "I've taken pains to ensure I write of my time and that I write representing myself and people who are like me. It sounds such a wank thing to say, but I need to get some headaches going to write about them." Naturally it wouldn't take very long to develop them.

Winehouse's research for her new album would take place in the gloomy but familiar reverie of love lost yet again, guided by an overflowing vintage jukebox crammed with rock, punk, soul, and blues, but also studded with gems from the Motown and New York Brill Building academies and with inspiring lectures by Emotion Specialists from the '50s and '60s, among them the renowned professor of lofty pain, Carole King.

She would study the creative curriculum established by those shimmering all-girl groups such as the Angels, the Crystals, the Shirelles, the Dixie-Cups, the Chiffons, the Supremes, the Shangri-Las, and the leaders of the pack, Phil Spector's Ronettes. Fronted by the incendiary young singer who would eventually herself become known as the original bad-girl of pop music, Ronnie Spector, they especially hit home with the forlorn young singer. As Winehouse succinctly explained to the *Times* later on, "I like old sixties heartbreak songs, girl group comfort music, songs you can sing into a bottle of whisky." These were the aura echoes that consoled her and inspired her to write again.

Winehouse stretched back into the classical world of pop music to breathe dynamic new life into her own next creative direction. For her, that classical period was the late 1950s throughout the 1960s and on into the early 1970s; its primary god was Phil Spector, and its goddesses were the all-girl groups living high up on the Mount Olympus of his brilliant and innovative Wall of Sound production technique. Its principle motif was the heartbreaking torch song Winehouse would now stylistically embrace to perfection.

Oddly enough, the *Back to Black* album is almost as much about Phil Spector, his brilliant wife and victim Ronnie, and his blistering Wall of Sound production technique as it is about Amy Winehouse. This is especially so because it was largely Mark Ronson who gave the album its signature sound. She was spiritually inspired by the bright and shiny sad songs Spector wrote and produced and was emotionally moved by the fashion style and sheer *oomph* of Ronnie and the Ronettes. Ronson was just as moved by the technical analog virtuosity of Spector's musical and recording skills, and he strategically applied them to her new album like a virtuoso surgeon.

In his excellent study of Spector and his historic influence, *He's a Rebel: Rock and Roll's Legendary Producer,* Mark Ribowsky opens his own examination of the producer as artist with a single salient fact: "Phil Spector, a little man with a Napoleon complex, faced his Waterloo in early 1966." By then, Spector had all but played out his welcome on the world music stage and needed to craft a new masterwork to stem the rising tide of changes in musical taste swirling around him. His history was already something for which he was rightly considered a musical deity, so much so that almost fifty years later he would encourage Amy Winehouse and Mark Ronson to religiously move into the sonic-church that Phil built.

Phil Spector's contribution to the future of music was his gifted use of pop arrangements clearly designed for white audiences and sung by voices who were in some cases blacker in tone that even Motown could muster, and of well-tempered jazz musicians as his pop posse, most notably the famous Wrecking Crew session players I've alluded to already, such as Hal Blaine and Carol Kaye. He then processed it all through a cataclysm of overwhelming audio affect that could paralyze the mind while freeing the heart.

The key female *dramatis persona* in these miniature Mozartian teen symphonies was Ronnie Spector, whose passionate paeans to pained love would elevate Amy and levitate the very jukebox pub in which Winehouse was lingering in 2005 while wondering what to do with both her personal and musical life and also how to cope with her huge newfound fame. As we now know, she decided to convert to the church of Spector and the Ronettes.

Ribowsky has more than adequately characterized the magic of the sound Spector invented—a sound so powerful and seductive that it would still haunt producers for the next half-century, especially the one that Amy was then woozily leaning on. "Phil Spector did overdub background vocals on his records to create a swirl of voices that aped his instrumental tracks," he writes, "but his love was *live* music, a rhythm section blaring and wailing its brains out the way great jazz combos did."

At Gold Star Sound Studios in Hollywood, a titanic rhythm section of the kind Spector had become famous for—four guitars, three basses, three pianos, two drums, and a small army of percussion—became one as only it could in a live, massed monolith. The room, Gold Star's Studio A, was saturated with sine waves; they bounced off the walls and the low celling and came tumbling out of two echo chambers before bing sucked into a tape machine.

When mixed down, the sound was not of this earth, without melody as we know it. It was a mood, a feel, aural poetry, and sheer rock-and-roll heaven. Even the ludicrous teenage themes of Spector's early records sound like the "Ride of the Valkyries" elevated to Valhalla by the tide of inspired commotion that was the Wall of Sound, or, as Spector himself would have preferred, "a Wagnerian approach to rock and roll, little symphonies for kids." This was a nearly ideal description of what would later become *Back to Black*.

Phil Spector had been born in the big band era of 1940 and by twenty-five had already changed the face of popular music forever with a stream of hits that topped the charts twenty-seven times from 1961 to 1965. He literally churned out hits such as the Ronettes' "Be My Baby," "Walking in the Rain," and "Baby I Love You"; Darlene Love's "Today I Met the Boy I'm Going to Marry"; Bob. B. Soxx and the Blue Jeans' "Zip-a-Dee-Doo-Dah" and "Not Too Young to Get Married"; the Crystals' "Da Doo Ron Ron," "Then He Kissed Me," and "He's a Rebel"; and, most tellingly for Amy, perhaps, the Righteous Brothers' "You've Lost That Lovin' Feelin'." That last one may have been her personal epiphany.

Perhaps most impressive was Spector's own debut song, which he wrote, produced, and co-sang at the tender age of sixteen, "To Know Him Is to Love Him." Equally revealing are the lyrics to "He's a Rebel," the song used as the title of Ribowsky's warts-and-all biography and the tune that could have totally summed up Winehouse's own misguided affections when she searched for, found, and lost the nameless shadow lover she would write about in *Back to Black*.

"Spector was a visionary, not a revolutionary," Ribowsky clarifies, "He didn't change the system, he used it. Entering a world in which a rock-and-roll recording session meant a small band—guitar, piano, bass, drum—playing simple-minded arrangements, Spector didn't invent a new rock and roll, he simply multiplied the old, using the same simple arrangements but with more and more instruments." This was, remember, in the relatively primitive days long before today's sampling and digital layering. "The Wall of Sound is often thought of as the height of sophistication, and in a way it is, as an example of a technology that engendered a new sound. It was crazy for Spector to cram two dozen instruments into his studio but in his hands the aural effect was a tool of purpose."

In Tom Wolfe's famous *New York Herald Tribune* profile, "The First Tycoon of Teen," in 1965 during a period just then undergoing the seismic musical shifts of the Beatles' *Rubber Soul*, Spector was already having to defend his deceptively simple song-writing approach to operating as the American Mozart. "I get a little angry when people say it's bad music. This music has a kind of spontaneity that doesn't exist in any other kind of music, and it's what is here now. It's unfair to classify it as rock and roll and condemn it. It has limited chord changes and people are always saying the lyrics are banal and why doesn't anybody write lyrics like Cole Porter anymore, but we don't have any presidents like Lincoln anymore either. You know? It's very today. Actually it's more like the blues. It's pop blues." Pop blues would also become perhaps the best term ever to describe *Back to Black*.

■ ■ ■

Few people were able to manufacture hit records quite the way Phil Spector was, and to say he had his finger on the pulse of popular culture at the time might be an understatement: he simply *was* that pulse. In a comparable way, albeit for a very brief time and during the making of a single record, Ronson and Winehouse would be the same thing: a kind of thermometer taking the temperature of the times.

A recent book on the arcane mechanics of making pop music hits happen is very instructive in this regard. *The Song Machine: Inside the Hit Factory* by John Seabrook seems to pick up where Simon Frith left off in his own visionary studies of the industrialization of popular music back in the '70s and '80s. His updated report on the evolution of the pop machine also peripherally demonstrates what made Amy Winehouse sound so special when she arrived on the *Back to Bedlam* scene. Her work clearly moved in the opposite direction stylistically, and yet it surprisingly still garnered the same huge payoff commercially, which was quite a paradoxical achievement back then, and still is today.

What's useful in Seabrook's book is the insight that today's music industry has highly mechanized marketing techniques that far surpass the automated methods some used to disdain in the Brill Building and Motown traditions. The author points out that the hardcore factory approach of today's pop kingdom far exceeds those old-time exemplars, and he accurately uses Taylor Swift as the ideal example of a radically soulless but utterly successful machine-style for the steady production of hits. He also identifies Cheiron Studios as the most influential manufacturing system for most of the late twentieth century hits that inspire many of today's hits almost invisibly, nearly as a practical functioning part of their technical DNA.

Most important here is the myth of sincerity and authenticity operating in the work of such diverse artists as Swift, Nicki Minaj, Pink, Celine Dion, Kylie Minogue, Rihanna, Kesha, Katy Perry, and Carly Rae Jepson, and even to some extent the still-reigning queen of mechano-pop, Madonna. They all proffer an illusion that they're performing for us alone in a once-in-a-lifetime show that is in reality just one stop on a seemingly endless world tour.

For Josh O'Kane, reviewing Seabrook's book in the *Globe and Mail*, this magic trick involves refining the art of pop for maximum listener gratification, which of course includes meeting all appetites and expectations at once and thus eliminating any surprises, through the deft handling of a "pop architect." Producers today work in the shadow of these hit-architects, the first ones obviously being Phil Spector, Brian Wilson, and George Martin, but they also have a new age of digital tricks up their sleeve as well, what O'Kane calls "the industrialization of 'track-and-hook songwriting,' where a producer creates a beat and chord progression and ships it to hook writers or 'topliners' to figure out the best melody for it. This shift away from the earlier hit-factories' traditional melody-and-lyric model has streamlined the creation of pop and it's also why so many songs sound so similar. Industrialization can be revolutionary but it's built on the acceptance of going through the motions."

Both O'Kane and Seabrook draw our attention to the reason why so often the song remains the same—a fact that also highlights what made both Mark Ronson and Salaam Remi's production styles so refreshing and Winehouse's songs themselves so arrestingly original. Ronson is already on record as acknowledging his stellar role as a *beatmaster* and how he had grown weary of chasing beats for a living instead of making music in a more organic manner. Even though he grew up in the shadow of the shadow of the first hit factories, and even though he admittedly heard in Amy's plaintive defiance the perfect pop hook, he still opted for a time-tested visceral route to arriving at their shared destination together. Among other things, that was why he eschewed the use of sampling and instead went directly to the gritty analog source of Daptone Records for this gold and Grammy generating mega-hit with his savant star. It was also how he methodically surfed her wild wave of contemporary passion crashing into classical restraint and captured its essence on good old-fashioned tape.

■ ■ ■

Nearly half a century after Phil Spector's triumphant reign over the pop charts, Ronson, witnessing what Daptone's Gabriel Roth and the Dap-Kings were doing in their crammed little Spector-like Bushwick studio, had his own personal illumination and realized that if he combined that tight session unit and analog vibe with his own ultra-digital, hi-tech DJ pyrotechnics, he just might be able to produce something openly emulating it in a grand homage. Even better yet, he could channel that raw energy and sonic spirit into a neo-pop/blues landmark.

But if Spector was the technical holy grail for Ronson, it was Ronnie Spector and the Ronettes who fulfilled that stylistic function for Winehouse. The Ronettes were the *crème de la crème* among the many other girl groups who were bleating and gyrating their way through heartbreaking episodes in their love lives. They did it in a way that didn't just make the pain go away or make it better but instead made it perfect and almost transcendental, even if it stayed with you forever.

Ronnie was and is simply sublime. If you look quickly at her in 1964, at the height of the Ronettes' fame, you could easily mistake her for a deeply suntanned Amy. And, of course, it goes without saying that the messages of songs like "Baby I Love You" and especially "The Best Part of Breakin'

Up" spoke deeply and personally to the young white British songwriter searching for a new way to be fully herself, whoever that might be. In retrospect, she would become the pagan writer of "Tears Dry on Their Own," "Love Is a Losing Game" and "Wake Up Alone," and she did it by echoing the aura of the Ronettes.

Ronnie Spector, née Veronica Bennett, was born in 1943 in New York to an African American father and a Cherokee mother and was encouraged at an early age to sing along with her sister Estelle and her cousin Nedra Talley, all of whom would also become Ronettes. Forty years after the Ronettes released "Born to Be Together" and "Is This What I Get For Loving You?," Amy Winehouse, lounging in that pub in London, would have her own moment of nearly sacred awakening—one that still shakes us to the marrow in "You Know I'm No Good."

If you watch videos of these Ronette songs in performance, especially the second one offered up on a British version of *American Bandstand* in 1965, you'll have your own intensely transformative experience as well. Especially if you then quickly hop through time to one of Amy performing "Some Unholy War." Indeed, your mouth will probably fall open almost as wide as your ears.

In a pleasant twist of fate, the Ronettes were inducted into the Rock and Roll Hall of Fame in 2007, in between the release of the *Back to Black* album and its recognition with five Grammy Awards. In a strange way, the awards were also honoring Phil and Ronnie Spector as well, though their life together was anything but as harmonious as the magic music they made in muse-like unison together.

In 2011, Ronnie Spector spoke to *Rolling Stone* magazine about Winehouse and her fate. "Damn it. Don't become like I was thirty years ago. Every time I looked at her it was like I was looking at myself. She had my beehive, my eyeliner, my attitude. She has such a great soul in her voice and her lyrics were so amazing I couldn't help but sing one of her songs. I was so happy to see an artist like Amy because she reminded me of my youth. And she loved girl groups. I thought she would carry on."

Listen to Ronnie's up-tempo dance version of "Back to Black," recorded with songwriter/producer Richard Gottehrer and hip-hop producer Phenom, and there will be tears in your eyes as well. Don't worry: they dry on their own. It's like listening to a vocal séance. Hearing the female soul being defiantly voiced by Ronnie Spector or Amy Winehouse gives a startling new definition to what femininity is supposed to mean.

Even if Amy Winehouse created only one great album, it is one whose roots and origins are still worthy of being explored by future musicologists, despite the fact that her entire life's body of work can be tucked into your shirt pocket. Her second album is still the ideal embodiment of Spector's futuristic concept of "pop blues," and he would have loved it. No reports have emerged from prison, where he's serving a life term for a pointless murder, on what his reaction may have been to their stylistic homage to his purple majesty by Ronson and Winehouse.

Mojo magazine's Colin Irwin hit the target perfectly with his characterization of the female blues voice as "a husky instrument that lingered on syllables like honey oozing off a spoon . . . the torch singers of the '50s, such as Sarah Vaughn and Ella Fitzgerald, held American men spellbound and came to represent the genre." The bluesy torch song would be lovingly handled again and again by great female singers on into the '60s and '70s, right up to those churning and burning Sharon Jones incantations with the Dap-Kings.

The torch would be just as boldly carried on by a sad young Winehouse, but possibly the trouble girls who carried it most efficiently—perhaps even most provocatively for our purposes, and thus the most Ronson-pertinent—were those booming and echoing girl groups banging off Spector's Wall of Sound. The white embodiment of that sexy ethos was never more palpable than when cascading out of the Shangri-Las, a Caucasian counterpart to the Ronettes, and it was especially *their* impact on the young lovelorn Winehouse that was crystallized so deliciously in her second album. It's a kind of irresistibly burnt emotional crème brûlée following the same recording recipes. It was the steady stream of steaming-hot singles from girl groups like the Shangri-Las, but also the Chantels, the Crystals, and Darlene Love who donated the movie soundtrack to many an adolescent fantasy for boys and girls alike. They all shared a special sound that would inspire Ronson to inspire Winehouse and then us decades later. That girl-group sound which so captivated, mesmerized, and haunted Winehouse, a sound recorded so brilliantly by Spector for Ronnie and by Berry Gordy for Diana Ross and the Supremes, can best be summarized as a big booming sound: atmospheric, echoing, reverberating, shimmering, sweet, dark, brooding, dangerous, and ultimately hyper-melodramatic.

Melodrama in its pure musical form, those songs are almost an opera of desires denied, deferred, or derailed. Songs like "Chains" by the Cookies, "Please Mr. Postman" by the Marvelettes, and "Baby It's You" by the Shirelles were already the national anthem of every tinny radio in every sweaty car across America even before the Beatles made them stadium anthems. And this is the basic ethos personified so well by *Back to Black*, especially on its operatic title track and on its heartbreaking aria, "Love Is a Losing Game."

It was hardly a *new* game, of course. The spiritually anguished sound of the girl group subculture that so entranced Winehouse was probably first introduced into American music in about 1958 with a song called "Maybe," written by Richard Barrett of the Valentines. It immediately set the gold standard for mini-operas about desperately trying to win back someone you've lost all through the next two decades and for that matter right up until its penultimate Winehouse séance-like reprise in 2006.

An army of girl-group symphonies would have been pouring out of Amy's jukebox in between her two albums and would have soaked deep in to her songwriting skills as it shifted away from jazz and toward girl-soul power. Her setlist would definitely have included the Angels' "My Boyfriend's Back"; the Chiffons' "He's So Fine," "One Fine Day," and "Sweet Talkin' Guy"; the Cookies' "Don't Say Nothin' Bad (About My Baby)"; the Dixie Cups' "Chapel of Love"; the Jaynetts' "Sally, Go Round the Roses"; the Paris Sisters' "I Love How You Love Me"; the Shangri-Las' "I Can Never Go Home Anymore"; the Toys' "A Lovers Concerto"; and the Shirelles' string of brilliantly dark hits, "Will You Love Me Tomorrow?," "Dedicated to the One I Love," "Mama Said," "Baby It's You," "Soldier Boy," and "Foolish Little Girl."

A close listen to these mini-symphonic melodramas will provide all the evidence required to place *Back to Black* in the proper perspective and to confirm the strange magic of this permanently young lady's spooky gift. Amy Winehouse's savant-like abilities might have been of so primitive a variety that she herself may not have known how she managed to pull it off. But we'll always be able to know the true stature of her accomplishment just by listening closely to it, and we'll never be able to forget the depth of our musical loss. It's almost a personal affront to lose a musical artist of her caliber.

5

RECORDING A MASTERPIECE

Mark Ronson, the Producer as Artist

"When I went into the studio I created a sound that I wanted to hear."
Phil Spector to Jann S. Wenner, *Rolling Stone*, November 1, 1969

Mark Ronson was characteristically humble back in 2010 when he was asked by Polly Lavin of *Ibiza Voice* how he responded to his sudden ascent as a highly acclaimed creative force in the music industry. "I think I'm mainly a producer *before* I'm an artist," he said. "You have to be able to collaborate with people well and pull the best out of them. When you're producing a record you might have ideas that you have to think are good but at the end of the day it's that band or that singer's album so you kind of have to take a backseat."

Working with the Dap-Kings on *Back to Black* resulted in another important discovery. "There was a band that sounded like my favorite records," he continued. "I realized I never need to go back and sample again."

By emphasizing the role of Ronson and the Dap-Kings, I'm in no way diminishing the artful contributions made by Salaam Remi to this record. In addition to his helpful insights into the role of the producer as artist, he had some pertinent thoughts on empowering Amy Winehouse, which he shared with the *Score* when asked to reflect on the stark stylistic transition she made from her first to her second record.

"Most people, when they know the producer's name, they know their name because they're an artist," he said. "So it's kind of like them being marketed as artists. I want you to buy Amy but I don't want you to buy Amy because it's *that* sound, because to me that plays the artist out. We need the artists as vehicles to go for the longer way. 'Cause most producers have come and gone, quickly, unless they made an artist who was bigger than them. Those producers made a difference." Indeed, Remi made all the difference to us even knowing Winehouse at all.

When Winehouse's agent and manager, Raye Cosbert, initially approached Darcus Beese at his Island Records office, carrying with him her roughed-out musings in verse and chorus, hoping to start the process of making her much-anticipated second album, he quite logically assumed that Remi and his *Frank* collaborator, Commissioner Gordon, would be paired again at the production helm. But he was surprised to hear that Beese and his boss wanted the young singer to meet another up-and-coming musician and producer, the New York–based Ronson, an EMI artist already under contract, and one then heavily favored by his label. Guy Moot would later tell *Music Week* that the two most pivotal moments in Winehouse's career were her signing with Cosbert as her new manager and her exposure to Ronson as her new producer-collaborator. He must also have been a little nervous about pairing the singer with Remi again, given how much she professed to loathe her debut album *Frank*.

Winehouse was writing very slowly at best, since she was not exactly at an emotional high point in her personal life; as she confided to *Beats Bar* in 2006, she only had a few scraps of ideas for songs and really only got into a groove when she met and hit it off instantly with her new producer and co-writer. Their primary bond was of course over Phil Spector's '60s girl groups and the '60s Motown sound they both loved. Interviewed for a 2007 *Rolling Stone* article, Ronson explained their creative destination succinctly: "The reason that everyone goes back to those Motown records is that there were amazing musicians playing together in a room, and that's what we tried to do." An ironic assertion in the end, given that he would assemble the key Winehouse tracks like a sonic mosaic, with the band and the singer operating on totally different continents.

Thus began the singer's ping-pong travels between London and New York, alternating with visits to Remi's Instrument Zoo in Miami, where the hip-hop specialist was following the same analog map as Ronson was using, recreating (or perhaps reincarnating) the snap, crackle, and pop of vinyl. Remi recorded the singer crooning in his living room while he was tracking in the upstairs bedroom, in a manner reminiscent of the way Don Van Vliet was recorded by Frank Zappa to enshrine his outsider-classic *Trout Mask Replica* in 1969. In the case of ultra-insider Winehouse, the vintage feel was not just being simulated: it was being actualized.

■ ■ ■

Sometimes it can be shocking how little time it really takes to invent something timeless. As Bud Scoppa once so ironically opined, the creative process works in mysterious ways. For *Hits Daily Double* he reprised what he called the series of heady decisions that led to the inspiration, creation, production, and delivery of the dark demon child known as *Back to Black*. The moment of "conception" for what he called the virtual soundtrack of the year 2007 was the now-infamous exchange between the newly introduced Winehouse and Ronson after shooting some pool together as they walked back to his Allido studio in Lower Manhattan.

"When she did this 'talk to the hand' thing," Ronson told Scoppa, "I said that was really hooky. We didn't give it much thought." After his initial reaction and suggestion that she go write a song based on talking to the hand, she played him what she'd come up with, and he responded with his typically laconic "cool," suggesting they put some hand claps here and there and perhaps a minor chord in the verse to make it a bit *jangly*. And that, according to Ronson, "That was it." Ronson worked up the arrangement after Winehouse went away for the night, and she returned to sing over it the next day. He had added drums, guitar, and keyboards to enhance the groove, while Winehouse's vocal "hit the hook with a vengeance."

Later on, when Ronson played his original demo to Scoppa in the studio, it seemed that even at that early raw stage it was clearly a natural born pop hit. In order to make his intuition about the song's potential a reality, however, he needed a certain authentic vibe to flesh out the feeling suggested by Winehouse's attitude. He wanted the feel of vintage R&B records, and he found it lurking in a gritty Brooklyn studio.

Ronson later famously remarked that the Dap-Kings were already making the kind of sounds he used to sample when he was first DJ'ing back in the '90s, a stage in his mostly cyber-based career when he would regularly purchase expensive vinyl recordings in order to sample maybe a single four-bar drum loop. This was the beginning of his rebirth as a musician and producer. Once he discovered that the drums used on Daptone Records were tracked on just one mic, he was converted to using one-inch 16-track tape, a key ingredient to attaining an accurate recreation of the Motown snare sound: one mic, magnetic tape, and tons of reverb. "I wouldn't have known how to make a record like that a year ago," he candidly admitted.

During a 2010 interview at the Red Bull Academy in London, Ronson further revealed the extent of his almost religious conversion to analog tape production after expressing some appreciation for Winehouse's first record, but only from the digital perspective of playing one of her debut songs where she (or producer Remi) had sampled sonic fragments from Nas's "Made You Look" during his DJ sets. Someone had told him he should meet "this girl Amy" who was a great singer, and when he did they hit it off so well that he tried to create a track that might connect with her enthusiastic passion for '60s jukebox pop. Incredibly, he was trying hard to *woo* her.

"I went into my studio and came up with that piano line that sounded a little bit generic but wasn't a total rip-off, it just summed up that era, the Shangri-La's, songs like 'Walking in the Sand.' Then, I'm not a drummer but I can loop myself in Pro Tools—I did a little kick drum that went 'boom, tch, boom, boom, tch.' That's all I had, the rough thing of the keys." The next day, after coating the whole thing in spring reverb, he played it to Winehouse.

"What do you think of this?" he asked.

"Yeah, I love it," she replied. Her reactions were always immediate and visceral, and they were always right.

During her extended stay, Winehouse would work for a few hours at a time, singing Ronson the intense lines of free verse that sounded like they'd been ripped from the pages of a young girl's private journal (because they had been), and he would unearth the magical foundation over and under which he would later layer in the Daptone Label groove of the Dap-Kings all on his own, once she had returned to England.

Jeff Mao of Red Bull enquired further about this serendipity in the studio: how it seemed like a departure from the typical process (putting it mildly) of playing a track for a singer and building it from the ground up, from nothing. The key question was how long this novel approach could take if you have an elaborate string orchestration and big sections with tempo changes throughout. Did it become overly complicated to orchestrate the changes that add to the dynamic of a song such as "Back to Black," he wondered, and to make us feel that the arrangement is somehow *breathing* by itself?

The sound on the whole record is of course a *big* sound, so managing scale could become an issue: how to stay on the right side of big without becoming crowded, noisy or bombastic. Though he has often professed his love of the big pop recording sound of Spector and others, he is smart enough to realize than managing such a sonic avalanche requires both skill and restraint. Especially in today's high-technology digital realm, there's always a danger of endlessly adding on instrumentation that could obscure the vocalist's craft, so Ronson was careful and judicious about not becoming overly dependent on programs such as Pro Tools. Instead, he was artfully reaching back to the '60s, where everyone was more attentive to the arrangements, and he managed to pull off the feat of recording the rhythm tracks in only five days. Then he wanted to add strings.

The very existence of strings and lush orchestration on the album is a bit of a surprise to those who know the somewhat fixed ideas Winehouse had about her desire for grit and street cred and her heated opposition to anything that might appear inflated or romantic. From the get-go, Ronson faced a battle with the mercurial singer over his orchestral arrangements, and had to work to convince her that they wouldn't turn her into Mariah Carey, as she feared. He reminded her that it was the string arrangements that made her favorite Shangri-La songs so unusual.

Finally an exasperated Ronson declared that *he* would pay for the orchestra himself, and if she didn't like it they could always just take it off. Winehouse emphatically squealed that he shouldn't "waste his fucking money!" and that she just wouldn't have it.

Amazingly, Ronson did the arrangements secretly, on his own, and only played them to her during the mixing process, praying that it wouldn't result in a creative flare-up. Luckily for Ronson—who knew that omitting them would have ruined the record—Winehouse jumped up and hugged him once she realized how good his judgment had been. And that was that: sometimes, great producers have to trick artists into doing their best work, almost in spite of themselves.

Luckily for Winehouse, given the emotional tightrope she was walking, with Ronson's inspiring guidance her music was about to become almost ideal in its resonance with the hybrid age we lived in during the first decade of the twenty-first century. Even more fortunate for all of us, the album that would result from her collaboration with two gifted producers and a hot studio session and live performing band, plus her ability to channel spookily realistic soul music in the molten Daptone vernacular, would be a stunning album.

Winehouse's authentic identification with the big production values of analog sound and the glorious heartache of its '60s girl groups, mixed with her startling honesty in personal storytelling, all conspired to manifest a near perfect collection of torch songs. It was one for the ages, despite the difficulties she faced and the grim backstory to its recording and mixing. Regardless of any personal challenges she may have had to deal with while collaborating with her new producer, in his capable hands the technical side of things was going swimmingly.

Ronson was simultaneously summoning up his beloved '60s and '70s funk-soul sound, especially the magic of Victor "Ticklah" Axelrod, whose stellar piano and shiny Wurlitzer action would enliven "Rehab," "Love Is a Losing Game," "Some Unholy War," and "Back to Black" itself. And at the end of this creative conveyor belt was Darcus Beese back in London, recognizing instantly that almost despite herself the young singer had made something astonishing happen, largely due to his own decision to merge the talents of a funkmaster with a popmaster. So, in a way, he deserved the pat on the back he was already giving himself when he heard even the first raw taped results.

What Beese also realized, of course, was that almost every song on the album had "hit single" lights flashing all around it. He was right, and Winehouse was equally right to boast to the *Daily Mail*, "Music is the only thing I have with real dignity in my life. That's the one area in my life where I can hold my head up and say, 'No one can touch me.'" That degree of outlandish confidence is obviously essential if an artist, even a very young one, is ever going to climb to the top of sugar mountain, although staying up there was quite another matter altogether.

As challenging as her apprenticeship in the music industry turned out to be, we certainly can't say she didn't have all the professional help any artist could ever hope to receive. When it comes to creative producers who mentor you technically while also providing an almost therapeutic environment for you to artistically deal with your demons on a daily basis, both her recording guides were practically manna from heaven.

Ronson and Remi remain massive players on the music scene today precisely because they altered the whole life of a young recording artist, and they accomplished that risky feat largely by being highly creative artists themselves. Yet even fellow artists sometimes need to work hard at making the right creative connections at the right time. And, as I've also suggested, sometimes producers need to almost *trick* artists into making the best choices for their work to be successful at all levels.

Winehouse has admitted that "Rehab," for instance, started as a silly remark that took Ronson's fancy and then morphed into the catchy pop song she claimed took her about five minutes to write (but five months for Ronson to turn into a pop hit). I do tend to emphasize Ronson and the Dap-Kings in this whole process because it was his role to maintain the sonic umbrella that unifies the album's eclectic range of material, and because theirs is the signature instrumental style that established her alluring brand worldwide both in concerts and on videos. It was definitely Ronson's pivotal creative role in New York that really made *Back to Black* happen at all: she simply never would have made it without him. In short, he *made* her make it.

But even if we grant Mark Ronson his self-deprecating charm (one of his more appealing features), not only is he an artist in his own right, he is also a *great* artist, and one who was singularly responsible for making the Winehouse musical miracle happen in quite the way that it did. Apart from both personal and professional support and mentorship, it was his brilliant audio craftsmanship that made the whole album into a deeply moving picture of painted sounds that tell a gripping emotional story.

Yet how on earth did someone make grief on steroids sound so incredibly beautiful? Apart from Winehouse's own remarkable voice, her visceral response to music, and her uncanny sense of timing and coordination, the question leads us to the inherent artistry of the record producer's integral role in the transformation of her feelings into forms.

■ ■ ■

What exactly do producers do? Apart from the obvious technical prowess required to capture the essence of a performing artist live on record, their principal purpose is to tattoo a dream, to transfer an artist's fondest wishes into a palpable form that we can all hold in our hands and position between our ears. They musically tattoo that dream onto our hearts, so to speak, and if they're really talented and lucky, they can also tattoo it onto the rapidly changing history of music.

Especially in the digital twenty-first century, some producers have themselves come to be perceived as gifted artists, and are often portrayed as conceptually creative composers who utilize their singers, writers, and musicians as skillfully, imaginatively, and dominantly as they twist the dials and push the buttons on their mixing boards. Truly, some producer/artists excavate the music of others like archaeological sites from which to extract sounds, beats, or portions of hooks and then incorporate them into their own original compositions as a kind of aural collage.

This sampling technique is not only musically valid and legitimate: it's similar to the appropriation and collage techniques popular in contemporary visual art for at least the last century. As Ronson explained to NPR in 2015, "Sampling isn't about hijacking nostalgia wholesale, it's about inserting yourself into the narrative of a song while also pushing that story forward." Unless, that is, you discover that it works even better to just travel to the *actual* archaeological site itself and get the indigenous population there to assist you in finding the material you're looking for. As he has also explained, doing that would turn out to be his creative epiphany: why sample or simulate something when you can access the real thing? In Ronson's case, the real thing was the Dap-Kings.

■ ■ ■

Like most prospectors who discover a goldmine, *Frank* producer Salaam Remi quickly had to share his mother lode with another panhandler downriver in order to fully mine the vein and bring it to the marketplace for precious metals. Remi was still on the scene, of course, and he would share production duties for the follow-up, but it was most certainly Mark Ronson who would shoot skyward on the tail of the comet Winehouse suddenly become. Queen Grammy would soon be smiling on him again, and indeed, by 2016 Ronson himself had also become pop music royalty.

Back when he was producing *Back to Black*, Ronson was still only a fledgling musician himself, a young producer and active DJ at the time of meeting the artist who seems to have singlehandedly resurrected his somewhat flagging career. (He's admitted to suffering from what we might term "beat fatigue"). He was hardly an untested sound artist, however, having crafted prior albums for Sean Paul, Macy Gray, and Lily Allen, as well as all of these other brand names in 2006: Christina Aguilera, Robbie Williams, Ghostface Killah, and Rhymefest.

His creative partnership with Remi would result in that special chemical compound of two gifted audio artists combining forces to make up what used to be found in the single individual production masters of the old school analog golden age. It also meant a special brand of unalloyed collaborative magic, and his borrowed recording style and sensibility is exactly what *Back to Black* called for. By the time they quickly bonded, Winehouse, like Ronson, had also become creatively besotted by her favorite girl groups from the Phil Spector age of river deep mountain high: architectural echo, doubled instrumentation, opulent reverb, and multiple layers of bold orchestra cake smothered with pounds of sonic icing.

Only eight years older than she when they collaborated (but now a ripe old forty-one), Ronson had released one album of his own, *Here Comes the Fuzz,* which failed to set the world on fire, prompting his label, Elektra Records, to drop him. Multi-talented and super-ambitious—perhaps even overly so—for that record he had written all the songs, created the charts, played the guitar, keyboards, and bass, and technically crafted the sound itself. The metaphor is unavoidable. Ronson is the equivalent of a musical Swiss Army knife: singer, songwriter, DJ, beat hustler, dance-club artist, musician, producer, arranger, orchestrator, mentor, therapist.

There was one other key difference between producers of the twenty-first century such as Remi and Ronson and those golden age producers of the twentieth century, such as Spector, Martin, or Kramer, whom they emulated. This was the fact that the new generation often also co-wrote songs for their artists, frequently sang backup vocals, and even played instruments on their records, making the overall creative collaboration even more intimate and intense.

While Remi would produce five of the songs on *Back to Black*, Ronson produced the other six, and their creative/technical partnership with each other was just as fruitful and blessed as the one they both shared with their brilliant but troubled troubadour. Together, they merged like two corporations in order to cook up her sonic dream soup, and as such they were suddenly also both conceptual performance artists themselves much more than mere producers in the true Tony Visconti mode.

Ronson's own second album, *Version*, a collection of masterful covers, was well received commercially and critically—mostly, he has admitted, as a result of his Winehouse gig. After guiding Winehouse through the difficult birthing of her second album, he did in fact set the world on fire, working subsequently with Adele and Bruno Mars, Lily Allen and Paul McCartney, among many others. He hasn't stopped climbing since, and Winehouse's skewed and outsized gifts were at least part of the fuel that would smoothly run his creative engine for years afterward. He was clearly off to a flying start after co-producing one of the first undeniable landmark albums of the twenty-first century. Even now, ten years later, I don't think there's yet been another album to match its purity of sound, its clarity of instrumentation, its curated narrative finesse, or its heights and depths of sheer human emotion pressure cooked into perfect pop songs.

Ronson's third studio album, *Record Collection*, was released in September of 2010 and peaked at No. 2 in the UK. By 2014, he had earned his first mutual UK and US No. 1 single with "Uptown Funk," featuring vocals from Bruno Mars, which in 2015 won the BRIT Award for "British Single of the Year." His fourth studio album, *Uptown Special*, was released in January of that year, becoming his first number one UK album. It obviously didn't hurt him one little bit to be associated with the tortured tornado called Winehouse (apart from the personal hurt, of course, of losing his and Remi's resident genius to her losing game).

■ ■ ■

Like Remi, Ronson was born into a highly musical family and exposed to rock majesties at a very young age. His stepfather was Mick Jones, the guitarist from the pop group Foreigner—not a brilliant pop group but certainly proficient and prolific enough—and a good conduit to the kind of aristocracy that can rapidly accelerate a young musician's career appetites and aspirations. At the age of eight, Ronson moved with his family to New York City, where he lived on the Upper West Side. One of his boyhood friends was Sean Ono Lennon, son of you-know-who, and he continued moving in just such rarefied circles as a young adult.

Also, like both Winehouse and Remi, Ronson was something of a musical prodigy, and early on he'd begun to act out his future industry fantasies at the gritty street and dance club level which was the reality school attended by so many of his young musical peers. While still a student at New York University, he'd already become a major fixture on the rave/dance club scene and Downtown hip-hop universe. He quickly made a name for himself as a highly flexible and stylistically articulate DJ, partially helping to re-define the role of DJ as an actual musical genre veering aesthetically toward compositional collage rather than merely what it was in the good old days: a person who played records.

It was fully ten years before his fateful hearing of *Frank* that he created a persona as a musical mutation leader, a genre-bending mix-master, and someone who was clearly going to make the eventual leap into writing and producing his own records rather than being content with mixing and matching the songs and dance records of others. Nikka Costa's manager heard one of Ronson's DJ sets and introduced the two musicians, who hit it off sufficiently for Ronson to produce Costa's song "Everybody Got Their Something."

This was a new age when individual songs, artfully produced, rather than whole albums considered as artworks, would move to the forefront of the music industry, which had increased its pace of product production and star-making machinery even more radically than it had in the corporate-driven '70s, '80s, and '90s, which were plenty fast already. Now it was supersonic. And while focusing our attention on what the fateful musical encounter between Winehouse, Remi, and Ronson meant to the artist and producers in question, it's also important to understand that by this time the business side of music had acknowledged what previously had only been realized by the creative artists themselves: in many important cases, the producers really made the music what it was.

The point to emphasize here is just how young all of these artists were (both Winehouse and her tag-team producers) and just how fast things were moving in the early twenty-first century, an accelerated age when someone like the admittedly talented Ronson could be making sounds for Tommy Hilfiger commercials one day, making records of his own the next, and then producing a masterpiece for a young genius soon afterward.

The best producers were now also artists of a sort themselves, using as their primary instruments first and foremost the voices and songs of their clients but also the orchestra of the studio mixing board as a special technical tool that didn't just capture the sounds emitted by singer/songwriters, as it did in bygone eras. Now they partially *created* an incarnation of the musical art which itself wouldn't have existed without their skilled intervention and their own personal, often very idiosyncratic sonic sensibilities.

The incendiary and insane artist-producers Joe Meek and Phil Spector were probably the first to alert us to this evolutionary change, creating for themselves an overall executive role, later evolved even further by producers operating at an ultimate level of combined technical virtuosity and musical mastery. As we've also seen, Spector's recording artistry would inspire Ronson to make *Back to Black* the enhanced and elevated listening experience that captivates us at such an almost primal level. In fact, his sonic styling would make *Black* a haunting example of primal therapy in musical form.

■ ■ ■

Prior to the ascent of rap and hip hop and their genre-disrupting entry into the musical mainstream with their absorption into pop music proper, and prior to the supremacy and virtuosity of the Beatles with their technical reconfiguring of the singer/songwriter process, the music producer was usually a white middle-aged man in a crisp suit and tie, maybe even a white lab coat.

These music trends changed all that, and suddenly former technicians became artist/producers—a special creative breed that continues to rule the industry roost in our hybridized pop universe. Phil Spector, George Martin, and Brian Wilson were key emissaries in the advent of the producer as artist-collaborator. Salaam Remi and Mark Ronson, among others, are the inheritors of their technical, artistic, and management innovations. And *Back to Black* is one of the best examples of what can result from the right mix of all the necessary recipe ingredients: writer, singer, mentor, engineer, producer, mixer. The final product feels at times deceptively effortless, like all great works of art feel: as if they had always existed.

Before the current era of this cross-fertilization between specialties, styles, genres, and techniques, the role of producer was historically that of overseer and project manager, capturing the fleeting medium of recording musicians playing live in the studio within a controlled environment designed to contour those live sounds. More poetically, perhaps, they were similar to medieval alchemists in that they transformed the base metal of their performers into a rare earth element hopefully capable of garnering Grammy gold and platinum—the only kind of precious metals that really matter in the music industry.

The producer performs multiple and crucial tasks, from selecting ideas for initiating projects in the first place to curating the songs and musicians almost as an editor, to coaching and guiding the artists while managing their sessions, and of course the overall direction of the entire process, from concept to completion, including mixing, engineering, and mastering the finished product.

Ronson neatly clarified his creative role and industry affiliations to *Performing Songwriter* magazine back in 2011. "I was always a big fan of the classic producer/arranger and always doing things backwards," he said. "Part of it came from my love of big band arrangements, like Quincy Jones's instrumental things. A big part also came from the Dap-Kings, who played all over Amy's record. Other than a few retro artists, nobody was using them in pop music, except for little hooks here and there."

In a way, the producer as artist is also similar to a film director, with each gig being an example of that *movie for the ears* metaphor. The sonic engineers and technical mixing-masters could even be compared to the cinematographer who distills the essence of what a film director wants to tell as his or her story through photographic images. This could be why Winehouse's album is so cinematic in its scope, feeling, and scale, and why in parts it has the rich texture of an almost biblical epic.

The digital collage technique Ronson was used to using would change overnight, however, when he encountered a certain revivalist groove. Having first tried using "every plug-in trick in the modern world" to try to make their work sound suitably retro, he had another idea: "Why not just get the Dap-Kings to play it? So I left a lot of the technical side of things to Gabe [Roth] because he really understands getting those sounds. That's why all of Amy's tracks were recorded to tape."

The technical side of his prowess in the studio is an intriguing amalgamation of making music himself, playing it for dancers in clubs, and creatively producing it for another artist. When Ronson embarked to the Daptone funk-soul studio to begin layering the near mystical cake of *Back to Black*, he found himself going back in time to excavate the landscape of sound in a way totally new to him: the allure of actual magnetic recording tape.

For *Back to Black*, Ronson obviously wanted to craft a retro-soul style, and, as we've seen, he succeeded marvelously, though largely by borrowing the existing heavily analog groove of that Daptone magic. Many producers these days are discovering more and more that tape is as superior to digital recording techniques as mono formats are superior to the marketing hoax of stereophonic sound that first loomed in the late '60s. Stereo was a ploy that we all naively bought in to, having been trained by all industries to believe that newness and the latest technologies must somehow be more advanced. They're not.

Working with the fabulous Dap-Kings in Bushwick Brooklyn, twenty-first century sonic wizard Ronson had discovered the magic of twentieth century analog tape for the first time in his young life. "They have an old Studer 16-track one-inch tape machine and a Trident desk," he told *Sound on Sound*. "After I worked with them in their studio, I realized the difference when you're recording to tape. It got me inspired and I'm gonna try to get a desk and tape machine for my studio now."

In other words, he was now traveling back in time to the greatness of George Martin's Beatle domain, and even further back into Phil Spector's sonic walls. Most people of his age, he admitted, knew nothing of tape, and probably never would, "unless they have some sort of weird experience where someone shows it to them. It's kind of a shame, because if you're going for any kind of warm '60s or '70s sound, whether it's Stevie Wonder, or Bowie, or Zeppelin, or Motown, or whatever, that tape sound is an integral part of those records." (It's also now a big part of his own post-Amy records.)

As he revealed in his exchange with MTV's James Montgomery, an integral part of that sound is contained in the "warm, rounded drums" that identify Ronson's own productions and brand them with that signature sensation of raw '70s funk merged with sophisticated hip-hop sensibilities. He now likes to carry it on as a kind of mystical secret passed on to him by arcane master craftsmen from another age.

The drummer here was the Dap-Kings' own Homer Steinweiss, probably the most gifted player since Charlie Watts or Mick Fleetwood, who gave the material that necessary deep groove specially ordained by the studio angels. As Ronson admitted to *Sound on Sound*, he simply went into the band's studio and used the same setup they had deployed on their own records. ("They'd probably kill me if I gave their secrets away as to how they got their sounds.") That warm, heavy drum tone was also a huge part of Ringo Starr's greatness and he achieved that sound partly through producer George Martin's brilliant decision to fold thick felt blankets into Starr's drums to "heavy-up" the tone. Once heard, never forgotten.

Subtlety is a quality often missing in the digital age, and Ronson, a child of the computer thinking and listening age if ever there was one, absorbed this esoteric knowledge from his senior analog mentors and merged it laterally with his own gift for contemporary postmodern techniques such as Pro Tools and an Akai MPC300—"the hip-hop standard"—which he uses to program beats.

Never mind his software fetish; Ronson's personal hardware

store is an even more impressive laboratory, out of which he cooked his dream soup for Winehouse. His Allido studio is a museum of synthesizers and vintage keyboards that are still busily alive, featuring collectors items such as a Moog Voyager, Roland Juno 106, Nord Electro, Hohner Clavinet D6, his beloved Rhodes, upright pianos, and a world weary Wurlitzer. For less technically inclined readers, this brief litany is rather important since it indicates the skill and proficiency that was necessary for him to achieve the stunning sound landscapes that populated the *Back to Black* sessions. These are the ingredients that elevate it as an artifact up to the level of an influential aesthetic accomplishment of the highest order: they raise it up to a work of art operating at the third degree of mastery.

■ ■ ■

After his near religious experience in the Dap-Kings' cavernous working-class studio, Ronson's newfound love for the analog dimension found expression in a blending of digital and old-school sounds for his ongoing recording projects, for which he merged his Technics SL-1200 turntables with a Rane TTM54 mixer. When he does his increasingly less frequent live work, he still incorporates old-world sonics; when using guitars, he tends to avoid pedals in favor of high-end amps. To achieve a degree of technical mastery, not to mention the magical ability to capture Winehouse's live essence on tape and eventually on disc, Ronson delved deep into an alchemy of machines and methods. As he explained to *Sound on Sound,* his arsenal of Pro Tools plug-in included Line 6's Amp Farm ("good and quick if you want to throw an idea down"), Echo Farm ("for the old-school delays"), and Digidesign's Lo-Fi ("to take the bit rate down and just get things a bit crusty").

He recorded three of the horn players from the Dap-Kings together for the '60s-sounding metallics on *Back to Black*, crowding baritone, tenor, and trumpet around a single Royer ribbon mic. (When doing the orchestrations at Metropolis in London, he used seven tenor saxophones playing at the same time, all miked individually.)

According to Ronson, another equally important aspect to the delicately nuanced aural mix of *Back to Black* was his voyage to yet another notable studio, this time over home on Winehouse's home turf, the historic Studio B at Metropolis Studios in West London. Located in Chiswick in a converted power station and co-founded by Gary Langan, Carey Taylor, and Karin Clayton in 1989, the studio has both new technology and vintage production capacities, which would have appealed to the history-seeking Ronson. He found plenty of nostalgic echoes in its fabled B room, the second tracking room commonly used for album sessions at any stage of record production, from conception to tracking and mixing.

Metropolis, considered Europe's premiere recording, production, mixing, and engineering site, with four analog consoles for mixing productions at its disposal, proved to be the ideal location for Ronson's *secret* addition of brass and strings to the foundational tracks he'd laid down with the Dap-Kings back in Bushwick. With top of the line in-house engineers such as Sam Wheat, Liam Nolan, Paul Norris, Stuart Hawkes, and Ben Rhodes, Metropolis had been an integral part of sound creation for huge bands such as Queen, U2, Stone Roses, and Paul McCartney, and for artists as diverse as Michael Jackson, Scott Walker, Rihanna, Lady Gaga, and Lauryn Hill. To that roster of stars would soon be added the name of Amy Winehouse, who while still then a considerably lesser-known young newcomer clearly already had the diva persona down pat.

This highlights one specific detail of working with Winehouse that was something of a challenge, although it proved useful in the end: her well known impatient bluntness, with which an idea would be completely dissed and dumped if it wasn't working out after twenty minutes. This proved rather

fore the storm: Winehouse at her Camden, London, home in 2004, after the release
Frank but prior to *Back to Black*. (*Mark/NBCP Camera Press*)

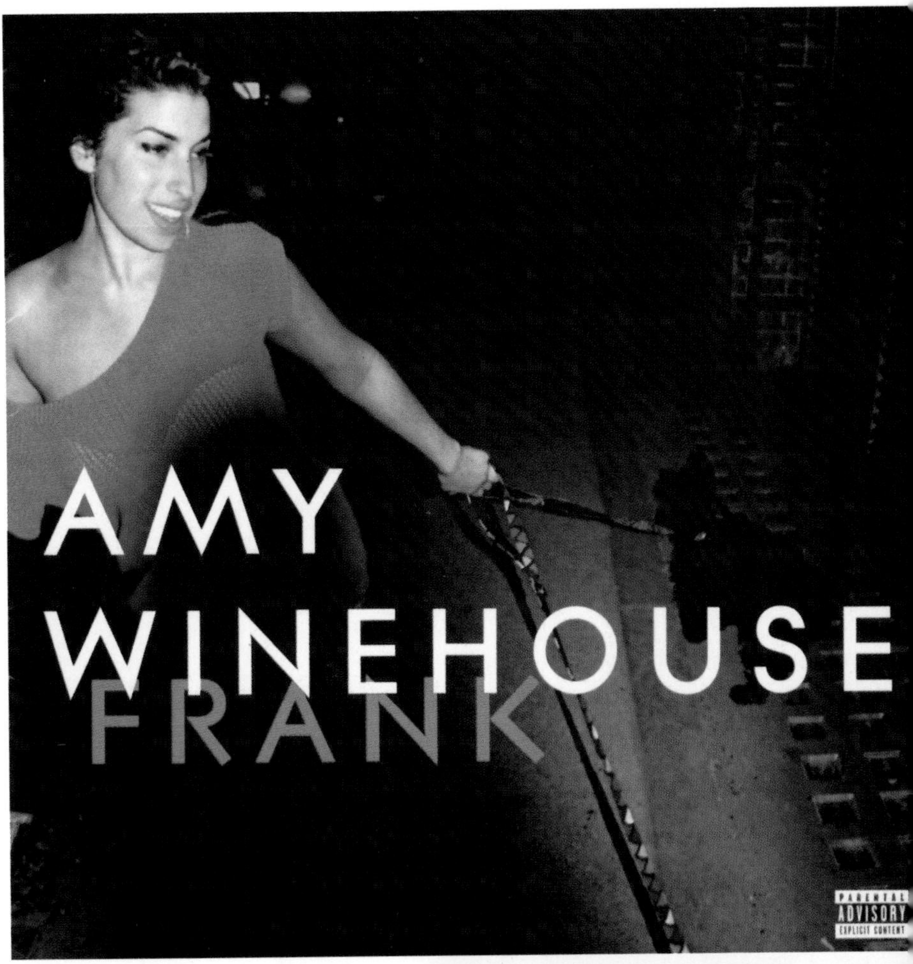

Freshman debut album: *Frank* was released on October 20, 2003, by Island Records. *(Author's collection)*

Salaam Remi, early mentor, producer of *Frank*, and co-producer of *Back to Black*, in New York, January 14, 2015. *(Johnny Nunez/Getty Images)*

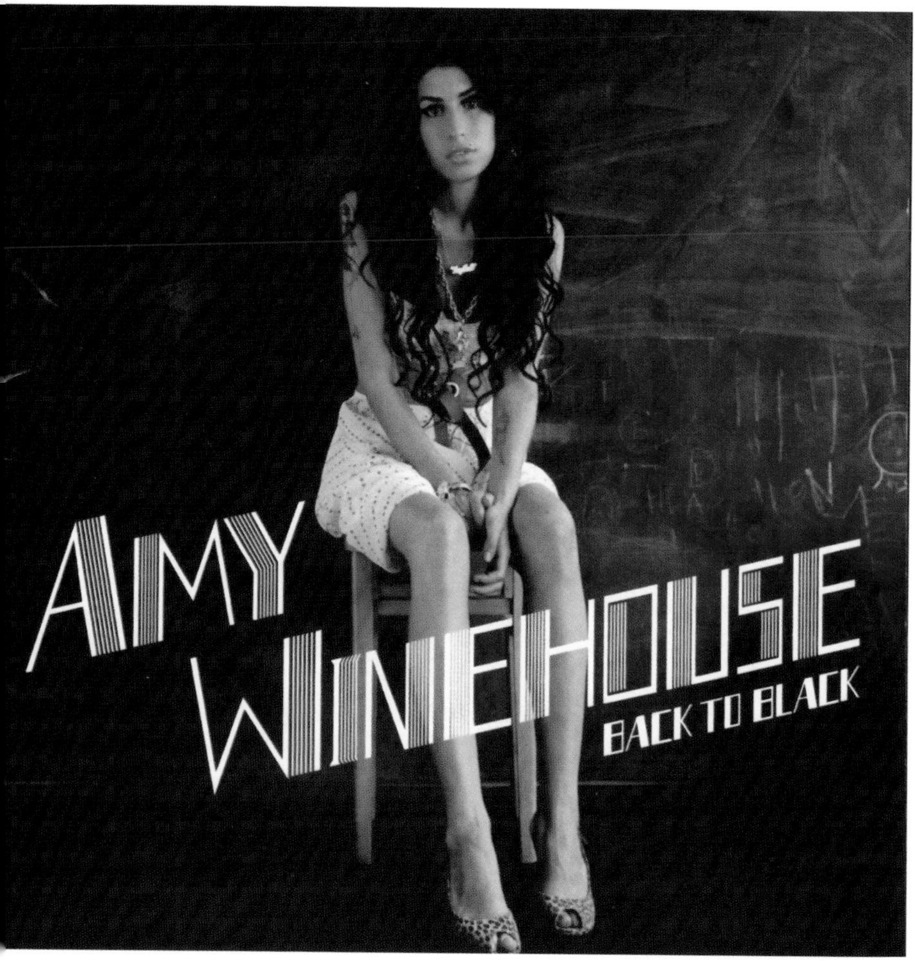

phomore sequel album: *Back to Black* was released on October 27, 2006, by Island
ecords. *(Author's collection)*

Mark Ronson, producer of *Back to Black,* at the MTV Awards, October 25, 2015. *(Dave Hogan/Getty Images)*

Producer Phil Spector with Ronnie Spector of the Ronettes at Gold Star Studios, Los Angeles, January 1 1963. *(Ray Avery/Getty Images)*

Lady Day" passed the torch on to "Lady Night": Billie Holiday, New York, December 957. (*Michael Ochs Archives/Getty Images*)

Anita O'Day, the ultra-Amy incarnation of her day, 1957. *(Photofest)*

The queen of the girl-group songs and Amy's spiritual godmother: Carole King, 1961. *(Photofest)*

The Shangri-Las—the white counterparts to the Ronettes and a huge influence on Amy's style and sensibility—in 1970. *(Michael Ochs Archives/Getty Images)*

he Dap-Kings grooving in concert. *(Getty Images)*

he Demonic Diva in full flight, live at the Empire, London, May 29, 2007.
ɟus Stewart/Getty Images)

Performing with Mark Ronson at the BRIT Awards, February 20, 2008.
(JM International/Getty Images)

Close enough to touch: performing with Mark Ronson at the 100 Club, London, July 6, 2010. *(Samir Hussein/Getty Images)*

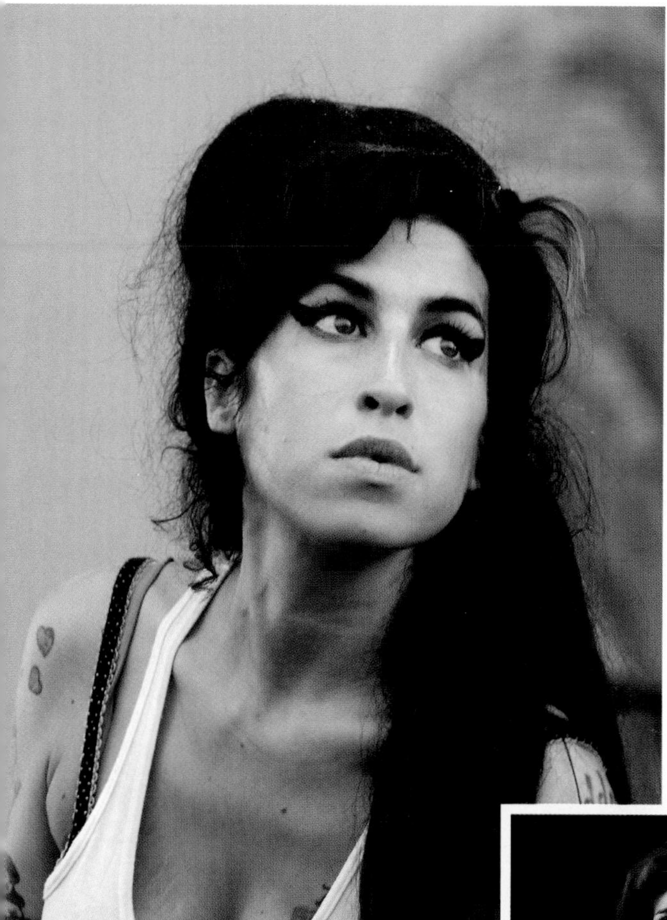

eflective: at the Isle of Wight Festival, Eng-
nd, June 9, 2007. *(Jo Hale/Getty Images)*

Rough Trade: performing at the V Festival Hylands Park, Chelmsford, August 17, 2008. *(Simone Joyner/Getty Images)*

Performing on *The Tonight Show*, 2007. *(Photofest)*

Sultry: performing at the BRIT Awards, London, February 14, 2007. *(Dave Hogan/Getty Images)*

ost-grad thesis album: *Lioness* was released posthumously on December 2, 2011, by
land Records. *(Author's collection)*

Pausing: the singer outside Magistrates' Court in London in 2009.
(Shaun Curry/Getty Images)

difficult to adjust to for professionals used to walking a diplomatic tightrope in order to fully accommodate each other's creative quirks.

As her producer, Ronson often found that an artist like Winehouse knows instantly if something is not working the way she wants it. After a while, he began to realize that there really isn't any point in being overly diplomatic, and that a songwriter of her skills has enough basic instinct to know what feels real for her. Winehouse wasn't exactly one to waste words, and her bluntness became her brand.

Toward the end of their personal and professional relationship, when Winehouse was close to getting clean and almost beginning to sound like her old self again, she and Ronson had a brief but intense falling out, followed by a reunion and return to form. The sudden distance was caused by her reading some comments he made in an interview about their working method together: that she would come in with rough songs she wrote on guitar, and that it was *his* job was to come up with polished rhythm arrangements and orchestrations and to figure out what the band was going to do musically. This was, of course, completely accurate.

In response to the interview that appeared to diminish her role in the record they made together, Winehouse had angrily messaged him, "One album I write and *you* take half the credit!" A tweeted text message couldn't ever really convey her wicked, tongue-in-cheek wit in person, however since the tone of her always biting, sarcastic humor and seductive irony was bound to be lost in print alone. However, it was still a telling attack, and it also secretly acknowledged Ronson's central role in her legend.

It's fair to say that his honest depiction of their collaboration genuinely angered and embarrassed her. But the alienation of affection didn't last very long; in fact, having long since become almost like siblings, it quickly rolled off both their backs. According to Ronson, they already had some time penciled in to go back into the studio again in October 2011. He was shocked by her sudden passing that July, just like all the rest of us were shocked, though of course we can always be shocked by something so momentous without necessarily being surprised by it at all.

■ ■ ■

For the intricate process of mixing records, Mark Ronson likes to let certain specialists do the final tweaking and balancing. His favorite mixing engineers are usually Serban Ghena and Tom Elmhirst, whose credits include Goldfrapp, Paolo Nutini, and Joss Stone. Of course, Elmhirst is also the mix master behind the majestic *Back to Black*, and he's much in demand for good reason: the recording industry loves a winner, and his proven pedigree is that of a time-tested thoroughbred.

Born in 1971—the year the Grammy Awards were first broadcast live on television—Elmhirst would win his first of many Grammys thirty-seven years later for the making of "Rehab," as "Record of the Year," and *Back to Black* as "Best Pop Vocal Album of the Year," in 2008. He's the best of both worlds: old-school engineer and new age mixer. As Ronson recalled, he would, for example, layer Dap-Kings drummer Homer Steinweiss's playing with "other kicks and snares . . . just to make it a bit more modern, without ruining the subtly of the live playing."

Like all the best technical masters in the recording industry, he likes to quietly stay working in the background and let his artful albums do all the talking for him.

Tom Elmhirst first rose to prominence at the SARM studios in London (operated by Chris Blackwell, the founder of Island Records) under the mentorship of the great Trevor Horn, affectionately known by many as the inventor of the 1980s. This tutelage is most evident in Elmhirst's own preference for analog mixing boards and systems but also in his skill at absorbing the ever-evolving technologies that led him to the use of digital recording methods. He was therefore the logical choice when Ronson, after being blown away by Sharon Jones and the Dap-Kings and enlightened by Daptone's old-school tape techniques, wanted to emulate her style and their sound in a retro homage that has since achieved historic proportions.

Elmhirst described to Paul Tingen of *Sound on Sound* how he managed to "massage" the Dap-Kings' '60s-soul vibe to create the ultimate ironically radio-friendly song, "Rehab," during the *Back to Black* sessions: "Mixing is something that you either have or you don't. . . . I enjoy mixing most when I stop thinking about what I'm doing . . . if what's coming out of the speakers sound good, then I'm not bothered."

Almost a minimalist master of his audio craft, he's evolved an increasingly economical approach to the art of sound, its transmission, and its recording, as well demonstrated by his preference for what he called "tightly organized edit windows that fit on a single screen, so I don't have to scroll." This is because scrolling or searching for something would distract him from the immediacy he seeks, moment by moment. Psychologists refer to this as the "flow state," a creative frame of mind that is utterly unconscious, intuitive, and instinctual, and which makes time disappear altogether, so that the task at hand is hardly considered to be work anymore.

Elmhirst has expressed a nonchalant lack of concern for whether he's working at 8-bit or 96-bit rates (meaning the number of bits of actual audio information contained in a sample, thus impacting the resolution of the overall sound). The storage of sonic information controls how the sounds will be clearer, how vocals can seem cleaner, and how there will less (or no) noise in the end product. He lets his own ears do the talking again, in other words, and if something sounds right to him then it is right, period.

Elmhirst's attitude to his craft is as modest and understated as the music he mixes. Although he can, if pressed, wax rhapsodic about the relative merits of 24K versus 96K, as someone who clearly cares deeply about sound quality, his main obsession is creative flexibility when it comes to mixing any given song. He puts this down to listening quietly and enhancing his mixing agility, and it demonstrates the degree to which his primary interest is musical rather than strictly technical.

As complex as it all might be for the technical layman—and I'm one of them—it's useful to know that acres of time has been spent "getting it right" before any of us gets to sit down, relax, and listen when we drop in to visit the aural environment he created for "Rehab." More likely, of course, we're often up swaying around the room because of the ideal combination of song, singer, band, producer, and engineer that made it possible for all of us to simply gorge ourselves at the sumptuous buffet they've cooked up together.

Given the results we can all hear in the final mix, he obviously worked hard to get it just right, to find the proper balance that honors the song. As he modestly put it to *Sound on Sound* magazine, "It takes time, but it all comes together in the end." "Rehab" is a good song to stay with as we try to follow his mixing process, not because it is the most notorious track on the album (since this book is more concerned with the brilliant songwriting, gorgeous music, and technical prowess than with the soap opera surrounding it) but more because it offers such a complex and sophisticated layering of old-school styles with supersonic technical equipment, massively towering instrumentation and hugely moving vocals. In other words, it is the Sistine Chapel of sound recording—a work by virtuosos moving in unison and together manifesting something so beautifully seamless it feels otherworldly.

Sometimes even the producer and the mixing engineer don't see eye-to-eye, or ear-to-ear, on all the details of the sound they're striving for. When Elmhirst first received Ronson's original mixes of "You Know I'm No Good," "Rehab," and "Love Is a Losing Game," for instance, the producer's mixes were more radical in terms of panning, and almost Beatle-esque in terms of the separation of instruments.

The engineer liked the fact that since they were recorded at Daptone Records using Dap-Kings technology, they had captured the drums, piano, guitar, and bass all live in one room, with lots of spill between the instruments. What this did was manifest that retro, '60s soul and R&B vibe, which of course is exactly what the Kings specialize in, and why Ronson called upon them in the first place. Elmhirst felt his brief was to focus on keeping the mix sparse but still keeping the beats up to date, so that the results would work well on contemporary radio without losing any of their nostalgic feel.

For the lead vocals, for instance, Elmhirst used plenty of hardware processing, and Winehouse's lead voice was treated with surgical EQ from WavesQ10, Great British Spring Reverb and EMT plate reverb. But even though he had access to and mastery over the latest hi-tech toys, Elmhirst is in no way what we might call a techno-snob, especially since his career has bridged the gap between the analog and the digital centuries. Speaking to *Sound on Sound*, he pointed out the difference between mixers and their contrasting approaches to vocal styles. As an example of these subtle differences, a comparative listen to the tracks mixed by Gary Noble will demonstrate the presence or absence of equalization on the voice.

Elmhirst's intention in applying equalization—the process of adjusting the balance between frequency components within an electronic signal—was to brighten up her voice a little, to add a little air to it. The end result—for him, Amy, and us—was a much more controlled vocal sound.

Late in the evening of the first day of mixing "Rehab," he pretty much held the vocal in the track all the time, performing the mix with the instrumental tracks and vocal tracks flowing at the same time, constantly tweaking it, bit by bit, probably in ways only a canary would be able to register, but in ways which would still impact all of us emotionally. Maybe even subliminally.

The same degree of fetishistic tinkering occurred with the drums, bass, timpani, and piano. Elmhirst used Vari-fi, for example, not as a way to speed things up or slow things down at microscopic levels that might make insects dance, but to give some of the sounds what he called a "smaller, more concise frequency spectrum."

He felt fortunate to have started in the music business during the last days of analog, at SARM with Chris Blackwell, where he worked on two-inch tapes and learned how to count bars, drop in to the mix manually, and be disciplined when track-laying. Working with tape, he explained to *Sound on Sound*, had become something of a lost art in the digital age.

The listening audience was the beneficiary of his good fortune and early training, with a great album being the final product of a long and complex collaborative mixing process. The main purpose of talented mixers is to become familiar with, condense, and organize the musical material that they are presented with by the producer, after he or she guides the artist through her paces in delivering whatever song is in the works. As Elmhirst clarified further, "It's not the technical side that matters, it's whether what comes out of the speakers sounds good." The understatement of the truly gifted.

■ ■ ■

These days, with the advent of technological advances that are light years away from the universe of Phil Spector, Brian Wilson, or George Martin, producers are now also often so musically adept themselves as arrangers, singer/songwriters, or musicians in their own right that they collaborate to a far higher degree with the artists they produce than they might have in days gone by. This leads to heady creative collaboration in the studio laboratory, best evidenced by great talents such as Rick Rubin, Daniel Lanois, Brian Eno, Salaam Remi, or Mark Ronson, to name but a few who play a crucial role in our narrative.

The eventual evolution of independent studios liberated everyone, theoretically, from the creatively confining domain of the factory enterprise model, with former record-company employees now operating their own rogue production systems themselves. This intimate creative context then made the whole process more direct and immediate and also much closer to the musical street itself, where the rest of us live and listen.

This new "producer as artist" motif also allows such a multitalented individual—a rarified Spector wizard, let's say—to perform all of these roles at the same time. Their work often even includes the co-writing and sometimes the elemental live in-studio performance contributions that gave their productions a signature style.

The technically analog preferences of gifted musical artists such as Jack White and his White Stripes in the hard rock/blues genre or the Dap-Kings in the blues/soul genre are prime examples of a post-digital "get back" mentality. As mentioned earlier, and in particular, the revivalist (not retro) recording techniques of Daptone Records would open Ronson and Remi's minds and ears to the "future" of occasionally looking backward instead of always rushing forward. Combining such back with forth was their consummate gift and also the secret skill that made *Back to Black* both so distinctive and influential.

Ronson was especially adept at applying analog techniques to his digital bag of tricks. As Ronson later explained, in an interview with National Public Radio, "At the time Amy and I were working on the demos for *Back to Black*, and I was using whatever computer tricks I could. They have plug-ins for your computer to make things sound old or whatever it is. And I played Amy the recording of Sharon Jones. And I said, 'How good is this? We should get these guys to play these demos.'"

Equally distinctive was the beautiful simplicity of the Remi and Ronson signature styles, separately and fused together—a grafting process that would give *Back to Black* such a powerful architectural structure of Supremes-style walls containing a carefully handcrafted furniture micro-world for her personal style hybrids. In actuality, wedding hip hop with soul and girl groups was the key to the pop kingdom for all concerned.

The fact that hip hop had emerged as such a dominant mainstream musical style is nothing short of amazing given its outlaw origins and rogue technical childhood. The term is often credited to the legendary rapper Keith Cowboy, who was part of the brilliant madness of Grandmaster Flash and the Furious Five. But it's equally believed to originate in the curiously kitsch crossover genre known of disco-rap-funk, a wild musical mutation that spawned a huge tidal wave of diverse rap-oriented attitudes and stylistic variations in the mid-'70s.

Its first usage as a subculture term affiliated with the urban poetry scene and the social sources that birthed it was by Afrika Bambaataa, the visionary founder of the Universal Zulu Nation. The first time "hip hop" appeared in print journalism—an ironically validating factor, given its original aggressive outsider status—was in a *Village Voice* article by Steven Hager, who would later write an early, influential history of hip-hop style in 1984. The emerging digital domain then loomed large in the sudden evolution of a style that would eventually envelop the anti–Spice Girl herself via Remi's own early musical upbringing.

Kurtis Blow was probably the first hip-hop artist to utilize a digital sampler in the manner later to be fully absorbed into the mainstream. Remi, of course, was the son of famed studio musician Van Gibbs, who played with Blow in the '80s and allowed his all-of-fifteen-year-old son Salaam to play keyboards on Blow's 1986 release *Kingdom Blow*. Salaam hit the ground running: he starting to mix records in the late '80s and by 1992 had fully produced a record by the hip-hop group known as Zhigge.

It was his superior hip-hop skills, merged with Ronson's gifted dance, rave, and '60s girl-group fetish, that would cross-pollinate into the exotic but short-lived flower we now remember as the white soul singer who took the world by storm before being swept away by her own doomed internal weather.

But the making of *Back to Black* didn't just consist of the incredibly fast ten-day period when Ronson had Winehouse to himself in the studio crafting raw and often acoustic demos, or even the heady five brief months during 2006 when it was assembled by him from recorded fragments separated by an ocean. In a very real sense, its actual history is comprised of the sixty years of pop music that preceded her sudden rise to prominence. The arcane musical menu Ronson wove together into so impressive a mosaic is still even more startling ten years later because of the almost supernatural ease of its conception. Often it was a matter of pure chance (which, as we now know well, is the fool's name for fate.)

As Ronson later remarked to *Performing Songwriter* of "Love Is a Losing Game," "We had done a recording of it with just her singing, accompanied by acoustic guitar, and I'd become so attached to it that we felt there was no way we could top that emotionally. But there was a part of me that still wanted to hear the sonic of reverbed drums in the background." The way he delicately handled and evolved her often *very* rough ideas and feelings into a finished product of such subtlety and sophistication is nothing short of breathtaking.

The results he concocted were even more impressive because he seemed to do it all from the heart, deciding early on that he and they needed to disregard the industry standards, the tastemakers, the critics or even their own peer musicians.

"We were just sitting in a little room in my studio and making the music we wanted," he told *Performing Songwriter*. When Ronson asked her what she wanted the record to sound like, Winehouse played him tracks by the Shangri-Las and Earl and the Cadillacs. "My job was to take [her] back into this era we were both infatuated with," Ronson added.

An equally absorbent sponge for past post-musical history, especially that of the Spectorized girl groups of the '60s, Ronson was perhaps the ideal collaborator for Remi and Winehouse. That said, his own personal music could never have compared with the album he would help Winehouse to create, and without wishing to diminish his considerable talents I think he'd be the first to agree that we may not be talking about him at all today if not for her.

As Ronson explained to Q-Tip, in an article for *Interview Magazine*, they met just at the time when he was beginning to feel burned out digitally. "I [didn't] want to be beat-hustling for the next ten years," he said. "It was about that time that I stopped really caring about what anybody else wanted or what was commercial, or what I thought I should be doing." When he started working with the Dap-Kings, he added, "it all just clicked," while on meeting Winehouse "there was just instantly this bond there, like you just meet some people and you get each other right away. She was so charming, and charismatic and funny." There was definitely a sense of something special and predestined about it. Other artists can only dream about this degree of fate stepping in, and even if it does it must happen mostly only once in a lifetime. The same is true with the remarkably brief but intimate studio experience they shared together.

There was clearly an uplifting sense of destiny in the air when Ronson recorded the first versions of these tracks in his Mercer Street studio before heading to Daptone to play the demos for the Dap-Kings. Winehouse had already gone back to England, and the young producer was on his own. By his own account, he was a little bit terrified—no, make that petrified—since it was to be the first time he had ever got in front of a band and directed them.

Especially daunting was the Dap-Kings' long history as a working crew, their proficiency at their instruments, and their seniority over him, and Ronson definitely detected some degree of suspicion on their part at first. In truth, not only were they like a crew, they also had the honed studio finesse of Spector's Wrecking Crew, as Ronson knew well. He also knew right away that they were what he needed for his creative liaison with Amy and that their sound was what would make it a truly meaningful record in the most authentic way possible. That first day recording together was, he later said, "like having an out-of-body experience . . . I knew right there that this was the sound I wanted to make for the next ten years."

Indeed, all the music he's created in the following ten years has carried the imprint of his fate-drenched encounter with both Winehouse and the Dap-Kings. When he won two Grammys for "Uptown Funk" in February 2016, I half expected him to thank Amy Winehouse for making it possible, and I'm only half kidding. He's that much a part of her legacy.

■ ■ ■

Earlier, I asked the question, "What does a producer do?" I have since outlined the basic facets that make some producers artists in their own right. Now the question is, "What does the producer-as-artist really do?" This means examining the meaning of the art of "thinking in sounds."

Mark Ronson crafted a florid flavor too complex to ever isolate easily, a strangely delicate sonic soufflé, the synchronistic *something* that made *Back to Black* what it still is. The early century arrival of digital audio workstation technologies further allowed the artisanal producer-as-artist the ability to assume and absorb more creative skills and technical functions than even the grandiose Phil Spector could have imagined for himself.

Eventually these technologies turned producers into a new kind of film director, crafting miniature aural movies for the individual songs that grace and enhance the artistic status of a formerly humble pop record album. Pop has to be ultra-eclectic for it to be pop at all, and the cross-section of tunes Ronson has produced—from Ghostface Killah to Foreigner, Lil Wayne to Paul McCartney—is so diverse it shimmers.

With Ronson, the producer-as-artist reached new and even dizzier heights, and the artifact he, Remi, and Winehouse left behind is the archaeological evidence of an entertainment empire he helped to build. By becoming tangled up in blue together, they left a kind of obscure pyramid on the landscape of popular culture and like those other ancient builders, people in the future may well wonder if their artifact was built by otherworldly beings. In a way, it was.

I tend to identify such brilliant production masters as agent provocateurs (from the original French for *illicit agents*) who in the generic sense of the term are also on hand to serve as midwives. They expand their original producer function of managing the project into a larger and richer creative capacity for challenging and even *provoking* the artist into making something better than themselves. Something higher, deeper and further ahead than their self-defined limits might otherwise allow. Both Remi and Ronson served this provocateur function well, separately at first and then fused together to fully capitalize on the living musical history lesson Amy Winehouse had become.

The final results, especially in the case of Ronson's vast, Spector-like sounds, are immense indeed, and they're highlighted by his skill for making a record something way more than merely the sum of its separate parts. Luckily, the volatile singer was able to be much more proud of her second album than her first, and maybe even more proud of surviving its difficult birth process, thanks to this talented team of musical midwives.

The word virtuoso is not misplaced in describing this talent for playing the studio itself as if it were Remi and Ronson's own musical instrument, within which the singer and her songs were collaged seamlessly onto the platform provided by a supremely gifted back-up band and smoothly distilled through Tom Elmhirst's magic mixing board.

All the best producers are easily identified by an obsessive-compulsive urge to polish the perfect sound. Clearly the best professional asset a producer can also have is an inherent musical talent to align with and superimpose on the work of their client. Remi and Ronson were both able to technically master the music of their temperamental and troubled young artist and contribute something all their own to making her recording into a work of art.

There was, however, a fourth member of this magical musical crew to greatly acknowledge here, and that's the multi-talented Gabriel Roth himself. Roth, who produces under the name Bosco Mann, is the co-founder of Daptone Records and also the writer, arranger, bass player, and producer of Sharon Jones and the Dap-Kings, and would win a Grammy Award for his sound engineering work on *Back to Black*. He is in fact the Mark Ronson of the Dap-Kings, and *he* was, after all, the crucial elixir that Ronson turned to when he wanted that raw vintage authenticity.

Roth admitted to Saki Knafo, in a December 2008 profile piece for the *New York Times Magazine*, that he had some reservations when he was first approached by Ronson to play behind Amy Winehouse, then just "a twenty-two-year-old white jazz-club performer." Having heard the Dap-Kings' cover version of Stevie Wonder's "Uptight (Everything's Alright)," however, Ronson knew instantly that he'd found the sound he'd not only been searching for but also trying desperately to imitate and simulate digitally.

Roth had to pause to seriously reflect on this job offer. Considering how stellar the results were, it may surprise some listeners and readers to discover that Roth was not initially enamored with Winehouse's music, finding it "a little too angsty and self-involved" for his taste. But being an astute bandleader, and not wanting to deprive his group of a decent payday, he figured this was an easy gig for a band that had honed its chops as stalwart "second-generation soul men." In retrospect, and given the sales bonanza the record created, the label got a phenomenal deal by offering the seasoned R&B instrumentalists a whopping $350 per musician per song.

The album they played on would of course go on to sell and make millions, would take them away from their longtime frontline singer Sharon Jones temporarily while they went out on the Winehouse global concert tour, and would garner Roth his first and only framed platinum record.

Roth remained true to his analog tape roots and distrustful of fancy digital technology: "Look, show me a computer that sounds as good as a tape machine and I'll use it." At the same encounter, the *Times* interviewer also noticed, when he visited the historic Daptone Studio, that Roth displayed his framed platinum selling record in his studio's decrepit downstairs bathroom, propped up against the wall, a few inches from the toilet. Wherever he may choose to display it, five Grammys later it was pretty obvious that Planet Earth liked what it heard coming out of its speakers, and it was obsessive-compulsive geniuses like Salaam Remi, Mark Ronson, Tom Elmhirst, and Gabriel Roth who made our ears dance around the room.

■ ■ ■

Once the album was crafted and created, it would be up to the singer herself to personally deliver it for us by dancing around the world to the sudden and nearly overwhelming acclaim unleashed by Amy-mania. Her own version of a retro-British invasion would be every bit as unusual an event as she was a performer. This aspect of her trajectory also brings us by circuitous navigation to perhaps her greatest challenge of all.

Even once you release a great album, there's still a big shock in store for an artist like Amy Winehouse. Now, you have to be healthy enough, or at least strong enough, to go out and stand on concert stages across the planet to *give the people what they want,* over and over and over again.

6

AMY THE PERFORMANCE ARTIST

Back to Black Onstage

"Fame is a series of misunderstandings surrounding a person's name."
—Joni Mitchell to Jian Ghomeshi, *Q*, CBC Radio, 2013

All of us naturally think of concert tours as entertainment, and of course they are, but in reality they're primarily extensions of the record industry, and often take the form of a live presentation of an album release. Stage performances permit, allow or demand of the artist that they embody their new record and deliver a personal evocation of it.

Since her ascent to musical acclaim and her rise to global public recognition were so speeded-up, even Amy Winehouse didn't fully realize that she'd almost accidentally joined the stellar ranks of pop stardom. She'd invaded a rarefied territory occupied by Shania Twain and Whitney Houston; she now resided in a zone of our pop celebrity culture stratosphere usually reserved for a Cher or a Madonna. How truly odd and scary that must have seemed to her.

The key word here is "accidentally." This wasn't her intention or desire, or even her wildest dream, and she's on record as believing that pop itself was kind of a dirty word in her mouth as an *artist*. Having fled the ranks of young retro-jazz singers and embraced an earthier retro-soul feel, it never occurred to her that the audience for her sad diary entries would become so huge that almost overnight a weird Winehouse fetish was happening.

It also certainly never occurred to her that pop stardom was suddenly being bestowed on her in a way that demanded ever larger and larger concert venues to accommodate the armies of Amy-lovers who identified so strongly with her messages of personal loss and lament. Everyone on the planet, it seemed, wanted to see and hear her perform this album.

As early as the month after *Back to Black*'s release in October 2006, Winehouse was interviewed by a British TV host who asked her if her new record was more *accessible* than her first one, since anything jazz related was always considered off-putting for the general public. She seemed perplexed, pausing before responding, "Well, it's a *little* more accessible, but it's certainly not *poppy*!" with a disdainful sniff emphasizing that supposedly lightweight category.

In an interview excerpted from Asif Kapadia's documentary on the singer, Winehouse's friend and pianist Sam Beste recalled how, much to her surprise, she'd become a commercially successful star—something she clearly abhorred. But it probably never dawned on her that she'd soon be so huge a hit that eventually she'd actually be contacting Salaam Remi, begging him to get back together to help her *return* to her roots and do something more jazzy again. She may also have been similarly encouraged by the extreme kindness, patience, and generosity shown to her by Tony Bennett during the occasionally nerve-wracking process of recording their final duet together. On record as declaring that she had one of the greatest jazz voices he'd ever heard, he also counseled her that brilliant jazz voices like hers aren't at their best in front of screaming fans in gigantic venues.

It's true: something strange happens to a performer like Winehouse when their popularity demands grandiose stadium-sized concert venues. The attempt to translate her intimate diaries into rock-scale spectacles was surely doomed from the start, especially when her vulnerable delivery style couldn't possibly just *expand* on demand to satisfy that amount of sheer pop extravaganza. Looking at her performances as the audience hunger for her presence increased exponentially is a crash course in career implosion. Her music always came across as (to paraphrase David Axelrod) an MRI of her soul, so how could it possibly benefit from being amplified up to monumental scales? Well, it couldn't.

In this context it's especially useful to remember that both concert tours and music videos are virtual-reality tentacles of a record itself; they're designed to raise and perpetuate awareness of artists and sell their records. This is an artist who was in distress before making the album, in distress while making it, and in distress during its busy promotional campaigns. As she herself admitted so boldly, her odds were stacked.

As we've seen, the *Back to Black* album must be an example of one of the most swiftly created and celebrated pop artifacts in music history, given the rapid evolution of Ronson's relationship with the singer, his inheritance of her roughly hewn songs for arrangement, their recording and mixing in New York and Miami, its pressing and release, and, ultimately, the promotional tour designed to conquer the world.

In the *Back to Black* concerts—except for the earliest ones in England—emotional entropy soon became the key narrative. In physics, a loss of energy suggests that mega-stars known as black holes can't last forever but rather will evaporate slowly, and in her case, she did it live onstage. A ten-date British tour had been planned to start the ball rolling at the Liverpool Academy 2 on November 10, 2006, but since her live licks were slightly rusty after the album's difficult birthing and an almost ten-month hiatus from the stage since her last tours for *Frank*, it was deemed strategically sound to do some more manageable "loosening-up" dates to get the singer back in gear to promote *Black*.

Ten months is a long time in the arts, where performers count in dog years, so it was a sound move to dust off her delivery via three prior dates, starting in Bristol, at the Fleece, on September 10. This first show marked the beginning of the media's distraction from her musical material to her appearance and behavior—a shift that would grow in proportion as her challenges expanded before our eyes. The *Daily Telegraph*, not the most musically savvy paper of record, actually went so far as to comment, "Overall the music is still less interesting than Winehouse herself. She is even more striking than before."

This of course must be one of the most egregious errors of judgment we've ever heard, given that her music had achieved a new level of composition, arrangement, recording, and delivery that the press likely hadn't encountered since who knows who.

No one could have been prepared for the stunning new image she presented live onstage.

Bristol was her first live test performance in almost a year, with fresh and shockingly confessional songs that all our ears probably needed time to adjust to. So it was especially disheartening for a local newspaper, the *Argus*, to remark of her concert at Concorde 2 in Brighton shortly afterward, "She seemed self-consciously disembodied from her old songs and fluffed her lines more than a couple of times."

Of course she was disembodied from her earlier songs: she wasn't even the same singer/songwriter who composed them, and she sure wasn't the same performer who had delivered them. In his bio, Mick O'Shea accurately notes that though she'd been working with her producers for half a year, she literally hadn't been performing at all, but she was building up her stage presence with each live appearance. This was evidenced by the more coherent rendering she gave at the Bloomsbury Ballroom in London, in the last of her three pre-tour "warm-ups."

Although the music press immediately twigged that her vocal style had matured and acquired considerably more subtlety in the years between her first and second albums, and also that her source material was even more autobiographical and harrowingly personal in nature, few seemed to register the perhaps insurmountable challenge of reliving the primal pain of her broken relationship onstage publicly over and over again. Despite that challenge, and ready or not, it was full steam ahead. Once she'd mastered a new live style for her new material, Winehouse was prepared (more or less) for the gigantic tours that would make her into a household name. Her tour schedule would be a grueling one, and by the time her show at the Academy 2 in Liverpool finally arrived, so too had the consequences of her full-fledged demonic diva persona, along with the public rumors of bad behavior that would soon overtake her.

After a hugely popular show at Leeds Wardrobe the day after Liverpool, she quickly rushed up to Glasgow for a perfectly situated small auditorium gig at Oran Mor (Gaelic for big song), then on to Koko in London's Camden Town. Two nights later she was onstage at the Birmingham Academy and being pursued by her shadow side even more gravely as she began her show by borrowing some lipstick from an audience member and asking the crowd to hold on for a moment while she put on her "blow-job lips." Her voice was already starting to show the strain and her biggest tours hadn't even started in earnest. She joked that if she ruined her voice then her arch nemesis, Katie Melua, could always stand in for her. This certainly didn't bode well for her upcoming invasion of America.

The night after Birmingham, Winehouse appeared at the Manchester Academy 2, where she had sufficient difficulties getting into gear that they trailed her to her next night's gig at Norwich, which was followed by Cambridge Junction on November 20, and then to Bristol for her Carling Academy show (the one where she shared with the audience the news that she was "still here, still standing"). Three days later, she was back in London for the Little Noise Sessions at the Union Chapel in Islington. In December 2006 she floated over to Belfast for a short promo stint and then on to Dublin for an appearance at the Ambassador Theatre.

The action just never stopped, and no one around her seemed to notice that she wasn't quite keeping up. Just as the British press was starting to write about her challenges, Amy was off to New York for a promotional visit to stimulate awareness about the upcoming American release of the album. It was then that she would make her now-legendary appearance at Joe's Pub (actually a nightclub), where she stunned both audience and press with her soulful spirit and funky brilliance. America was about to be taken by storm. And Winehouse herself was about to be deluged with attention.

"Just wheel me onstage," she purred to all and sundry. The *Village Voice* characterized her appearance this way: "Backed by a taut ten-piece band, the Dap-Kings, she hit the tiny stage like a tatted-up Ronette from hell, complete with thick black eyeliner, fabulously ratted bouffant weaves, and a skintight strapless cocktail dress." For *Spin* magazine, she was "a quintessential Bond-girl from the Sean Connery era." And in the midst of all the press attention, she started giving those shockingly honest interviews to platforms like *Entertainment Weekly* and the *Washington Post* in which she openly declared the laundry list of psychological difficulties she had suffered while growing up and admitted to still having as a sudden star.

But *still* no one let such deep psychic revelations get in the way of enjoying her retro party-girl image, mostly because she was just so incredibly refreshing and so disarmingly different from every other super-polished performer on the planet. One solitary British voice was the *Independent*, which chided, "The disjunction between the kind of venue that success brings and the intimate nature of what she actually does cripples the show. Her success may be dragging Amy

Winehouse into inappropriate places, but that's the price of making pop music this good."

■■■

Winehouse's seemingly endless concert tour—which was actually only just beginning, and would continue on headlong into her 2008 Grammy Award wins—marched to Southampton, on February 18, 2007, then back to London, for an Astoria show, then to the varied Academy shows, then to Newcastle's Northumbria University, then back to Glasgow and on to Sheffield and Nottingham, and back to London again. Another thirteen-date US tour was scheduled for the end of April. But then the cancelations started; first only a few, later on many, and eventually all.

Late April saw her careening across US stages in San Francisco, Indio, Colorado, Minneapolis, Chicago, Philadelphia, Boston, and New York; in Holland, Germany, Sweden, Norway, Belgium, and France; and then yet more back in London. By June 14, "Rehab" had risen to the *Billboard* Hot 100's Top Ten. Then even more high-profile music industry awards started to be showered on her shaking shoulders.

On August 21 it was announced that after a slew of random cancelations here and there along the way, her entire upcoming American tour of big theaters, important outdoor festivals, and even the "Central Park in the Dark" event was being canceled as the singer was being hospitalized for a variety of unsavory ailments euphemistically lumped together as "exhaustion." There was no looking back from this vantage point, only looking down.

Since life can only be lived forward but can only be understood backward, luckily our retrospective position is always more favorable than that of the subject of a narrative while they're embroiled in actually living their story. Looking back ten years later is easy, and it's plain to see what made some of her concerts so exciting and exceptional and some of her videos so vivid and memorable, at least in the early stages of her meteoric ascent. Equally clear is how unusual her relationship with her musicians was, and so too the interplay between their interpretation of her music professionally and their interaction personally.

For example, guitarist Binky Griptite and Amy Winehouse had a special bond made perhaps even more exceptional as a result of the fact that they had each contributed sections of her songs to the other only via recordings, without having met personally. Using his considerable studio wizardry, Mark Ronson had recorded them separately and then played back the vocal and instrumental sounds with each of them singing or playing along to the other already on tape. So their ability to be perfectly in sync was all the more remarkable, both on a track like "Valerie," made *after Back to Black* came out (and the first time they ever met), and in their later grooving in unison for live concert performances to support her album on tour.

On January 16, 2007, Winehouse and the Dap-Kings took to the stage for their first ever live performance together, which was also her American debut. As Amy Linden wrote for the *Village Voice*, "By the end of the gig, everyone knew that Winehouse, all 85 pounds or so of her, had smacked R&B back to life. In four-inch pumps. The intimate pub was filled with unabashed love, and she knew it. She sounded great but acted like she didn't believe it. It made me fear that Amy had the talent to be a star, but might not have the strength."

For his part, Griptite was philosophical about his interaction with the new hit artist. "When we played 'Fuck Me Pumps,' I'd just learned the song that day!" he told the *Village Voice* in 2015. "It starts with an unaccompanied guitar part. I blew the fourth chord and had to start over. On the mic, she says, 'You're fired!' I cringe and start the song again." He felt better about it when, later in the set, Winehouse made a mistake of her own. "That happened every time she and I did duo gigs. We took turns fucking up, and would laugh it off later."

As Hilary Hughes observed, also in the *Voice*, "That night marked the beginning of the big headlines and the big, brutal spotlight that suddenly turned its merciless light on the singer." While Joe's Pub set the scene for Winehouse's introduction to the American industry, for Griptite it was also a reality check. The Dap-Kings, and Daptone at large, were very much independent and not part of the major-label world. Working with Winehouse was "a case study in the music business." But while some of his bandmates were "not as into" the idea of playing with a major-label act, Griptite was philosophical about it. "We got to play great music with great people, and we had great fun, but it's not the same as being in the machine, you know?"

Speaking of being "in the machine," it's surprising, given how radically she lived, just how old fashioned and bare bones a live Winehouse concert performance could be. Not old fashioned in the sense of her so-called retro style, but in the basic presentation itself: a post-feminist chick in a tight dress and sharp heels on a simple stage swaying with a large old-school ensemble feverishly cooking behind her. No big light shows; no theatrical props, stage set, or costumes; no special effects. In point of fact, she was her own special effect; anything else would have been superfluous.

■ ■ ■

At first, when we try to imagine an artist doing something like 143 public concerts as part of a demanding global schedule under the blinding media limelight, as Winehouse did, it can certainly seem like a high number of physical and emotional appearances—at least to regular mortals like us. But our perspective can be clarified somewhat when we realize the huge number of concerts delivered by other musical immortals, especially some who are still busy stoking their fires today. For example: the Rolling Stones are up to a total of 2,200 concerts and counting; Bob Dylan is at 3,100; the Grateful Dead (whose fiftieth anniversary farewell tour took place in 2015) peaked at around 2,400.

Nevertheless, Winehouse's tours as a whirling diva were sumptuous affairs carved down to the bare essentials, just her and a superb backup band, with the Dap-Kings almost as visually entertaining as she was. Eventually, audiences that started as small as they should have been would grow as huge as they needed to be. Then, finally, they grew bigger than they should have been.

What becomes clear when we examine the living documents these performances represent, especially in the case of the turbulent and accelerated living pace of an Amy Winehouse, is that performing a great work can often be just as challenging as creating one in the first place. From August 16, 2003, until December 19, 2004, Winehouse played seventeen concerts in support of her debut album, subsequent to which she played one hundred and twenty six concerts to promote the new material from *Back to Black*. These appearances occasionally referenced both records but eventually focused solely on *Black*, probably as a result of both audience demand and record promotion, as well as her own well publicized disdain for her first recorded outing.

The erstwhile Ms. Winehouse was not by any stretch of the imagination a lazy performer. In fact, if anything, she had the opposite challenge: an astronomical inability to pull back on the reins and get some much-needed rest. Of course, by 2009 and through all of 2010 she was already attempting to mount a valiant battle against the forces conspiring against her future success; no extensive performances took place during that draining hiatus.

However brief her activity as a live stage performer, several of her concert dates are among the most polished, captivating, and compelling examples of sharing a musical gift with complete strangers ever rendered. They demonstrated a degree of sincerity and authenticity almost unrivaled in popular music culture, so therefore they're the concerts worth discussing in some detail.

Foremost among these is Winehouse's stellar appearance at the South by Southwest Festival in Austin, Texas, in 2007. SXSW is a mixture of film, interactive, and music gatherings and conferences that takes place every March, with live music concerts running for five days and featuring a wide range of contemporary artists. With its eclectic blend of mediums and formats, it's the largest such registrant-based festival of its kind in the world, an event inaugurated in 1987, its name playing on the reverse of the Alfred Hitchcock movie.

As a result of its mixed-media concept, the music featured is also presented within a larger cultural context of films and technology, and as such it attracts quite a different blend of attendees from the average pop or rock concert. The music portion of the festival has an average attendance of 29,000 and is known as a launching pad for alternative talent that subsequently hits it big in the mainstream. The Hanson brothers were brought there by their father in 1994 in the hopes of getting attention, which they received from A&R executive Chris Sabec, who became their manager and got them signed to Mercury Records; John Mayer's 2000 appearance led to his signing with his first major label, Aware Records; the Polyphonic Spree achieved prominence after appearing there in 2002; James Blunt was first discovered by producer Linda Perry while performing to a small crowd at SXSW 2004, and would go on to become almost as popular, albeit briefly, as Winehouse did on a much huger scale.

Amy Winehouse gave a relatively intimate series of performances at the Texas festival in March 2007 at a time when she was still well known only in England, and as her first big-format showcase in America (the corporate stint at Joe's Pub was minute by comparison), SXSW to be an ideal launching pad for her special talents. In addition to her appearance on the main stage, a small indoor acoustic set that included the title song from *Back to Black*, casually presented by the singer in jeans with a single guitarist, proved to be the perfect introduction of the singer to the continent. She was healthy, if not entirely happy, relatively clean, and utterly mesmerizing for the tiny Bourbon Rocks audience, whose members appeared completely stunned by her breathtaking beauty and powerful song skills.

She also did an excellent version of "Me and Mr. Jones," slowed down incredibly to a snail's pace, with her full band in flight. This was the perfect venue for her intimate skills, ideal in scale and temperament for her undeniable strengths: small-to-medium-sized listening groups, similar to a jazz club in volume, personal enough for her to banter quietly with and sing softly to without straining her vocal chords to reach the top and back of giant rock stadiums or huge festival fields.

Equally impressive were her SXSW appearances at the Levi's/*Fader* Magazine Party and the La Zona Rosa venue, where she delivered spine-tingling versions of "Rehab" and "Wake Up Alone"—renditions that were both heartbreaking and awe-inspiring declarations of an unworldly skill and an innate technique beyond anything even an accomplished senior artist can be formally taught. Clearly, talent like hers couldn't be learned; it came from beyond.

Only a month later, on May 28, 2007, Winehouse graced the intimate stage of the Shepherd's Bush Empire in London, another venue that seemed ideal for her talents. Originally built in 1903 by renowned theatre architect Frank Matcham for impresario Oswald Stoll, this little theater was once operated by BBC Television as a broadcasting/performance venue.

Its capacity since 1995 has been almost 2,400 seats, which is the absolutely perfect scale for a musical artist of Winehouse's style and substance. Anything much larger, such as the venues ten times that size where she appeared later on in support of *Back to Black*, only lose the essential ambience and interplay between performer and audience that would have been the key ingredient to any quintessential Winehouse presentation.

In reality, of course, around 240 people clustered around a circular stage where she didn't have to shout or undergo dramatic rock-style amplification would have been even better, but this charming little neighborhood theater space could still simulate the sensation of seeing a great vocalist with a tight band in a local bar or nightclub. That's why the documentary film made of her performance there, released by Island Records in November of 2007, comes across as being so magical in practically all respects. It's half documentary film, half music video, and the two halves merge very well to deliver something intimate yet grandiose at the same time.

I Told You I Was Trouble: Amy Winehouse Live in London captures her proverbial live lightning in a bottle (no pun intended), and as a film document of her superior skills at delivering songs that chilled your spine, it's still a lasting testament to her innate abilities. It ranks as one of the finest achievements in both live performance and the filming of a concert for commercial release. This despite the fact that the event had to be rescheduled twice due to "personal difficulties" (an ongoing theme of both her music and her life).

The most shocking part of the performance is a rather pleasant one that leaves the viewer shaking his or her head in bewilderment as we hear the singer talking in her normal speaking voice. Hearing her switch quickly back and forth from her blurring, clipped cockney accent, with its occasionally incomprehensible jumble of vowels, to her astonishing, accent-less angelic howl as she sings her songs, is quite breathtaking. It just boggles the mind how a person with her personal speech patterns could also have a jazz/blues/soul voice that swooped with such animal ease across deep and heartfelt lyrics—after which she would cheekily grin and revert back to her everyday rude, slangy self with a daft chuckle.

Winehouse is in her element here, commanding the crowd with her finest blend of charming sass, saucy spunk, and sheer inexplicable musical talent. And of course the Dap-Kings, the best studio and live backup band since the Wrecking Crew and the J.B.'s, are pounding away behind her. On occasion they almost steal the show; or, at least to my mind, they borrow it briefly.

Watching Winehouse performing live in a concert, or even in a video of one, is maybe the best way to deconstruct her inscrutable allure. When we listen to her record on our own, we're treated to that movie for our ears in a way that depends only on our own mood and imagination, but viewing her in full flight and delivery allows us some space and time to actually study the science of what she did so well. The Shepherd's Bush Empire show was a nearly perfect vintage 2007 gig for this still relatively fresh young singer, before America transformed her into a bona-fide superstar and a casualty of her own popularity.

As with most of her concerts, the set list remained fairly fixed; she did after all only have two albums from which to choose songs to perform, while the audience appetite for certain songs in a certain order was already ravenous. She did include a few non-Amy songs in the set—a smart move on her part, and one she may have benefited from expanding as a performance concept, since having a handful of songs by others that inspired her may have helped varnish the fact that she was surfing a long wave and didn't just drop onto the planet from nowhere. A couple of Carole King, Roberta Flack, or Phil Spector songs, for instance, would have been downright utopian.

Winehouse opens her London show with "Addicted," and though it's one of the weakest songs from the UK release of *Back to Black* (from which the North American market was thankfully spared), it's still diverting to see the band and its amazing dancing dudes rollicking along with her. She inexplicably ends the song by apologizing for something inaudible before picking up a large tumbler of what appears to be milk and briefly walking away, only to appear again instantly, running with her beverage to the microphone again just in time to begin to sing "Just Friends," finally putting her glass on the floor and starting her signature sashaying dancing.

She gestures to her family beaming in the balcony and leaps into a lighthearted *Frank* song, "Cherry," a love song to her guitar, before launching into the majestic gem that the audience really all came to hear, "Back to Black," but not before also generously plugging her best girlfriend's music. The spine tingles. As sad as it is, it was what she was sent to earth to do. She thanks the audience somewhat inarticulately, shares a story about biting down on an ice cube and injuring her tooth, shows the crowd her teeth, and even mouths "I love you" to the figure in the balcony who inspired (or caused) her to write all these songs in the first place. (That moment in the concert chills the spine too, though mostly for other, non-musical reasons.)

"Wake Up Alone" follows in its dark wake and adds a bit of Spector spice to proceedings, by which point her energy starts to flag slightly, until the Supremes spirit of "Tears Dry on Their Own" lifts her back up and pushes her forward into "He Can Only Hold Her / Doo Wop (That Thing)," a warning to all lovers that many guys and some girls are only about one single unnamed but familiar thing. She sweetly plugs her two backup singer dudes, Zalon and Ade, after this one, probably just to grab a breather for herself.

A brief respite from the darkness follows as she returns to

the *Frank* energy of "Fuck Me Pumps," smiling and laughing at the audience's loud thrill at its opening, as if genuinely surprised at their worship. A sip from another large tumbler, this time filled with a red fluid, lubricates her slowly descending pace and starts off her giant hair-flipping regime. Her voice now seems to be coming from another body, her facial expressions suggesting that she really is actually somewhere else, that location probably involving the increasingly distracting presence in the balcony, at which she begins grinning and making funny faces. But suddenly she plunges further down into her séance-like manner of delivery with "Some Unholy War," and then feels like a crop-dusting plane swooping low over one of the saddest songs in music history, "Love Is a Losing Game." This song, she declares, "wrote itself," but paradoxically it wrote her. For some reason this tune, delivered here even more slowly than on the album itself, brings the whole concert to a much higher level, one that seems to stretch out infinitely and leaves her in tears and embarrassed. "Thanks for not leaving during that song," she whispers. "I'm serious."

Luckily, the superbly up-tempo Zutons song "Valerie" comes next, reminding us of the girly '60s vibe she so gorgeously evokes with every breath. She returns to the milk glass and sings "Hey Little Rich Girl" by the Specials (whose great drummer, John Bradbury, passed away in 2016), providing another brief emotional detour into their bouncy ska-land before sheepishly jumping into her new national anthem. The crowd erupts at the opening chords of "Rehab."

"My voice has gone shitty now," she says. "If you don't like it, I won't give you your money back, I'll give you a kiss on the cheek. I better shut up now. I'm in trouble now." When we hear that wonky accent again, it only enhances our amazement when her incomparably soulful singing voice begins to seep out of her fragile frame. "You Know I'm No Good," the second saddest song in history, tattoos her brand onto the shared heart of the audience; she owns them by this point, even though they may not be fully aware that she doesn't own herself. The spotlight owns her. She squirms in its tightening grip. The viewer can feel it. She pretends to leave the stage after taunting the audience that she will only *say* the show is over, but that's the way the business works; she'll actually be back. As if they didn't already know.

After the obligatory clapping for more, she's back to introduce her band and then celebrate her friend Nasir Jones, aka Nas, with a terrifically fun and slippery version of "Me and Mr. Jones." Then, to close the evening on an upward note, she performs the rollicking Toots and the Maytals hit "Monkey Man." Her vibrant stage presence gives the word "intimacy" a whole new meaning; her band is incredibly tight, and by the end of the concert, so is she, but tight in a very loose, musical way.

■ ■ ■

The Shepherd's Bush Empire show was an early and impressive example of Amy's brilliance personified live in performance. Soon afterward, she would appear at the famous Isle of Wight Festival, which took place from June 8–10, 2007, reprising her Empire show in a magnified and amplified-up rock-festival scale, exploring the same set list in what had already become, for her, a ritualized and largely unconscious activity.

Two weeks later, she appeared at the Glastonbury Festival in Pilton on June 22, 2007, the latest installment of the communal musical gathering more or less modeled on the late-'60s and early '70s template of eclectic outdoor rock concerts with drastically diverse performers, fashioned in England by followers of the American hippie ethos of Woodstock and Monterey. (Since the first festival in 1970, it has grown in popularity and latterly boasts an attendance of upward of 175,000 people over a five-day period.) Winehouse would appear at Glastonbury three times in total: as a debutante in 2004, in her *Back to Black* incarnation in 2007, and again in 2008 during her world-domination tour, when she was involved in a filmed altercation with one of the fans who got too close for her comfort.

After the ideal Empire concert in its modest but familiar theater setting, Winehouse was now beginning to mesmerize ever-expanding audiences with her short and brilliant pop sagas. She performed twice at Glastonbury that summer, first during the daytime and then again at night. Luckily for us, both of her festival sets were filmed by the BBC and provide a stirring document of just how captivating a live performer Winehouse could be, despite all her personal challenges.

For the daytime concert, after emerging from behind a curtain that she coquettishly used to pretend to polish her shoes—not high heels now but comfy runners—she opens with the obligatory "Addicted." Since we're in the domain of the daylight rock concert, her beehive is gone, her frilly little dress and sharp heels are replaced with jeans and a dangling belt, and she exudes a more casual and much less seductively transfixing energy. Nevertheless, it's still a magical concert performance, and one that follows the basic set formula she would deliver for almost the next four grueling years on the road. The crowd has swelled to approximately ten thousand raucous nightclub patrons and is now spread across a communal but swollen listening landscape that can't possibly fully or properly hear her magic, let alone embrace the curious and exotic vibe that had propelled her up to this level of stardom. But they don't care, and neither do we, because she's still Amy at this point, and she manages to quell her customary bad nerves and slowly succeed in transmitting her spell out across this vast crowd filled with squirming adoration.

Though the daylight of the big outdoor field in the windy sun is slightly less kind to her appearance in close-up than a dark spot-lit hall, few if any audience members will see her that close anyway (at least until they see the later concert footage, which reveals some degree of her health challenges). Instead, they are buoyed by the reggae-fied version of "Just Friends" and the just plain refried rendition of "He Can Only Hold Her," which both somehow seem to come across as accidental soul tributes to Sharon Jones.

The English rain begins to pelt down on the crowd but they still manage to generate considerable enthusiasm as the singer again begins to sip from her usual huge tumbler of red fluid and relaunch a vocally charged version of "Cherry" that allows her to demonstrate her rather idiosyncratic dance moves for the drenched but happy crowd. A sea of umbrellas starts to sway as the vibe shifts gears into "Back to Black," which she delivers at a slightly quicker pace, almost as if to lift her own spirits above and beyond the emblematic song that has clearly already started to weigh her down.

Her spoken explanation of the meaning of "Wake Up Alone" is that we can all control our thoughts and feelings through the day, but at night alone in bed we lose the illusion of control and plunge into our own true selves. As if on cue, the sun emerges from the clouds over the muddy field and people begin dancing merrily, completely oblivious to the actual content of this mournful song. A curious example of how profound suffering can be transformed into a consumer product, this tune is one of the great mysteries of pop music in general, and of Winehouse's torch songs in particular.

The best example of this irony follows her next introduction, in which she says, "I didn't believe in [love] anymore when I wrote this," at which point she chokes up, wipes away a tear, and points a finger at her temple as if to shoot herself. The band slides into "Love Is a Losing Game" and the singer gives a heartfelt interpretation of a hurt that's deep beyond belief.

Again that cockney accent charms the crowd: "How ya feelin'? You aww right?" And again we wonder, how could *this* voice belong to the gigantic spirit that transcended definition while singing that song? As we try to figure out this puzzle, "Fuck Me Pumps" returns to lift her spirits into a satirical stance where at least for a moment she's singing about someone other than herself. Even better is the reggae-drenched rendition of Sam Cooke's "Cupid" that follows. It's another song that pleads for love, but in a more hopeful and tongue-in-cheek manner. The same is true of "Hey Little Rich Girl," the Specials' ska-flavored ode, and Toots and the Maytals' "Monkey Man," which offers a brief respite from her sorrows and seems to allow her a bit of time to physically and psychically prepare for the upcoming inevitable return to form. As she toasts the crowd by holding aloft her huge red tumbler, the heavy bassline of "You Know I'm No Good" requires her to climb back in and out of her dark goldmine. The smiles of the crowd as they sing along provide yet further inexplicable evidence of the odd emotional link Winehouse offered to people: she built a bridge allowing them to walk, or dance, right into her broken heart.

The crowd goes veritably nuts when her "*no, no, no*" refrain announces "Rehab's" anthemic beat, after which she introduces her band and finally closes the show with the relatively joyous ode to friendship of "Me and Mr. Jones" and the paradoxically happy Zutons letter-from-jail hit "Valerie."

For the night concert that same day, she sports a new outfit and a new energy; it's the same set, but the two performances are as different as, well, night and day. Gone are the jeans, sneakers, dangling belt, and casual daytime vibe, replaced by a bright red miniskirt, glittery black tank top, staggering heels, and a beehive hairdo that seems to have a life of its own. Somewhere in the afternoon, it seems, she has picked up some alien energy infusion of unknown origin. She performs the whole second set in a more idealized, adult, and almost X-rated version. It is splendid beyond words.

■ ■ ■

In what must have felt like a hop, a skip, and a jump, Winehouse then headlined the Eurockéennes festival in Belfort, France, on June 29, 2007. Prior to her taking the stage, the large Gallic audience of Amy-worshippers was treated to a loud and spirited recording of "He's So Fine," the shimmering Ronnie Mack song so delightfully rendered by her ancestral spirit-girls, the Chiffons, in 1963 (by now all but impossible not to hear without also superimposing George Harrison's lovely but pirated "My Sweet Lord" melody over it). This was followed by the circus-like high-wire drumroll that customarily calls forth her specter, with a Dap-King MC shouting, "Ladies and gentlemen, Miss Amy Winehouse!"

This time she was in casual tank top T-shirt, black jeans, and white ballet shoes, and slipped instantly into her finest squirm-mode to deliver "Addicted" (with its secret sample of the 1965"s "Sugar Pie Honey Bunch" by the Four Tops) and kick start the parade marching toward "Me and Mr. Jones," with the prerequisite roller-coaster ride of up and down songs wedged in between. By now, however, each live concert had become an ordeal, its star running on automatic pilot but almost empty of fuel.

Her splendid headlining stint at the Lollapalooza festival in Grant Park, Chicago, on August 5, 2007, offered a strong reprise and powerful demonstration of why she became the pop giant she did, even though by now the audience was beginning to perceive the strain caused by pulling herself across the now fully memorialized emotional territory of *Back to Black*'s riveting setlist. But she was still in fine form and strongly buoyed, at least on the outside, by the monumental recognition she was receiving.

That fall, she appeared live at Alcatraz in Milan, Italy, on October 26, 2007, giving one of her best concerts. Architectural beehive wrapped in a colorful scarf, garishly tattooed limbs wildly flailing, she was still in fine form vocally but physically starting to show a little of the inevitable strain of opening herself up night after night in a different city or country. Watching footage from several performances in a row, with documentary subtitles in either French or Italian, or whatever other language, once again reinforces the weirdly universal human appeal of her amazing talent. But two years after the *Back to Black* album's release, her third appearance at Glastonbury brought our attention to a more darkly sultry, consciously sexy (or sexist) delivery of the same set material, with the singer poured into a sparkling one-piece cocktail dress, sporting even more towering heels, and with a Lady Day–inspired flower arrangement in her hair. Instead of Billie Holiday's gardenia, Lady Night has three cocktail umbrellas stuck into her beehive, which from a distance must have still looked like flowers.

Her voice still works marvelously here, despite the fact that she may have been fueled by some sort of subterranean octane throughout the gig, but her articulation of lyrics has begun to falter slightly, and her remarkable voice frequently dips in and out of a wordless animal growl. She straps on a handsome white vintage electric guitar for "Some Unholy War," but it's there more as a stage prop than anything else, and possibly to help her remain vertical. It does still look good on her, even if she frequently forgets to strum it, let alone to play it. This is unfortunate, since in fact she had developed considerable guitar skills early on in her youthful arrival and career ascent, with her roughed-up guitar delivery being the quality that first entranced Mark Ronson and inspired him to collaborate with her and amplify her songs up to Spector-scale.

Another performance error was her decision to end the concert by trying to interact directly with the audience while singing "Rehab," leaving the stage and wandering through the first few rows of worshipful but frenzied fans, many of whom practically grope her. She angrily punches one of them in retaliation for something thrown her way; most of the others seem utterly unaware that she's turning the formerly ironic tongue-in-cheek song lyrics into accidental self-parody.

This gig was followed by an appearance at the T in the Park Festival in Scotland on July 13, 2008, which would be described by one attendee, from the *Daily Telegraph*, as thirty-five minutes and nineteen seconds of sheer bliss. The roaring audience agreed, although they may not have noticed, as one can plainly see in the concert film footage, that she was now regularly replacing certain lyrics with guttural snarls instead of words. If we console ourselves by likening this technique to what Van Morrison once called the "inarticulate speech of the heart" then it almost works. Almost.

■■■

The performances described above were some of the supreme trouble girl's most opulent and captivating live concert appearances on an increasingly global stage. Those performed after late 2008 and early 2009 were sorrowful spectacles best left to others who specialize in pathology to analyze. If you're a fan of her remarkable music, you may want to avoid looking at her later dates altogether. Gone was that sparkling Amy of more hopeful, promising days and going, going quickly was the sad shadow she generously left behind for us to celebrate a decade later.

It *was* her party, though, and she could leave if she wanted to. But even if she did leave the world stage way too soon, at least she also left us some great home movies of her hit songs to remember her by.

7

BABY, YOU CAN FILM MY SONG

Back to Black on Video

"The downside of videos is that it will put my vision in front of other people, so they might not get the chance to create their own."
—Carole King to Diane Rehm, NPR Music, 2009

Just as with live concert performances, videos of individual songs offer a filmed evocation of their narrative and have become essential in today's pop-cultural domain. They're also often the only remaining visual evidence of an artist's creative activity after they're gone. Amy Winehouse's handful of videos now lingers on here among us as a captivating kind of ghostly archival visual evidence of her music.

Oh to have been a studio fly on that wall of sound during the fabrication of this album. Oh to have been present in the audience for her live concert tours while she was still in her prime. It would have been akin to seeing Brian Wilson perform live in his prime—for different stylistic reasons, of course. But the next best thing to seeing her live is to watch her perform her songs on film in videos evoking those cheeky narratives.

The film critic Geoff Pevere once curated a program celebrating the relationship between pop music and movies that emphasized how intimately the two are tied together in our cultural imagination. *Sound and Vision: Watching Popular Music* explores both musical feature films and music video in a way that reveals how embedded one is in the other, while his program notes go on to declare, "There is no pop music without pictures." By this he means that all our ideas about the sounds we love are intimately wedded to images we've derived from both pop history and our own personal experience of the music we listen to. This especially includes the music videos we love to watch of Winehouse being wicked.

"When Al Jolson broke the sound barrier with *The Jazz Singer*, he brought audiences down the road to today's infinitely accessible YouTube online jukebox," Pevere explains. "Now, we don't just expect our pop music to look as good as it sounds, we demand it." Surely few recording artists were more photogenic than Amy Winehouse in her prime, or even after it, for that matter. She was just tailor made for the current age of rapidly transmitted images of popular music on screen, sometimes even to her detriment of course, yet always in a mesmerizing manner. "From the advent of early sound, it seems like the technology was invented so we could hear music. If the camera worships the face, the microphone adores the singer."

Music videos have from the very beginning been mostly about youth culture, but every so often a singer comes along who reclaims the medium for adults. Winehouse was one of those. In the digital age, she was also a goddess of the instant availability of sound and vision married perfectly together, just as she was an unbridled queen of that infamous domain celebrating raw and immediate gratification in any and all forms. She was instant karma personified.

According to Pevere, "Music video slaps the pop wallpaper on for good: we can watch and listen to music anywhere at anytime and carry infinitely replenished audio and video jukeboxes in our pockets." The mobility of today's musical delivery systems, especially the art of video, might be the ideal vehicle for an artist such as Amy Winehouse. Image-wise, her creative agenda of making old-school music in a new-age format was perfectly suited to what Pevere has called "the ubiquitous culture of picture pop."

Earthy and somewhat naïve, Winehouse was also an untutored and totally natural anti-movie star, weaving the paradoxical power of Edith Piaf and Diana Ross together into an utterly unique carpet that only she could stand on. Her presentation of herself on film and in videos wasn't just acting in an "I'm not acting" style, because she really wasn't acting. It was the ultimate method actor motif, and it worked effectively for driving her video vehicles forward and for succeeding as the most ideal picture-pop queen since Madonna.

Although it may be crass to call them television commercials for advertising albums, that description of music videos is not that far from the truth. In the same way that concert tours complement album sales and promotion, music videos complement concert tours, and they do of course take place in the context of television (or more likely on computers these days). They're simultaneously both the appetizers and the desserts for the entrée dish of the main album.

In an informative *New York Times* article on the release last year of a Blu-ray DVD boxed set of Beatles videos, Alan Light placed the video art form in a context at once both creative and commercial. His "Baby You Can Film My Song" explained how the Beatles turned to videos when touring live became too difficult. Michael Lindsay-Hogg was the director of many of the Beatles' videos, and he's noted that theirs was the only band historic enough to single-handedly kick-start the music video revolution, even though the visual arts industry surrounding their production wouldn't fully take flight for another twenty years. As Light explained, "Before, a band would have to go on all these television shows," he said, "and it was really time-intensive. The Beatles were powerful enough that the band's manager Brian Epstein could say: if you want the Beatles, you'll take this film clip." Eventually, as we've seen, the making of videos would be embraced by Hollywood itself, often with big-name directors doing the honors.

It was of course too late historically for Winehouse to substitute filmed documents of her songs for live performances, since the twin deities of concerts and videos had by her time become pillars of the recording industry as we know it today. Since touring was such a draining drag for her, she would have if she could have. Either way, she's left us some splendid footage evoking her storytelling motif: videos that fit her songs like a glove.

Another useful guide for the history of the music video is Saul Austerlitz's *Money for Nothing: Music Video from the Beatles to the White Stripes*, which also positions the Fab Four at the center of the video vortex. His book chronicles the fact that although music promotional clips date back to the 1930s, again it was the Beatles who were "the first significant musical artists of the rock era to embrace having a visual component to their work. They showed that a video doesn't just have to be a camera focused on a person at a microphone or with a guitar, or set story or theme—it was more about the quality of the visuals. They really laid the groundwork for what came in the next decades." The group also created the ideal creative context for the loosely narrative and dream-like imagery that would work so well in the case of Winehouse's evocative torch songs.

The term "music video" is said to have been coined by J. P. Richardson, the DJ better known as the Big Bopper, in 1959. He was undoubtedly using it to describe one of the first ever videos to portray a filmed narrative involving a singer interpreting their song: Elvis Presley's "Jailhouse Rock" (1957). As archaic and primitive as it was, it's still one of the finest examples of how a charismatic pop star can transform his or her image instantly by making a short promotional movie. A color version of that song clip was then widely distributed as a short excerpt performance to promote all things Elvis.

The first extensive experiments in musical film vignettes, like most of the innovations in pop music after the 1960s, involved the Beatles, initially with Richard Lester's mock documentary *Hard Day's Night* in '64, and then *Help!* in '65, where the opening title sequence is practically the unintentional template for every music video made since. The song performances inserted into the film launched a conceptual revolution, and in 1965 the Beatles started making short promotional song clips, known back then as "filmed-inserts," for distribution and broadcast around the world as a means of communicating the songs' content cinematically.

In one single night that year, a young director named Joe McGrath shot ten different film clips for ten songs in one single sitting. Since no one knew that was impossible, and since it was after all the Beatles, the mega-shoot was done effortlessly. Instead of having the band showcase and mime to their hit song, these film clips involved all kinds of surreal configurations that evoked the songs without literally demonstrating or illustrating them. These were the first modern videos, and the first to employ the freeform narrative style evolving into the super-sophisticated features of the hot '80s music videos twenty years later, and eventually into those sultry Winehouse video-songs twenty years after that. In a 2015 article for the *Daily Telegraph*, "Did the Fab Four Invent Pop Video?," Neil McCormick emphasized the group's importance even further, pointing out that no other recording artists of the era accrued anything like the visual record of the Beatles. "There is a tendency to think of music videos as originating in the 1980s, the era of MTV and Michael Jackson's *Thriller*, when every major single would be accompanied by a short film, marrying music with visuals in ways intended to enhance the song and market the artist's image. But, like with so many pop innovations, the Beatles got there first."

Sir Lindsay-Hogg, who directed the videos for "Paperback Writer," "Rain," "Hey Jude," and "Revolution," has since explained, in an article for the *Daily Telegraph*, that this was simply par for the course with the Beatles: "They weren't thinking about the future; no one envisioned MTV. Society was changing and music was in the vanguard. I always thought that what they were doing would be part of the history of that time. Just to appear in public became a great hassle for them, so they had the inspired idea that maybe promo films could be made instead."

Eventually the technology advanced, as it usually did, solely to keep up with the Beatles' creative innovations, and the visual vocabulary of the music video as an art form was born, creating a competition for adventurous styles of delivery that has continued ever since. As McCormick notes, the Beatles' sense of style, as exhibited in the legendary 1967 promo films for "Strawberry Fields Forever" and "Penny Lane," clearly anticipated "the kind of special effects-laden, narratively abstract, stylistically bold videos with which modern stars routinely mould their image."

Indeed, the anti-star image of Amy Winehouse was perfectly suited to such intensely designed and elaborately staged mini-dramas. As I've also suggested, to a great degree some of her videos are similar to turgid 1950s Douglas Sirk films such as *A Time to Live and a Time to Die*. The German film director Rainer Werner Fassbinder, a master of cinematic feminine angst, would also have easily made spot-on Winehouse music videos if he were still around at the time. She would even become the ideal Fassbinder star-in-reverse type of performer to best capitalize visually on her particular charms and obvious musical skills, and to *sell* a song as if it were a painting in motion.

She was always an actress playing a role, a performer reenacting a theatrical script, and to accomplish her amazing and almost divine delivery style she obviously wore a vivid performance mask. The mask was used effectively onstage and also on video. Once you recognize that mask and see what it was designed to counteract both personally and professionally, her remarkable music suddenly comes into even greater focus. Indeed, it becomes even more miraculous, and it's especially well illustrated in her marvelous videos.

The challenge she faced was not just the shyness she combated but the fact that once she put that performing mask on, she couldn't take it off. She's also on record as stating that she realized early on that she might have to balance her personas carefully if she was ever hoping to survive any potential fame or celebrity. The 2015 documentary film *Amy* contains a clip of an interview from back when she was still an ambitious teenager and is asked if she expected to become famous. "Oh, no," she quickly answers, "not at all. I'd probably go mad if I did."

When it worked its magic live, that persona and performance mask was as magnificent a creative tool as any pop star had ever conjured, before or since. As is usual with all creative performance masks, hers had three sides: one on record, one onstage, and one in videos, all of which were necessary tools for supporting her primary art form, as captured in the studio.

■ ■ ■

In addition to writing about music, I often write about films, so it seems natural to approach the stunning visual image of Amy Winehouse cinematically and examine how and why she was portrayed so effectively onscreen in the medium of videos, which so saturate our picture-pop culture.

Once again, the surprising thing about her miniature marketing movies is how straightforward, old-fashioned, narrative-oriented, non-feminist, and emotionally melodramatic they are in their style, form, and content. They intentionally eschewed any Madonna-style, Katy Perry-esque, or Gaga-like special effects, largely because, as I've suggested, Winehouse was already her own living special effect to begin with.

To use a Hollywood phrase that seems most applicable in her case, the camera loved her; it ate her up, as they say, even though she was clearly an anti-star in every respect. She had the ability to appear both utterly fragile and superbly strong at the same time on camera—something like that tender Natalie Wood quality—and this paradox was at the heart of what made her so photogenic, so filmable, and so successful as a video star. The music video as we currently know it, both as an art form and commercial communications vehicle, only matured in 1981, two years before Winehouse was born. As a natural and intuitive raconteur, she would become adept at capitalizing visually on her image-brand, and she utilized her obvious musical skills to present each song as a tiny opera for the small screen.

We also can't forget, though, the perfectly reasonable claim made by the legendary Tony Bennett that *he* was really the one who invented the first music video when he was filmed walking through Hyde Park in London in 1956, with his song "Stranger in Paradise" played over the footage. The fact that it was sent to television stations in the US and featured on Dick Clark's *American Bandstand* has to make it something like the first promotional music video in history. He might be right. Who would want to argue with Tony Bennett? Certainly not me. Fifty-five years later, he would also make a delightful duet video (her last) with a worshipful Winehouse. He also, it seemed, totally worshipped her, and the video they made together is both tender and touching.

Like most pop mediums, the video art form quickly became a feverish competition to create not only the most innovative visual images but also the most controversial social content, frequently sexual and political in nature, as often championed by Michael Jackson or Madonna, Katy Perry or Lady Gaga. By comparison, Amy Winehouse's early videos evoking her *Frank* songs seem relatively tame, with the possible exception of the still rather innocent but cheeky lampoon of "Fuck Me Pumps."

But by the time her videos telling the stories in her diaristic sound-novel *Back to Black* began to appear, she would capture attention as a rare kind of filmed creature, delivering some of the most captivating and compelling *roles* ever filmed. This despite the fact that she didn't appear to be remotely conscious that she was actually acting a part. On film she was merely *being*, in front of us all, in a way that made it impossible for us to look away, for better or for worse.

Amy Winehouse had a mesmerizing live presence in her stage performances when she was at her peak, and her videos, like most examples of an art form designed to promote albums, were exceptionally well-crafted miniature movies with compelling narratives, within which the shy star could be captured in the process of celebrating her personal, penetrating form of storytelling. Her videos are gems of the medium, and she was the ideal pop star to take full advantage of the sultry audiovisual landscapes that her directors, especially the talented Phil Griffin, devised for her to strut across. Videos were simply the best art form for transmitting her provocative languidness into our living rooms.

In several of her music videos we witness an ironic combination of complete charm and total dread, so authentically narrated through the filmed images of her various directors that each one seems like a Hollywood achievement. The combination of all the disparate elements in her personality obviously contributed to her video mystique, and her videos manage to capture her paradoxical nature so effectively that they've already become technical standards in the medium of musical storytelling through an audiovisual language. Their sumptuous but simple imagery also influenced many others that followed.

Though her first three videos, "Stronger Than Me," "Take the Box," and "Fuck Me Pumps," are from the debutante Winehouse vintage, they definitely set the visual standard and cinematic narrative that would be expressed even more vividly later on in her mature artistic phase. It's hard for us not to feel that each of her videos is a short scene in a longer epic foreign movie in need of subtitles. Each one has a single female character enacting a series of vignettes that slowly reveal her true self over time, or at least the self she imagines is hers, until it feels epic in its emotional proportions.

"Rehab" (directed by Phil Griffin)

Starting with *Back to Black*, the later veteran Winehouse videos quickly began to assemble a ritual set of stylistic signatures that construct a kind of private film festival around the singer's strongest flaws, foibles, and character features. It's especially evident in her most important video, crafted through director Griffin's masterful take on her "national anthem" song, "Rehab," released in September 2006, one month in advance of the album.

Suddenly we're in for a rude awakening. The movie of her life now has an invisible cine-surtitle reading "three years later," and with its grittier video imagery, her second album has dropped not only on an unsuspecting music industry but also into the even more unprepared public arena of television.

Oh, the viewer gasps. I see. Things have changed.

That's putting it mildly, but even as a new, skinnier, frightened- and troubled-looking Winehouse starts to launch into her sad signature song on film, the viewer also instantly knows that, okay . . . *now* we're in the presence of something truly musically brilliant. In addition, her new visual image on film also seduces us instantly whether we want it to or not, via one of the smoothest and best-produced videos to ever sell a record.

Originally, Winehouse had a certain approach and style in mind for the video of her most famous song—a visual idea about which she was somewhat at odds (as usual) with her label when it came to deciding how best to capture the song's true essence. Even after a dozen or so visual treatments by different directors, they couldn't quite come to any agreement. Until, that is, a veteran video artist named Phil Griffin entered their field of vision. Having produced great visual sagas for stars such as Diana Ross, the Sugababes, and Atomic Kitten, he seemed to offer the right aesthetic vibe for interpreting Amy Winehouse's songs onscreen.

Griffin was introduced to Winehouse by her friend Tyler James, and would later tell MTV News how quickly they bonded (just like everyone else who ever met her, apparently). "I went out one night with my friend Tyler and Amy was there, and we talked about how women were filmed and how it's all flouncy and pretty-pretty and how I thought beauty should have an edge." Naturally, that edgy ethos instantly appealed to the raunchy singer, so she contacted her label and aggressively advocated on Griffin's behalf for him to be the maker of what would go on to be an award-winning piece of work. It was always hard to refuse an aggressive Amy.

Griffin convincingly pitched his idea to the label's head honchos: "'Amy wants performance, you want narrative—it's pulling in two directions.' So I needed to tread between the two and I came up with the concept of a 'postcard from rehab.' . . . You end up in a hospital cell; the band is there. There's no real narrative: it's all just postcards of the day you went to rehab . . . postcards from a girl in distress." Winehouse immediately loved the idea, having one of her usual instinctual reactions. Perhaps more unusually, so did her record label.

Griffin has said he believed that Winehouse was an artist at the same level as Diana Ross; he decided not to shift the perspective much, if at all, opting instead to let the camera linger on the singer's face as she delivered the lyrics in a deadpan manner directly into the camera's eye and directly at us, the voyeuristic viewers. "That's why I didn't move the camera and there aren't many mid-shots. It's all about wide shots and details, which reinforces the sense of portraiture."

Like most Winehouse ventures, the shoot lasted for only one day, after a styling meeting with Winehouse, during which Griffin expressed a fondness for her loosely fitting orange kimono as a point of departure. After that, the location scouts searched for a building with that same aesthetic, quickly finding an old, nostalgic-feeling structure with distressed surfaces of orange and green. It was a broken-down building at 32 Portland Place, London, with rust-covered and faded green walls that ideally suited Griffin's image sensibility.

Griffin was astute enough to realize that, given her retro-style and affection for melodrama, he would be best served to take an old-school cinematic perspective to match her old-school musical vibe. Thus he discussed the tonal details and color palette with his art director and cinematographer. In this sense, they actually followed the same formalist agenda as Winehouse's music producer, Mark Ronson, did when he settled on taking an old-school analog tape approach to the sound of the album itself.

The director then moved the singer and the band from one location to another through a series of decaying rooms. He was also a good judge of the immediacy of her character, choosing to have her singing directly to the camera, and by extension the viewers. He knew very well that with this particular artist, everything she did was instinctive, and therefore he was openly accepting of the fact that rather than being a video directed by Phil Griffin, it was a video portrait of Amy Winehouse by Phil Griffin. It was, in other words, a completely balanced creative collaboration. That's exactly what makes it work so perfectly as an artful music video telling one of the most compelling stories on *Back to Black*.

"You Know I'm No Good" (directed by Phil Griffin)

This same perfectly matched creative team followed up with the video for "You Know I'm No Good," which premiered on

VH1 on March 3, 2007, for which Griffin (who by then had grown quite close to the singer) and photography director Adam Frisch returned in fine form with another sparkling little melodrama that feels highly cinematic in its essential capture of her emotional volatility. The corporate brief: how does one convincingly convey a sense of zero self-esteem in moving images?

Shot primarily nearby Gibson Gardens and Chesholm Road in Stoke Newington, London, it was subsequently released to mass media channels in late November 2006. The seductive bass line, percussion, and rhythm slither along sinuously as the all-too-familiar video plot begins to unwind. The *fictional character* portrayed by Winehouse at first appears with yet another boyfriend, sitting in a stylized studio and being confronted by what seems to be a Polaroid of her latest compromising position of infidelity.

Again we're pulled through shifting, dreamlike scenes from the darkened studio, where the music starts to groove out from a retro reel-to-reel tape console, then on through her sultry clandestine lifestyle narrative in a shuffling of images that suits the mercurial actress's embodiment of the song's perennial motif of betrayal to a tee. This mini-film subsequently premiered on VH1 in early March 2007 and soon afterward aired on MTV's *Total Request Live*, but it was also shrewdly featured in a sneak preview for the AMC series *Mad Men*. It was a brilliant marketing maneuver: the song obviously and effortlessly encapsulated the essence our favorite advertising philanderer and further visually exemplified the singer's '60s style allegiances.

Here, the singer/actress demonstrates her extreme nonchalance and lack of loyalty or commitment to her distraught lover, who eventually walks away and leaves her to deliver her signature dollop of self-disdain. The video looks like a chapter of her earlier diary/novel video for "In My Bed," right down to the flashed image of two lusty men fighting over her, one white, the other black (a stylistic segue from the final frames of "Bed").

The Winehouse brand is in full force for this vignette of emotional disregard for either self or other as she pursues to its fullest extent the rank beauty of her mythically casual sexual lifestyle. She moves carelessly from studio to bar to bed to kitchen floor to bathtub to beyond belief, while her incredible voice intones that she's actually cheating herself, like she knew she would. This motif would return yet again in the skeletal remains of her mythical third album in a tawdry little ditty called "Between the Cheats," though clearly only as an unworthy fragment of debris that was left over from the magnificent sessions for *Back to Black*.

"Back to Black" (directed by Phil Griffin)

The video for the album's title track, released on April 30, 2007, was again crafted by Griffin and his able editor, Mark Alchin. Singing the greatest song of all from her great second album, Winehouse stuffs all three members of the Supremes and all three Ronettes into her skinny white frame to visually evoke the lyric. She had already created a timeless torch song out of its harrowing content; now she would collaborate on one of the most visually evocative music videos of her short career as an anti-movie star.

I'm not only saying this is a great pop song ideally portrayed, I'm claiming this is the greatest pop song since Diana Ross belted out "Stop! In the Name of Love" in 1965, or since the enigmatic Scott Walker moaned "The Sun Ain't Gonna Shine Anymore" in 1966. In addition, the short black-and-white neo-realist drama filmed by Griffin for the album's title track is perhaps the most effectively illustrated music video since Michael Jackson channeled the great Bob Fosse for his "Billie Jean" epic back in 1982.

An ideal combination of loosely structured and tightly edited, here Griffin finds the quintessential ambiguity lurking at the very core of Winehouse and her obvious talents. Ostensibly waiting around for a funeral procession to get under way, the members of her band are shown not performing but carrying instruments and mingling, presumably with friends and family, near a cavalcade of cars, waiting glumly while Winehouse sits perched in a big chair and begins her now famous lament.

Eventually she stops lip-syncing and joins the band as they all travel to the graveyard, each of them dropping flowers or handfuls of soil into a small hole in the ground. This little square hole is of course designed to specially fit the small box that can be seen traveling in the traditional glass-walled hearse on its way to the gravesite.

The mystery of the small coffin increases until it's lovingly lowered into its tiny enclosure and covered up. The box contains the singer's heart! But some of the inherent tenderness of this video was actually lost in an ironic way when, after the singer's passing in 2011, the last few shots of the gravestone itself were edited out, one assumes in a gesture of respect for the now-deceased superstar. But this removal of the final frames has the unintended effect of draining the video of its value as a visual document of the song, leaving it so ambiguous as to approach meaningless. This is because the final video frames in question showed the granite carved gravestone reading "Rest in Peace, the Heart of Amy Winehouse." Not her body, just her broken heart. Shades of Janis Joplin again.

This was obviously meant to echo the themes of the song—that she has been left brokenhearted by her relationship's demise so has buried her heart in its own private little grave—but without the inscription, the video suddenly loses some of its original poignancy and actually, accidentally now has an even more maudlin tone.

The one other stylistic loss caused by this editing out of aesthetic reality in deference to actuality would not however be lost on those of us who remember one of her songs from *Frank*. "Take the Box" is about an ex-lover removing all the gifts he'd given her when they broke up; now, in this case, "taking the box" could have poetically referred to the earth itself receiving the box containing the singer's own heart. In my view, retaining the final frame wouldn't have been disrespectful at all—more like reverential. The gravestone would have visually amplified even more the incredible fatality at play in Winehouse's overall narrative while also maintaining the artistic fidelity of a video that so beautifully evokes one of the finest torch songs in recent memory. As a matter of fact, this song and its video evocation are probably the Mount Everest of torch songs. Any attempts made by upcoming artists in this musical genre will have to take them in account, the same way young painters all have to face the legacy of Picasso.

"Tears Dry on Their Own" (directed by David LaChapelle)

A shift in sentiment and style is sometimes a good thing to keep things fresh, and such a shift would occur when Winehouse's next video was released August 13, 2006. Directed by David LaChapelle, it was produced by Ron Mohrhoff, with Dave Hussey as colorist. Best known as a super-slick specialist in high-fashion photography and advertising campaigns, LaChapelle was the perfect choice for this little video vignette, and his selection reminds us again that every music video is a miniature advertising campaign unto itself. He also later on shot a strong and heavily Amy-inspired video for Florence and the Machine's hit song "Spectrum," as well as clips for Macy Gray's "She Ain't Right for You" and Gwen Stefani and Eve's "Rich Girl." Like Griffin before him, LaChapelle was the right man for the job of interpreting Amy Winehouse visually.

A favorite video of a personal favorite song on *Back to*

Black, this mini-movie offers a strange twist on the notion of time healing all wounds. The actress intones that "you don't owe nothin' to me, but to walk away I have no capacity" as she struts past colorful buildings in her most towering beehive hairdo while the recurring musical mood follows her like both a lyrical and literal ghost.

The viewer is repeatedly brought back to her sunny, golden bedroom, with the actress sitting on her bed singing over some gorgeous close-ups of her still exquisite face. But we're eventually pulled back out to a more and more crowded sidewalk, which Winehouse strolls along almost absentmindedly while still cherishing her lost love. We return to her bedroom but now notice she's pulled her legs up to her chest to reveal a scarily skeletal frame. People bump into her during her passage along the hectic sidewalk; a loony approaches with an ominous sign that reads "the end is near"; lovers kiss behind her; a man tries to pick her up; suddenly it's night and dark outside and fighting couples are dragged into police vans as she swivels into the entrance to an inevitable bar.

This song could have been an ideal vehicle for the Supremes back in the day. In our age it's the perfect emblem for the Winehouse dilemma, with the short video chock full of bustling public interruptions until she finally arrives at her fully expected destination, a pub. The sense of public intrusion into private suffering is fully palpable, as intended.

"Love Is a Losing Game" (directed by Phil Griffin)

This video, released on December 10, 2007, is somewhat problematic. It was issued in two formats, a live version and a montage version, with no official director credit for either. Originally slated to be directed by the talented Phil Griffin and shot by his gifted director of photography, Adam Frisch, at Pinewood Studios, it was reportedly planned as another mini-melodrama. The video shoot was canceled after the real-life

Winehouse soap opera interfered and she didn't show up for filming—something that was starting to happen more and more frequently as time went on.

Instead, two alternate and unsatisfactory versions of the video were released: one is a montage of stills juxtaposed with live performance footage, the other comprised of Shepherd's Bush Empire concert footage (which was far preferable anyway). There are also other visual records of her performing this song, some far superior to either of these; one has her accompanied only by an electric piano/organ live in Austin, Texas, and is utterly moving in its depth of soul and delivery. Viewing that version is a much more satisfying visual experience.

"Just Friends" (directed by Anthony Mathile and Robert Semme)

The video for "Just Friends," from 2008, is not exactly a work of art, since unlike her other videos it's not a miniature movie narrative but rather a loosely edited collage of moments culled again from her Shepherd's Bush concert. Assembled in a montage of slightly evocative black-and-white tones, it has no coherent or cohesive visual language to speak of but is more of a patchwork quilt of images pulled together apparently at random over the song.

By this time Winehouse was so busy touring globally in support of the *Back to Black* record that she may not have had any time to deliver her actress video role by collaborating with a director, so the next best thing was a woven fabric of disparate footage. But the very tenderness of the song is lost amid the rough-and-tumble editing of elements that compete with rather than visually enhance the lyrics and instrumentation. So, while it may be a valuable relic, it is not nearly as fine a music video as her others.

"Body and Soul" (directed by Unjoo Moon)

The video for this duet with Tony Bennett, released on September 14, 2011, was directed by Unjoo Moon, who is practically Bennett's personal video documentarian, having shot around fifteen videos for the legendary singer, including an updated 2011 version of his "Stranger in Paradise" (the song Bennett claims was accompanied by the first original music video ever, made by him almost sixty years ago).

The video of the Bennett/Winehouse duet premiered two months after her passing, on the day that would have been her twenty-eighth birthday. In a classic call-and-response format, the song proceeds as a shared benediction between the living jazz vocal icon and one of his principal worshippers. It's clear that Bennett also greatly admired the young singer, having already called her the greatest jazz singer he'd ever heard, and I suspect he wasn't just being a nice guy.

Having performed and recorded with Sarah Vaughan and Anita O'Day, the two singers Winehouse most resembles in tone and temperament, Bennett was in a privileged position to wax rhapsodic about her considerable gifts. To MTV's *Buzzworthy*, Bennett said that she was "someone who knows how to intuitively improvise and make it believable and sing with humanity and soul and honesty, with no compromising. . . . Amy had that gift. She was the only one of all the contemporary artists that I've met through the years . . . she's the only one who was able to do it."

Part of the alluring charm of their encounter, apart from her looking deceptively healthy via professional makeup and being ecstatic at the chance to record with a personal idol, was the sheer magnetism and flirtatious energy that coursed between the two of them. Recorded in March of 2011, only four months before her hasty departure, this song had also been a favorite of both Billie Holiday and Dinah Washington, the two key artists the young Winehouse first found solace and inspiration in while growing up.

Delivering it so coquettishly with Bennett made her

extremely nervous (they had to restart the shoot four or five times when she repeatedly flubbed it and broke down in tears), but she still seemed satisfied with what she'd accomplished. While the video is not technically on a par with her earlier narrative styled mini-movies, this casual-feeling studio encounter, complete with hand-held sheets of lyrics, offers a tearful celebration of inter-generational greatness, pure and simple.

Yes, you'll cry, and you probably should. When they embrace at the end of this angelically shared song rendition it's hard not to. But the real importance of the duet for me is the revelation it contains: Winehouse wasn't imitating, copying, mimicking, or doing any kind of impersonation or impression of the female vocal giants of the past; she was an actual and literal distillation of their essence, like a superb wine that's decanted in order to cleanse it of sediment. The other thing that struck me while watching this video and listening to what is perhaps her ideal song was the slightly odd realization that all those earlier monumental vocalists find in Winehouse a weird kind of *balsamic reduction* of all their genres and styles. She clearly represents a ripening of multiple formal motifs, ratcheted up to an almost unbearable level of emotional intensity.

■ ■ ■

There are also a couple of other non-video videos that are worth observing, especially the MTV footage of a live version of her most infamous song. MTV being the home of commercial music films, it managed to accidentally render this one a music video by default. Although it wasn't intended for the usual video purposes, one of the best performances of the by-then monster song "Rehab" took place at the first *live* broadcast of the MTV Movie Awards on June 3, 2007. Winehouse was introduced by an over-the-top Bruce Willis (he had personally requested to do so) who graced the stage with a zonked-out attempt at pop cool—"Yippie-ki-yay, motherfuckers!"—and then brought out a seemingly fairly stable and secure Amy for a sterling live version of what was already her signature piece.

For MTV, the singer, and her Dap-Kings support band, this deft delivery was perfect in every respect. It was also one of the key publicity moments that ignited the Winehouse engine and caused the singer to roar even higher and deeper into the American pop culture of the day. In a sense it's poised somewhere between a concert performance and a music video, since it was filmed for MTV's audience and televised worldwide, and it provided us with a living embodiment of the song and the video they'd already so readily embraced as an iconic but fragile vessel of the times.

Winehouse's stunning cover version of "Will You Still Love Me Tomorrow?," first recorded in 2004 in one of her most glorious video renditions of a classic torcher, shows her off at her finest and displays her gifts at their strongest, even though she is, ironically, delivering someone else's song. Like many other fragments of her dazzling live performances during her short career, this one became a landmark video in its own right due to the sheer power of her vocal interpretation.

This one song's video performance alone will send chills up and down your spine. (In music, that's what spines are for.) Even though it was written by another artist from an earlier age, it might personify her mesmerizing talent in a manner that liberates her from her own identity, personality, character, and hubris and frees her to more comfortably display the full intensity of her industrial-strength gravitas without her having to really be herself. Since that in the end was always one of her most compelling challenges, for us to be able to see and hear that burden being lifted from her fragile shoulders may perhaps have been the best way to penetrate her strange magnetism.

An exceptionally compelling montage of images accompanies her utterly idealized version of this song, which was originally released by her heroines, the Shirelles, in 1960 and also again in 1971 by the song's original composer, the superb Carole King. Through a collage of still photos and fragments from other videos, the video builds to a gorgeous crescendo carried along by Winehouse's exquisitely fresh face and voice. It ends with a happy, young Amy on a British talk show, exclaiming how much fun she's having in her early career: "Yeah, I never want it to end." But as we now know so well, all good things must come to an end.

There are also some other very worthwhile Amy Winehouse videos comprising concert footage of the singer performing *Back to Black* songs live at the MTV Europe Music Awards in 2007; "Back to Black" live @onlive in 2008; "Rehab" at the Isle of Wight on June 9, 2007; "You Know I'm No Good" and "Rehab," live via satellite for the Grammys in February 2008; "Back to Black" and "Me and Mr. Jones" at Eurockéenes on March 28, 2008; "You Know I'm No Good" from Benicassim in 2007; "Wake Up Alone" in Madrid; "Love Is a Losing Game" at T in the Park in July 2007, the BRIT Awards in February 2008, and Rock in Rio in June 2008; the full Glastonbury concert from 2007; *Live at the BBC* from Porchester Hall in 2007; her performance at MTV's *45th at Night* with Mos Def in 2007; and a full concert filmed at De Yves in 2008.

Multiple video performances of the same song are actually very worthy of re-viewing and only add to her grandeur. These Winehouse videos are all the evidence you'll ever need that her rare soul-music power extended far beyond only telling her own personal stories. Clearly—or at least as clearly as I've been able to explore it—her musical mystery was so much more than the unfortunate, melodramatic narrative surrounding her.

8
TEN YEARS AFTER
Back to Winehouse—the Album as Storytelling

"Every bad situation is a blues song waiting to happen."
—Amy Winehouse to Simon Kelner, *GQ*, January 2007

Back to Black was released by Island Records on October 27, 2006. It has sold over twenty million worldwide copies and was awarded six Grammys in 2008: "Record of the Year," "Song of the Year," "Best Pop Vocal Album," "Best New Artist," "Best Female Pop Vocal Performance," and "Producer of the Year" (the latter for Mark Ronson). Winehouse became only the fifth female solo artist in history to receive five awards in one night, with another to follow posthumously. Exactly how this was accomplished may just remain a mystery. As a wise person once observed: wonderment can always exist without understanding. It certainly does here.

In the first week of its release, the album sold almost 45,000 copies in the UK, and by year's end it was certified platinum: something was in the pop cultural air and *Black* just seemed to capture its essence in a surprising way. Then, by the end of January 2007, after what seemed like mere moments since it dropped, the album achieved the dreamt of No. 1 spot on the British charts, and it would remain there on and off through the year, at one point lodging for twenty-seven weeks straight in the Top Ten. The word *zeitgeist* is certainly applicable here, and *Back to Black* seemingly personified it in a way reserved for only the most rarefied of pop artifacts.

By the time a second new year arrived, it was certified at five times platinum by industry watchers, indicating nearly two million copies moved. Much to its still-young author's chagrin, that acclaim would also relaunch her despised first album, which joined its haunted sibling in the top sales charts all over again and refused to go away. Naturally, the media, as well as the public, would make comparisons between both the records, and also the mirror opposite personas of their maker.

The *Daily Telegraph* was content to announce that Amy was "slamming the door on those laidback lounge influences and strutting into a gloriously ballsy, bell-ringing, bottle-swigging, doo-wop territory." A little over-the-top, perhaps, but certainly accurate. The *Observer* touted *Black* as "a starkly confessional album, as chiffon-light in parts as it is unflinching in others." The *New Musical Express* was the most spot on by characterizing it as "a tapestry of undeniable musical brilliance," declaring that *Back to Black* can be considered one of the most influential albums of the last ten years.

Those last phrases form the genesis for our present examination and provide the sole reason for taking the record so seriously as a singular artifact: it simply damn well deserves it. The *New Musical Express* was even more insightful when it interviewed the weary performer in the days immediately prior to the album's release, and when the slightly too cheery Krissi Murison fashioned it as the product of a clearly serious creative growth curve: "In the three years since becoming the nation's second favorite jazz warbler (the other supposedly being Winehouse's hated nemesis Katie Melua) she had undergone quite a transformation, resplendent in her war-paint makeup, necking jugs of cocktails and sporting a huge naked woman tattoo on her arm, she's every bit the outrageous pop icon that makes Lily Allen look like Mother Teresa."

Being the *NME* though, the effusive observations about style were also ameliorated by fair praise for her substance as an homage to '60s girl-groups, "sung through the pipes of

Aretha Franklin and the liver of Janis Joplin." Now there's a great line from any journalist.

To her own credit, the still extremely shy singer did at least as often as possible try to steer people's attention to where it should be, toward the music she made out of the mess she was in, like most great musicians: "I don't think people care about *me* . . . I made an album that I'm very proud of, and that's about it." She could also be rightly proud of the creative relationship she'd forged with the producers who made the album possible.

The making of *Back to Black* involved handcrafting a pop artifact through the complete absence of guile and the desire to tell you her stories, whether you wanted to hear them or not. Sometimes, on rare occasions, if your impact on the industry and audience is big enough, a legacy takes shape while you're still alive. In Winehouse's case, the impact of this album was immediate. As soon as the first notes of the opening track arrive, the rapt listener instantly knows that the jazzy chick of her debut has taken a hike, replaced by a darkly sultry and slightly scary apparition whose every song is also a life story. They may be the saddest stories ever told, but their telling is so artful that they make us all feel better.

Back to Black has both unpopular feelings and pop hooks aplenty, all seamlessly collaged together from almost ten different musical styles and traditions. I might even slightly misuse the term *avant-pop* to describe it, modifying it a little from Robert Christgau's original usage in the *Village Voice* back in the '70s. That advanced romance motif is why it will be remembered and played again and again, as long as there are broken or wounded hearts in the world who need its strangely soothing sonic bandages. As long as music lovers wonder at the mutant heart of music itself, and as long as music is the best way we all have of breaking the heart's anger, listeners will reach for it.

"Rehab" (3:35)

Written by Amy Winehouse. Produced by Mark Ronson. Mixed by Tom Elmhirst. Band arrangements by Gabriel Roth and Mark Ronson. Orchestra arrangements by Chris Elliot. Baritone saxophone: Dave Bishop, Ian Hendrickson-Smith. Bass guitar: Nick Movshon. Cello: Anthony Pleeth, Joely Koos, John Heley. Drums: Homer Steinweiss. Guitar: Binky Griptite, Thomas Brenneck. Harp: Helen Turnstall. Handclaps: Mark Ronson, Vaughan Merrick. Piano: Victor Axelrod. Percussion: Frank Ricotti. Tenor Saxophone: Jamie Talbot, Mike Smith, Neal Sugarman. Trombone: Richard Edwards. Trumpet: Dave Guy, Steve Sidwell. Viola: Boguslaw Kostecki, Chris Tombling, Liz Edwards, Everton nelson, Jonathan Rees, Mark Berrow, Peter Hanson, Tom Piggott-Smith, Warren Zielinski. Violin, orchestra leader: Perry Montague-Mason. Recorded at Chung King Studios and Daptone Studios, New York, and Metropolis Studios, London. (Sometimes it just takes an army.)

Songscript: Released as a single on October 23, 2006, Winehouse's signature song won three Grammy Awards: "Record of the Year," "Song of the Year," and "Best Female Pop Performance." It also won the Ivor Novello Award for "Best Contemporary Song." She had apparently written the key lyric line in one of her diary notebooks years before, but it was only when she quipped about it in a casual New York street conversation with producer Mark Ronson that it "came to life." What would have happened if he didn't respond the way he did?

Rolling Stone magazine acclaimed the song as a Motown-style hit about a lovesick bad girl testifying like Etta James, while *Billboard* saw it as Shirley Bassey meets Ella Fitzgerald and called it "a better buzz than a double-gin martini." It was also released as a huge hit single, with a B-side of "Do Me Good."

It's ranked no. 7 on *Rolling Stone*'s list of the one hundred best songs of 2007 and no. 94 on their 500 greatest songs of all time. *Time* magazine's Josh Tyrangiel declared that "it was impossible not to be seduced by her originality. Combine it with production by Mark Ronson that references four decades worth of soul music without *once* ripping it off and you've got the best song of 2007."

The song has also been covered copiously by other artists, most intriguingly by the Jolly Boys, a Jamaican Mento band, and has even been echoed strangely by a Rihanna song also called "Rehab" from 2008, in which she uses the term metaphorically to reference getting over a boyfriend as if he were an addiction or infectious medical condition. Too close for comfort, that one, but hardly at the same standard creatively.

The tune is of course totally tongue-in-cheek and also very Garbo-esque: I want to be left alone, but I want everyone to watch me being left alone. The listener knows something has dramatically changed from the nineteen-year-old who wrote *Frank* to the twenty-two-year-old who wrote *Back to Black*. It was also a curious mirror for the times we lived though, drenched in the Internet, suffocated by social media, bereft of solutions to social problems, and hell-bent on rearranging the deck furniture as the ship is going down.

"Rehab" is surely the hippest and happiest ironic call for help any of us had ever heard, even if it makes us cringe a little, ten years later. Most infamously, when she declares that she doesn't have the time to go for help—and that, besides, "her daddy thinks she's fine"—what at first seems like a song about the enabling of an equally self-destructive boyfriend takes on even more sinister tones when we realize it is her real-life paternal advisor that she's referring to.

The sound of this song, like the aural tapestry of the whole album, is such an evolutionary leap forward that it takes us aback at first, allowing us to experience agony and ecstasy simultaneously with nostalgia—which is perhaps often the purpose of great art in any medium—as the song begins to weave a prophetic kind of sonic dream that lulls us into a false sense of her defiant invincibility. But my interest here is in rehabilitating not the singer but her music, and that music is astonishingly brilliant and captivating, despite the dark, personal undertones lurking in the lyrics. She notes a preference for staying at home with the music of Ray Charles and Donny Hathaway as her sole companions, and she readily admits (in one of the sincerities the public loved her for) that yes, she's "been black" (as in blacked out), but when she returns from that little vacation, we'll all know about it. She openly declares that she doesn't want to drink again, but she just needs a friend (the bottle) and doesn't want to spend ten weeks out of action and have people *think* she's on the mend if she really isn't. Most revealing is her conclusion, where she reveals that this is not just foolish pride; it's merely a survival mechanism until her tears dry, presumably with the help of the darkness, suggesting that all her troubles were only temporary and just a response to her heartaches, which would, she assumed, have to end sooner or later. Wouldn't they?

Aura echo: This song contains gorgeous reflections of two great Lesley Gore songs from 1963. The first is "It's My Party," with its insistent refrain of "cry if I want to," sung three times, spookily resonates with Winehouse's "no, no, no," which culminates in the ultimate resistant if unspoken refrain: It's my life and I'll die if I want to. The second is even more evocative: "You Don't Own Me" contains the ultra-Amy anti-"Rehab" hook as Gore cries out "Don't tell me what to do, don't tell me what to say. You don't own me!"

"You Know I'm No Good" (4:17)

Written by Amy Winehouse. Produced by Mark Ronson. Mixed by Tom Elmhirst. Band arrangements by Gabriel Roth and Mark Ronson. Baritone saxophone: Ian Hendrickson-Smith. Bass guitar: Nick Movshon. Drums: Homer Steinweiss. Guitar: Binky Griptite, Thomas Brenneck. Tenor saxophone: Neil Sugarman.

Trumpet: Dave Guy. Piano, electric piano, Wurlitzer, handclaps: Victor Axelrod. Recorded by Vaughan Merrick and Mark Ronson. Recorded at Chung King, Daptone, and Metropolis. Released as a single on January 5, 2007, backed with "Monkey Man."

Songscript: This song was originally recorded as a solo track and has also been remixed by Wu-Tang Clan member Ghostface Killah. One of her most heartbreaking songs, it's harrowing in its emotionally personal and physically intimate revelations. Clearly identifying herself as a young woman with self-esteem issues and not afraid to confront them, at least in her art, she declaims with an ironic sort of pride, that she had cheated herself, just as she always did, and that she had warned her lover, and the rest of us, that she was trouble. Far from being the usual tale of a partner who cheated on her with someone else, this song magnifies the fact that she's cheated on herself, offering a troubled twist on the torch-song tradition, which was maybe one of the reasons the public related so deeply to her turmoil.

She plays both parts here, the offended and the offender, with the partner being a mere prop in the saga of her sinking. A musical gem of melancholic reflection, the singer performed this song, along with "Rehab," for the 50th Annual Grammy Awards via satellite from London, in a live rendition of heart-wrenchingly subtle beauty.

Aura echo: Embedded in the soul of this song is a whole generation of bad girl declarations. Eartha Kitt in 1953 purred that she wanted to spit tacks in "I Want to Be Evil." In "Bad Reputation," Joan Jett shrieked in 1980 that she didn't care if you think she's strange; "I ain't gonna change." And Patti Smith similarly growled in her 1975 gem "Gloria" that "Jesus died for somebody's sins, but not for mine!"

"Me and Mr. Jones" (2:33)

Written by Amy Winehouse. Produced by Salaam Remi. Recorded by Franklin Socorro, Glyder Disla, and Shomari Dillon. Mixed by Gary Noble and James Wisner. Trumpet, bass flugelhorn: Bruce Purse. Baritone saxophone, tenor saxophone, guitar: Vincent Henry. Drums, double bass, piano: Salaam Remi. Guitar, backing vocals: Amy Winehouse.

Songscript: Clearly referencing "Me and Mrs. Jones," the Kenny Gamble and Leon Huff composition originally recorded by Billy Paul in 1972, this song has the often-overlooked subtitle "Fuckery," a term aimed at anything that gets in the way or messes up her plans. Oddly Shakespearean in its tone, the word recurs at intervals with the basic question that adds to the song's weirdly formal, theatrical tone: "What kind of fuckery is this?" The Mr. Jones in question is the rap star Nas, whom she declares to be her "best black Jew" apart from Sammy Davis Jr.—another pop historical reference that takes her out of the run-of-the-mill millennial crowd.

"Nobody stands between me and my man" repeats the sentiment that not all of her relationships are or have to be of a romantic or physical nature. Naturally she fights with him as much as she would fight with a lover, but in the end her allegiance is to friendship over love, at least for as long as this bouncy tune unfolds.

This song is the first of four produced by Remi, though it occurs under the sonic umbrella of co-producer Ronson's analog fetish for strong sound walls. Remi has often remarked that going to him in Miami was for Winehouse a kind of restorative respite from the temptations of either London of New York, allowing her to concentrate only on her music instead of her other personal challenges. Another salient distinction of the Remi-produced tracks is the more basic and simple instrumentation, often focused on Amy's guitar and his bass, with only about eight musicians accompanying them rather than the twenty-one or so arranged in the Ronson army for her other songs.

Aura echo: "Me and Mr. Jones" perfectly parlays an intimate but supposedly platonic relationship first explored by Connie Francis in the incredibly innocent taunt of "Lipstick on Your Collar" from 1958 and also references the glorious girl-group themes of the Toys' 1965 recording "Lovers Concerto."

"Just Friends" (3:13)

Written by Amy Winehouse. Produced by Salaam Remi. Mixed by Gary Noble and James Wisner. Recorded by Franklin Socorro, Glyder Disla, and Shomari Dillon. Bass: Salaam Remi. Guitar, clarinet, bass clarinet: Vincent Henry. Drums: Troy Auxilly Wilson. Electric piano: organ: John Adams. Guitar: Amy Winehouse. Trumpet, flugelhorn: Bruce Purse.

Songscript: The second of Remi's productions from Miami adds a seductive pendulum swing toward and away from the key Ronson signatures on the album, providing a bit of a breather from the more heavy and melancholy introspection at work throughout. It ironically celebrates the core lament that a lover can never be a friend—at least not the lovers she seems to pick, or that pick her. Again she references her lover's competing partner, the one who has taken or is taking him away from her, and she pleads with us to tell her when a friendship between a man and a woman might be possible. She goes on to admit that the other woman will never love him the way she does, but they still need to find the time to face their situation together somehow. She was forever hoping to face her situation, while we simply get to face the music

Once again, and in a manner similar to "Me and Mr. Jones," the listener gets the embarrassing feeling of not only eavesdropping on someone's personal conversations but also guiltily reading their diary. Except, in this case, every diary entry is another amazing song.

Aura echo: Another shimmering image from Lesley Gore's 1964 album, the perfectly Winehouse-resonant *Lesley Gore*

Sings About Mixed-Up Hearts, "That's the Way Boys Are" explains love and loss in her epistle to male-female friendship. Frankie Lymon and the Teenagers posed the same eternal question in 1956 with "Why Do Fools Fall in Love?"

"Back to Black" (4:01)

Written by Amy Winehouse and Mark Ronson. Produced by Mark Ronson. Mixed by Tom Elmhirst and Matt Paul. Arranged by Gabriel Roth and Mark Ronson. Recorded by Mark Ronson and Vaughan Merrick. Orchestra arranger, conductor: Chris Elliott. Orchestra leader, violin: Perry Montague-Mason. Alto saxophone: Andy Mackintosh, Chris Davies. Baritone saxophone: Dave Bishop. Bass guitar: Nick Movshon. Cello: Anthony Pleeth, Joely Koos, John Heley. Drums: Homer Steinweiss. Engineers: Dom Morley, Jesse Gladstone, Mike Makowski. Guitar: Binky Griptite, Thomas Brenneck. Percussion: Frank Ricotti. Piano: Victor Axelrod. Tambourine: Mark Ronson. Tenor saxophone: Jamie Talbot. Viola: Bruce White, John Thorne, Kate Wilkinson, Rachel Bolt. Violin: Boguslaw Kostecki, Chris Tombling, Liz Edwards, Everton Nelson, Jonathan Rees, Mark Berrow, Peter Hanson. Tom Piggott-Smith, Warren Zielinksi. Released as a single on April 30, 2007, backed with "Valerie."

Songscript: The ultimate Phil Spector girl-group tribute and one that also channels the Supremes in a marvelous way without at all appearing to be copying their power; just another example of how her gift for fusing styles was authentic and sincere rather than aping or plagiarizing. But here, she's all three Supremes squashed into one teetering carnal creature of spooky power, a paradox and contradiction beyond compare when you consider what she's *actually* telling us all with so forceful a presence.

She's also all three Ronettes, all three Dixie Cups, all the Crystals, and all three Shirelles merged into a monument to infidelity and its ramifications. Her combination of ex-lover, current paramour, future husband, and ex-husband is the chief character in this little melodrama, of which she's merely the main dramatic protagonist. This song was of course largely sketched out by Ronson, along with "Rehab," during his initial brief encounter with Winehouse in New York, in swift and intuitive arrangements that transformed the singer's preliminary raw guitar solos into an unexpected tower of sound.

The plots of her stories are often well trodden but still sad paths: here, her ex-lover didn't leave her with the luxury of regret when he returned to his own ex-lover. This song is a declaration of her attempt to hold her head up high and try to live without the love of her life. She announces in no uncertain terms that she is once again playing a losing game where the odds are stacked against her: she will in all probability return to what she knows best: the blackout state, at first temporarily and later permanently. We get to listen in on the whole affair. Torch songs have never before reached either this level of intensity or intimacy. It's hard to imagine they ever will again.

Aura echo: Once again the profoundly alternative femininity of the young Lesley Gore is enshrined in this song, with both "Judy's Turn to Cry" and "She's a Fool" from 1963 capturing some of the tear-stained angst of the other-girl scenario.

"Love Is a Losing Game" (2:35)

Written by Amy Winehouse. Produced by Salaam Remi. Recorded by Mark Ronson and Vaughan Merrick. Mixed by Tom Elmhirst. Engineered by Dom Morley, Jesse Gladstone and Mike Makowski. Arranged by Gabriel Roth and Chris Elliott. Alto saxophone: Andy Mackintosh, Chris Davies. Baritone saxophone: Dave Bishop. Bass guitar: Nick Movshon. Cello: Anthony Pleeth, Joely Kloos, John Heley. Drums: Homer Steinweiss. Guitar: Binky Griptite, Thomas Brenneck. Harp:

Helen Tunstall. Percussion: Frank Ricotti. Piano: Victor Axelrod. Tenor saxophone: Jamie Talbot, Mike Smith. Trombone: Richard Edwards. Trumpet: Steve Sidwell. Viola: Bruce White, Jon Thorne, Katie Wilkinson, Rachel Bolt. Violin: Boguslaw Kostecki, Chris Tombling, Liz Edwards, Everton Nelson, Jonathan Rees, Mark Berrow, Peter Hanson, Tom Piggott-Smith, Warren Zielinski. Violin, Leader: Perry Montague-Mason. Released as a single on December 10, 2007.

Songscript: Again the restorative asylum offered by Remi in Miami seems to result in a tender ballad being made even more gripping. There are no departures here; the dramatis personae remains the same couple going through the same travails, but this song is so sadly resigned and touching that it rivals the deepest heartaches of Billie, Nina, Anita, Joni, Janis, and many others in its sheer compositional beauty and near existential delivery.

As the song is played out achingly by the band, love feels like a losing hand in a game with high stakes—too high in the end—and it is, she declares, more than she can tolerate. Her mind is scarred by the memories of her lost love, and she feels laughed at by the powers that be as she approaches the final frame of a movie over which she has lost control.

Never has a personal destiny been cast in so inevitable a shape, the idea that all hope is to be abandoned so predetermined. That abandonment is also sculpted through time, music, and performance, into yet another sonic monument to giving in, giving up, going on. While we listen in secretly from the other room, our ears pressed to the walls that are closing in around her, thinking perhaps of Beckett's own resignation, "I can't go on, I'll go on."

Aura echo: The great Connie Francis seems to be reincarnated here, in an echo of "Who's Sorry Now" from 1958, "Everybody's Somebody's Fool" from 1959, and especially her own youthful masterpiece, "Don't Break the Heart That Loves

You." For good measure, some of the Motown Supremes' vibe of "You Keep Me Hangin' On" saturates the shared theme of doomed game playing between the lovers.

"Love Is a Losing Game" (original demo version, 3:44)

Written by Amy Winehouse. Produced by Mark Ronson. Arranged by Gabriel Roth and Mark Ronson. Engineered by Dom Morley. Alto saxophone: Andy Mackintosh, Chris Davies. Baritone saxophone: Dave Bishop. Bass guitar: Nick Movshon. Drums: Homer Steinweiss. Mixed by Tom Elmhirst. Percussion: Frank Picotti. Piano: Victor Axelrod. Tenor saxophone: Jamie Talbot. Trombone: Richard Edwards. Violin, orchestra leader: Perry Montague-Mason.

Songscript: It's a demo, but like many of the Beatles' demos this one has a special quality that helps us understand where she was going and how she got there. The more basic and less-produced structure reveals an even deeper angst than the finished and more polished final product. It has the quality of an abstract feeling captured before it turns into a fully functional painting, a sketch, something like a plant seed we can watch grow, or in this case listen to, turning into a flower right in front of us. There's a time-lapse photography aspect to the way it would evolve into the later studio album version and, as such, it's actually a rare and useful artifact to have available for appreciating the finished recorded version.

Sean Michaels of the *Globe and Mail* shares my sentiments for the simple clarity of the unadorned and barely produced version of this sad song. "'For you I was a flame,' Amy Winehouse once sang. In this 2006 acoustic demo version we can hear the unshakeable calamity of it. We were reckless with our desire. We loved her for standing in the heart of the fire. Of course we did, and how could it have been otherwise? 'Love is a losing game,' she sings. But all I'm really certain of is that this need not be true."

"Tears Dry on Their Own" (3:07)

Written by Amy Winehouse, Nicholas Ashford, and Valerie Simpson. Produced by Salaam Remi. Mixed by Tom Elmhirst and Matt Paul. Recorded by Franklin Socorro, Glyder Disla, and Shomari Dillon. Trumpet, flugelhorn: Bruce Purse. Piano, bass, guitar: Salaam Remi. Backing vocals: Amy Winehouse. Baritone saxophone, tenor saxophone, alto saxophone, guitar, piano, celeste: Vincent Henry. Drums, tambourine: Troy Auxilly-Wilson. Released as a single on August 13, 2007.

Songscript: My personal favorite among all of Winehouse's great anti-anthems. A simple but powerful message, and one shared perhaps by women through the ages: why does she put so much priority on men, when life has so much more to offer besides their infidelity? In a curious way a coda to "What Is It About Men?," an earlier query from *Frank*, she again laments that, at first, in the early and exhilarating stages of romance, she still knew he really wasn't the one for her, and now in retrospect can't imagine why she became connected to him in the first place. In a sudden moment of rare clarity, she even admits that it's her own responsibility and the perennial "he didn't owe anything to her" still left her with no capacity to walk away.

If she had walked away, of course, there would have been no *Back to Black*, and we're naturally left wondering: was it all worth it? "We had to hit a wall," this sentiment being expressed in her music was the "inevitable withdrawal." But even if she stopped wanting him, a perspective still arrives on her doorstep: she'll be some next man's other woman soon. Sigh.

She knows she shouldn't play herself yet again, as in deceive herself with another version of the same thing. The ultimate dilemma of self-harming: why couldn't she be a better friend to herself, instead of depending on men for fulfillment? If only that were the case. Instead we're left with a perpetual refrain, sung with incredible charm. Strangely brave, the vulnerable song is a celebration of defiance: I won't wipe away my tears, I won't let the world see me do that. They can dry all by themselves. But unfortunately there are always more tears where these came from. She seemed to be a veritable fountain for them.

This song was the fourth single released from the album, on July 31, 2007, and one of its many charms is the sampled inclusion of a section from Marvin Gaye's Motown hit from 1967, "Ain't No Mountain High Enough," behind the singer's voice and underneath her melody. It links the past with the future in a marvelous Amy manner.

Aura echo: In addition to channeling some of Roberta Flack's tenderness from "Killing Me Softly" from 1973, this track also reaches back to Ronnie Spector and the Ronettes and the life lesson of "The Best Part of Breakin' Up (Is Makin' Up)" from 1964. There's a similar recurring thematic presence in Lesley Gore's "Out Here on My Own," written for the 1980 film *Fame*, which contains the ultra-Amy line, "I dry the tears I've never shown, I may not win but I can't be thrown."

"Tears Dry" (original version, 4:08)

Written by Amy Winehouse, Nickolas Ashford, and Valerie Simpson. Recorded by Glyder Disla and Frank Socorro at Instrument Zoo. Strings arranged by Tim Davies; Horns arranged by Vincent Henry. Guitar and drums: Salaam Remi. Organ, piano, Rhodes, synths: John Adams. Guitar, flute, saxophone: Vincent Henry. Background vocals: Zalon, Heshima, and Salaam Remi.

Songscript: This original version of the eventual and much better final track on *Black* was tentatively called "Darkness" and demonstrates a much more basic and simplistic approach. Written at Remi's Miami home over the period of a few weeks, the song contains a familiar observation about all she could ever be with her lover: "There's a darkness that we once knew and it's deep regret I've grown accustomed to." Originally planned as a dirge-like ballad, it was improved upon considerably by incorporating a juicy upbeat Motown vibe in keeping with the other Ronson-oriented pieces on the record.

This bare-bones version shows us not something superior in its simplicity but something evolutionary in its development, and is useful perhaps as an indication of how rough raw material can become magical through the process of musical interventions. But though it's an even sadder demo, it still hints at the production greatness of the later finished rendition of this song that made it to the polished album.

Aura echo: The feeling here is like nothing less than Brian Wilson's superb bare-bones solo versions of either "In My Room" or "Surf's Up," and almost as unbearably tender. Sometimes rough song demos manage to achieve an accidental greatness all their own.

"Wake Up Alone" (3:42)

Written by Amy Winehouse and Paul O'Duffy. Produced by Mark Ronson. Recorded by Mark Ronson and Vaughan Merrick. Mixed by Tom Elmhirst. Arranged by Gabriel Roth and Mark Ronson. Engineered by Jesse Gladstone and Mike Makowski. Bass guitar: Nick Movoshon. Drums: Homer Steinweiss. Guitar: Binky Griptite. Piano: Vincent Axelrod. Organ: John Adams.

Songscript: Another harrowing diary entry left open for the world to read, or listen to, as she declares that there's nowhere left to run; she's alone again, naturally. Dread soaked in soul is of course the best way to characterize her breathtaking music here, which has to be heard loud to be understood well. It's the *Finnegan's Wake* of soul music in that respect: reading the lyrics tells you nothing; hearing them float over the magic beat of the Dap-Kings tells you everything you'll ever want to know about the ambivalence of avant-garde romance.

Aura echo: The afterglow of romance abandoned and lamented ideally mirrors Roberta Flack's 1969 recording of "First Time Ever I Saw Your Face" and also two delightful echoes from the Supremes, "Where Did Our Love Go?" from 1964 and "Stop! In the Name of Love" from 1965.

"Wake Up Alone" (original recording, 4:32)

Written by Amy Winehouse and Paul O'Duffy. Arranged and recorded by Paul O'Duffy. Bass, vibes, and rhythm: Paul O'Duffy. Recorded at La Source Studios, London.

Songscript: A recycled version of the first song recorded for the *Black* sessions, in the form of a one-take demo recorded in March 2006 by O'Duffy. As a form of artistic archaeology it may have some historical value, maybe not so much as a hidden treasure as a rough sketch. It's a demo, after all. Unlike the polished version released on the initial album, this rough take is still highly revealing as a detailed roadmap to the later goldmine.

"Some Unholy War" (2:23)

Written by Amy Winehouse. Produced by Salaam Remi. Recorded by Franklin Socorro, Glyder Disla, and Somari Dillon. Mixed by Gary Noble and James Wisner. Drums, bass, guitar: Salaam Remi. Guitar: Vincent Henry. Guitar, backing vocals: Amy Winehouse.

Songscript: A spooky but spirited song and one of the few that appears at first to reference a world outside of her solipsistic love affair, as she imagines her man off fighting somewhere and how she would stand by him the way all faithful women support their soldier men. She refuses to let him go, as usual, and at his side, drunk on pride, they wait for the blow. It would come sooner than they expected.

This song, and by extension the whole record, has been called by some an urban take on Tammy Wynette's "Stand By

Your Man" for the twenty-first century, which makes it all the more ironic in its stance of torched soul support for a lost love interest. As a ballad, with its gentle guitar and strings hovering overhead, this has the feel of a Curtis Mayfield or Isley Brothers tune. It's hard to imagine that this mini-symphony really only cascades past us for a mere two minutes and twenty-two seconds, making it even shorter than most of Spector's own girl-group dirges.

Stripped down to the bare essentials instrumentally, the song also asks an intriguing question about putting it all down in words: who is she writing for in the end? Just the two of them alone, she concludes, her stomach standing still; it's like we're all reading her last will and testament, and we did seem to be doing just that. But she will battle until the bitter finale, "just me, my dignity, and this guitar case." Of course, we all know that she's writing it to and for us, the huge crowd listening to her laments in the other room.

Eventually the song detours to announce that her man was in fact fighting some "unholy war," but alas that war was really the one going on between the lovers, a nation of only two. Even so, she would still stand beside him; she would have died too; she may even have liked to do so. The unholy war is merely their private/public relationship, amplified to the scale of a state or international conflict.

Aura echo: The notion of standing up for your man was never rebirthed so effectively as in this statement of support that effectively reflects "Soldier Boy" by the Shirelles from 1962, with it's "I'll Be True to You" theme, and "Will You Still Love Me Tomorrow" from 1961. But tomorrow never knows.

"Some Unholy War" (down-tempo version, 3:16)

Written by Amy Winehouse. Produced by Salaam Remi. Mixed by Gary Noble and James Wisner. Recorded by Franklin Socorro. Organ: James Adams. Drums, bass, guitar: Salaam

Remi. Guitar: Vincent Henry. Guitar. Backing vocals: Amy Winehouse.

Songscript: By turning the tempo down she turns the message up, changing the song into a whole different ball of wax, transforming it from a romping declaration of endless support into a mournful litany for the lost "soldier." The war in her heart is the same, the battlefield remains, but the soldier now seems to return to her embrace suffering from the post-traumatic stress that had become part and parcel of her daily life in Amy-land.

Aura echo: This version is somewhat reminiscent of raw and unpolished Lennon demo songs, or even those he penned for his first primal therapy inspired solo album in 1970, such as "Working Class Hero."

"He Can Only Hold Her" (2:46)

Written by Amy Winehouse, John Harrison, Richard Poindexter, and Robert Poindexter. Produced by Mark Ronson. Mixed by Tom Elmhirst. Engineered by Dom Morley. Original demo produced by P-Nut. Recorded by Gabriel Roth, Dom Morley, Derek Pacuk, Matt Paul, and Vaughan Merrick. Finger snaps: Mark Ronson. Baritone saxophone: Cochemea Gastelum. Bass guitar: Nick Movshon. Percussion: Sam Koppelman. Drums: Homer Steinweiss. Guitar: Binky Griptite, Thomas Brenneck. Piano: Victor Axelrod. Tenor saxophone: Neal Sugarman.

Songscript: A strange song, possibly the strangest of her anti-anthems. If the "she" and "her" in the lyric is the singer, the song means one thing; if they're her partner's ex or current girlfriend, the one he went back to and thus made her go back to black, the song takes on quite a different complexion. While it's a hopeful and optimistic notion that the basic truth inside her can never die, even if her heart has been broken, in reality we all know that actually, what's inside her can die a hundred times. She's already told us so.

The female character in the song misses the man he longs to be but can't ever be, for one unspecified reason or another. It's a simple and ambiguous song, disguised by the customary brilliance of the instrumentals and the singer's gift for an arresting melody riding on a wave of stunning rhythm. In a sense, this one is the essence of what rhythm and blues is all about: a sadness seeking to find solace in the arms of our accelerated emotions. It's a perfect example of what the great Phil Spector once accurately defined as his pop blues. He may have invented it, but here Amy Winehouse embodies it powerfully.

Aura echo: Connie Francis crooning "Where the Boys Are" (someone waits for me), the Ronettes pleading "Be My Baby" in 1963, and the Dixie Cups chirping their anticipation in "Chapel of Love" in 1964 all feel like song ripples that sent shivers down the spine of Winehouse when she was writing this reflective jukebox ode.

"Addicted" (2:45)

Written by Amy Winehouse. Produced by Salaam Remi. Recorded by Franklin Socorro, Glyder Disla, and Shomari Dillon. Drums: Troy Auxilly-Wilson. Drums, bass: Salaam Remi. Electric piano, organ: John Adams. Guitar, backing vocals: Amy Winehouse. Guitar, saxophone: Vincent Henry. Trumpet, flugelhorn: Bruce Purse.

Songscript: Only the UK and Irish releases of *Back to Black* include this song, and that's probably a good thing, since to have this little complaint song as the final statement on an album that opens with "Rehab" might be too much to bear—a subliminal bookend that could have forced the point. The addiction in question here is the relatively harmless one of grass that she indulged in earlier before her dark paramour introduced her to his own preferred rituals of decay.

The basic message, delivered with her usual aplomb, is that weed gives her more solace than any man ever could, so her presumed roommate should leave her stash alone, since the singer would rather her girlfriend lose the man who's raiding her "stuff" than to be without it herself. "Tell your boyfriend next time he around, to buy his own weed and don't wear my shit down."

Though not my favorite Winehouse tune by a long shot, I still admire the way she incorporates the basic opening riff from the Four Tops' 1965 hit "I Can't Help Myself" in yet another ironic self-reference. While this is not one of her greatest songs, its inclusion as the ending salvo on the British *Back to Black* pressing did serve as a curious reminder of just how peculiar a performer she really was—something of a rare and near extinct breed who single-handedly engraved some obvious human verities onto our cultural consciousness by her sheer personal example.

Aura echo: Oddly enough, the song most embedded in this Winehouse tribute to her favorite herb is one by Peggy Lee devoted to her own favorite stimulant on an album of the same name in 1953, "Black Coffee." The emotional aroma is almost identical.

■ ■ ■

Posthumous record album releases are always a risky affair, fraught with the dangers of both crass commercialism and maudlin indulgence, and yet when the listening public loves an artist's work enough to refuse to live only with what they were officially given, such releases are all but inevitable. Janis Joplin's last completed album, *Pearl*, was released in 1971, three months after the singer's death, and went on to be her bestseller. Joy Division's second and last album, *Closer*, was released only two months after the suicide of their singer Ian Curtis in 1980. Michael Jackson's estate released the first of ten posthumous albums of so-called hidden treasures in 2009. John Lennon's demo of "Free as a Bird," finessed by

Paul, George, and Ringo for their 1995 *Anthology* album, became their first "new" Beatle song in twenty-five years. And of course, the tales of endlessly new old material from Jimi Hendrix and Tupac are legion.

With Amy Winehouse, however, we seem to have arrived at the full extent of her creative output, and maybe that's a good thing. In his liner notes to *Lioness: Hidden Treasures*, released on December 2, 2011, Salaam Remi recalls how difficult it was to pull off the release of a posthumous Winehouse album. "When I listened back to the tapes, you would hear some of the conversations in between takes . . . that was emotional. It has been hard, but it has also been an amazing thing. Amy was a gifted girl. I believe she has left something behind beyond her years. I'm blessed to be part of that process, to have known that person, and to continue her legacy with this album."

Elsewhere, Remi explained to the *New Musical Express* that this record would not be leading to another "Tupac situation," as he put it, lamenting the fact that since the rapper's death in 1996, a full seven posthumous "albums" have appeared on the market.

Remi's own personal justification for participating in the posthumous element of what he optimistically calls her legacy was to give focus to what, to him, was the most impressive and indisputable aspect of her character: just how creative this young woman really was, despite all her difficulties. "A lot of people, through the other antics that were going on with her personally, didn't get that she was at the very top of what she did. Coming to Miami was her escape from all of that, and her writing process could document her life, whether it was recording the pain of the loneliness, or her humor. It makes no sense for these songs to be sitting on a hard drive, just withering away."

For Mark Ronson, the posthumous release was a similar labor of love. He was devastated enough by her passing to enter into a kind of self-imposed exile and to avoid the media, which had already become overwhelming during her difficult last years. When he spoke to *GQ* magazine about his response to both her absence and *Lioness*, he was as guarded and circumspect as Remi had been about the subject of sending her few remaining scraps of sound out into the world so soon. He shared with Dan Hayman his need to shield himself from the scrutiny that had so haunted Amy throughout her final turbulent days and referred to his near-sibling bond with the young singer, formed after only a couple of days in the studio together and forged through the making of *Back to Black*, especially the epic "Rehab," which Hayman called "the confessional track that epitomized *Black*'s open-door policy," into her tragic challenges.

Ronson was reassured by Remi's presence on the project, given the latter's role as her collaborator from the beginning (shockingly only eight years earlier). He was soothed by their own creative parallel energies and moved by the global appetite for Amy, which couldn't quite be denied—or so it seemed. When speaking to *GQ*, he was clearly crushed by the memory that they had planned to go back into the studio the same month she passed away. "It was always a bit of an ongoing question in my head: if Amy and I worked together again, what should it sound like? But you kind of know what sounds good with Amy's voice. But who knows what it would have sounded like? She could have come up with a batch of songs that sounded completely different."

Lioness, which contains only two of the newly minted songs for that third album, was obviously a painful piece of work for both Ronson and Remi to participate in, but it was up to them, to make it work as well as possible as a cohesive expression of the material she left behind, before, during, and after *Black*. Ronson clearly felt that having her most consistent creative partner Remi on board, as well as the active cooperation of her family, tended to resolve any potential hesitation he may have felt about issuing posthumous material: "He [Remi] wouldn't let anything come out that he didn't think she would like. I certainly wouldn't either."

The Winehouse Estate authorized the release of the posthumous collection, telling Nick Levine of the *National* that if the family hadn't felt the album was up to the standards of both *Frank* and *Back to Black*, they would never have agreed to release it. Three tracks from it are pertinent to our appreciation of *Back to Black*, in that they were remaindered from the album and lingered on in a nascent state. They may or may not have matured into finished tracks for her long awaited follow up record but they do offer further archeological evidence of what she somehow managed to accomplish during her short career.

"Between the Cheats" (3:34)

Written by Amy Winehouse and Salaam Remi. Recorded by Glyder Disla at Instrument Zoo. Bass, guitar, drums and bells: Salaam Remi. Guitar and saxophone: Vincent Henry. Background vocals: Zalon and Heshima and Glen Lewis. Wurlitzer and Rhodes: John Adams. Strings arranged by Stephen Coleman.

Songscript: This song was developed with early mentor Salaam Remi as a potential item for Winehouse's mythical third album, but somehow it registers as a warmed-over leftover from *Back to Black*, since it doesn't strike out in any new direction at all, stylistically or lyrically. Instead it appears to recycle the same extremely world weary sensibility relating to two lovers who both cheat on each other but still maintain a strong bond (supposedly) in between their infidelities.

If the third album had continued to mine the same territory as the second, no matter how brilliantly recorded it might have been it would hardly have struck the global audience as evidence of an ongoing creative evolution. A been there, done that feeling and yawning response would have been likely, especially since the audience by that time would have known all too well the personal details and outcomes being referenced in the rather trite tune.

One of her weakest songs lyrically, it is hard to imagine the listener taking this song as seriously as any average Joni Mitchell torch song. The lyrics recycle some of the familiar "stand by your man" themes from *Back to Black*, though with less impact and aplomb, offering a warning to anyone who tries to come between her lover and her; their interference will not succeed, since there is a "winning secret" that bonds them, even though it is embedded "between the cheats." Alas, Phil Spector wrote better lyrics even before puberty, and this effort does not bode well as a standard bearer for a third, prayed-for Amy album. But we'll never know.

"Like Smoke" (featuring Nas, 4:38)

Written by Salaam Remi, Nasir Jones, and Amy Winehouse. Recorded by Frank Socorrow and Glyder Disla at Instrument Zoo. Strings arranged by Tim Davies. Horns arranged by Vincent Henry. Bass, drums, and guitar: Salaam Remi. Guitar: Vincent Henry. Bass and guitar: Dale Davies. Keyboards: James Poysner. Strings: the Czech Film Orchestra. Nas appears courtesy of Island Nas Records.

Songscript: Perhaps the flimsiest excuse for a song in the posthumous *Lioness* collection and really more of a brief scatting exercise of the sort she often used to warm up the voice before getting down to her *Black* business, this skeleton was later embellished by adding a Nas vocal and simulating what may have happened if they had ever actually recorded together. Another pale lyric leftover from the *Black* sensibility, it really should have been left in the drawer as a rough sketch for something that may or may not have made it onto the third album. Its recycling of some of her commonplace ambivalent attitudes about men—"Never wanted you to be my man, I just needed company—like smoke"—recalls some of her more innocent pothead perspectives from "Addicted."

"Will You Still Love Me Tomorrow" (4:23)

Written by Carole King and Gerry Goffin. Produced by Mark Ronson. Engineered by Gabriel Roth. Pro Tools editing by Vaughan Merrick. Drums: Homer Steinweiss. Bass: Nick Movshon. Guitar: Binky Griptite, Thomas Brenneck. Trumpet: Dave Guy. Tenor saxophone: Ian Hendrickson-Smith. Baritone saxophone: Cochema Gasteum. Piano: Victor Axelrod. Background vocals: Kevin Keys, Saundra Williams, Angele Blake. Orchestra led by Perry Montague-Mason. Arranged by Chris Elliott and Mark Ronson. Recorded at Daptone House, House of Soul.

Songscript: At least this has the Dap-Kings on it, and it's also one of the greatest Carole King songs from her blockbuster 1971 album *Tapestry*, the Grammy-winner for best album of that year. But it was actually first recorded in a speedier dance version back in 1961 by the Shirelles, one of the key Amy girl-group inspirations, to huge acclaim. A classic "answer" (or response) song, it was also covered by an army of earlier Amy templates such as the Chiffons and the Kestrels, and has also been beautifully interpreted by several other Amy precursors: Brenda Lee, Lesley Gore, Dusty Springfield, Jackie DeShannon, Sandy Posey, and the great Roberta Flack.

A younger Winehouse had originally recorded it in a slower and jazzier version in 2004 for the film *Bridget Jones: The Edge of Reason*, so it made perfect sense for the elder Amy to revisit it, especially given the pertinent lyrics: "Is this a lasting treasure, or just a moment's pleasure?" Cradled in the arms of Winehouse's voice, still powerfully evocative even in 2011, this song takes on poignant new meanings and conveys some of her deepest feelings of love and loss. It's a brilliant cover version of a song that was accidentally just made for her.

■ ■ ■

For the true fetishists among us, *Back to Black* was also released in a "Deluxe Edition," with bonus tracks, on January 1, 2007. It contains several gems worth considering in the context of this great pop album.

"Valerie" (3:54)

Written by Abi Harding, Boyan Chowdhury, Dave McCabe, Russ Pritchard, and Sean Payne. Engineered by Andrew Rogers. Guitar: Thomas Brenneck, Binky Griptite. Bass: Nick Movshon. Drums: Homer Steinweiss. Percussion: Amir Thompson. Trumpet: Dave Guy. Saxophone: Neil Sugarman. Baritone: Ian Hendrickson-Smith.

Songscript: Though written by the members of the Zutons, this is the perfect vehicle for Winehouse's own retro-soul vibe, especially since it shares her diaristic, hyper-personal focus on quotidian aspects of life with a lover, delving into one question after another about his/her absent heartthrob. An incredibly catchy and infectiously danceable tune, it's laced with the considerable irony of the admission that the singer's body is a mess as she returns home and pleads with her lover to "stop-making a fool out of me."

Winehouse met and played with the Dap-Kings for the very first time while recording this hit song. The original track is from the English band's 2006 album *Tired of Hanging Around*, for which it served as the ideal single release. In their hands it was a pleasant-enough ditty, well crafted and produced, with a clever video narrative and an old school '60s vibe of its own propelling it along merrily. But in the hands of the brilliant Mark Ronson and the haunting Amy Winehouse, especially in the live version later performed at the BRIT Awards in 2008, it becomes a totally different species of song, leaping suddenly into emotional warp-drive, with Winehouse barely able to contain herself in that skinny frame as she squirms through her finest Ronnie Spector impersonation.

Mark Ronson coaxed her into delivering a great rendition. "One afternoon in late 2006 I took Amy to Daptone Studios, where I had recorded all the backing tracks to 'Rehab' (among others)," Ronson told Q magazine in 2015. "She had been in England and had never seen the place or met these brilliant musicians who had played on her songs. There was a joyous feeling in the room and I thought we should try cutting a tune for an album I was working on. Amy picked 'Valerie.'"

The song crackles with a sheer joy absent in the original: Winehouse is swaying and twitching with her eyes mostly closed, bringing tears to your ears. It's incredible. It's everything about her that will so sorely be missed. A wild temporary spirit housed in a fragile container built to sing, but not built to survive.

"Cupid" (3:49)

Written by Sam Cooke. Produced by Mark Ronson. Mixed by Gary Noble. Music director: Dale Davis. Baritone Saxophone: Frank Walden. Drums: Rank Tontoh. Guitar: Hawi Gondwe, Robin Banerjee. Keyboards: Cyril McCammon. Tenor saxophone: Jim Hunt. Trumpet: Henry Collins. Additional vocals: Ade Omotayo, Zalon Thompson.

Songscript: A great Sam Cooke song from 1961, and a masterful choice for Winehouse to emulate. The only thing more amazing than her own gift for penning tenderly tragic songs was her uncanny ability to feel a powerful empathy for other songs she could have written herself and to deliver heartfelt versions of them. Like "Valerie," this cover of a historic soul gem fits perfectly on the deluxe *Black* release while also still being a conduit for the singer's own private narrative. He/she pleads to the Greek god of love to draw back his bow and let his arrow go, straight to the lover's heart, to please hear her cry, because though she doesn't want to bother a deity (who does?), she's in some distress; there's a danger of her losing all of her happiness (or what little of it there was left), and this can be fixed by the god of love's intervention on her behalf.

The song trails off in exasperated hopes and wishes and promises to love on "until eternity": doesn't he hear her, she asks, she needs him to help her, she confirms, and most tellingly declaims, "Cupid, don't fail me." Of course, since it's Amy, she delivers the plea in a shining reggae-fied Johnny Nash rendition that somehow works perfectly, once more proving she had certain undeniable but equally indefinable abilities as a medium. It's just pure magic, and one of the last couple of fragments from the *Back to Black* sessions to truly make the deluxe boxed set worth the investment.

"To Know Him Is to Love Him" (3:44)

Written by Phil Spector. Produced by Sam Gregory. Engineered by Matt Snowden.

Songscript: Well, it's a Phil Spector song and one of his best early odes to worshipping the wrong guy, and in his own personal case, the words first appeared on the tombstone of his dead father—a suicide that haunted Spector throughout his dark but hugely successful life. It was the first song he wrote, the first of his songs to become a huge hit at No. 1 in 1958, and the only one performed by a group of which he was an active member, the Teddy Bears. At two minutes and twenty seconds it is just about the most perfect of his teen symphonies and sums up worshipful love more succinctly than anything before or since.

As usual with Winehouse, when the song comes pouring out of her lips it takes on a whole new and pertinent meaning: "To know, know, know him, is to love, love, love him, just to see him smile, makes my life worthwhile." This acoustic version was recorded and released as the B-side to the 2007 single of "You Know I'm No Good."

It's advisable to find and watch the Teddy Bears' version with the spooky Phil Spector himself strumming along as a warped but gifted teenager who went on to invent the sonic techniques that eventually would inspire Mark Ronson to produce a masterpiece for Amy Winehouse. Then quickly switch to viewing her version and wait for the chills to stop running up and down your spine. Her voice on this track is especially otherworldly, almost unbearably tender, and more than enough to remind us of why we remember her. At the risk of sounding maudlin, to hear, hear, hear, her, is to love, love, love, her.

■ ■ ■

Perhaps not entirely surprisingly—despite the fact that Universal Records executive David Joseph valiantly declared that he had destroyed all extant demos, remixes, and unreleased tracks pertaining to his Winehouse empire—VH1 included at least nine unreleased tracks in a 2015 profile piece called *A Reminder of Amy Winehouse's Talent*. This followed the earlier off-the-grid release of a horde of rejected *Back to Black* and *Frank* material that today floats around the musical world like a cloud of mosquitoes zeroing in on a plate of leftover food in the back alley.

Of course, some bootlegs are goldmines in themselves, and in fact some of the Grateful Dead or Bob Dylan's bootlegs are among their best musical offerings. Perhaps the greatest bootlegs in history were the multiple discs of Brian Wilson's legendary *Smile* album from the time of his meltdown in 1967, which circulated privately among fetishists for some thirty-five years before he got around to finishing the album the way he'd originally planned, with the help of the Wondermints instead of his original and dysfunctional Beach Boy family.

The VH1 material was definitely not of that caliber by any means, but it still offers something salient for lovers of her sound and spirit, and covers the overlapping *Frank* and *Black* sensibilities in a way that temporarily satisfies your yearning for more (if not exactly fresh) Amy cuisine. "Long Day," "What It Is," "Trilby," and "When My Eyes" are outtakes from *Frank*, while "Procrastination," "Alcoholic Logic," "Beat the Point to Death," and "Close to the Front" offer alternatives to the *Black*-era menu. A bare bones demo version of "Losing Game" at least further demonstrates how close to the primitive brilliance of raw Lennon tracks prior to production polishing she really was, not in style but in terms of vulnerable self-revelation, and as such it has at least some archaeological value.

In addition to these shards, the Winehouse tracks cobbled together for the so called *Other Side of Amy Winehouse*, a larger bootleg compendium of vault debris, which came out privately in 2008 to capitalize on a gold rush then underway full steam, is also guaranteed to sustain your appetite for Winehouse nutritional supplements. The *Other Side* song list includes what the makers euphemistically call "B-sides, remixes, demos, and rarities," offering song detours into "Monkey Man," "Valerie (Live Lounge Version)," "Best Friends" (as an acoustic study), "Will You Still Love Me Tomorrow," "He Can Only Hold Her," "Do Me Good," "Fuck Me Pumps," "To Know Him Is to Love Him," "Round Midnight," "Back to Black (Zilla Rocca Remix)," "Best for Me (featuring Tyler James)," "Rehab (Desert Eagle Remix)," "I Should Care," "I Heard It Through the Grapevine," "No Good (Skeewiff Remix)," "Hey Little Rich Girl," "Back to Black (Rumble Strips Remix)," "Fuck Me Pumps (M. J. Cole Mix Edit)," "Get Over It," "You're Wondering Now," "Don't Go to Strangers," "Fools Gold," "Stronger Than Me (A Cappella version)," and "Beat It," a forgettable cover of the iconic Michael Jackson hit performed with Charlotte Church.

Though utterly without any rhyme or reason, order or flow, they are all still . . . well, some thirty or so tracks of Amy Winehouse lasting for 137 minutes and 18 seconds, and considering that you'll never likely hear another sound coming out of her, they may be a soothing balm for the Amy lover who just can't get enough. Close listening, however, clearly reveals why these tracks were outtakes or rejected B-sides, and the discerning listener is best advised to simply stick with the exquisite majesty of the actual *Back to Black* album itself.

The "Deluxe Edition" also has the advantage of being, well, deluxe, as in of higher quality and more expensive than other examples of its kind in name, and also somewhat luxurious. Though non-essential except perhaps for the Amy-lover on your gift list, it does contain period gems that are well worth a close listen. Her cover versions provide ample insight into the sublime torch sensibility of the singer and the roots that inspired her. These interpretative tunes clearly demonstrate Winehouse's strong link to the musical world she became such a huge part of for a short time. This singer may definitely have been a singularity. But she was certainly not alone.

In addition to reminding us of the long torch tradition she renewed so vitally, the songs on *Back to Black* also accidentally remind us of the verity of a remark by the wise playwright George Bernard Shaw: "There are two tragedies in life. One is not to get your heart's desire. The other is to get it."

■ ■ ■

The year 2015 marked the tenth anniversary of Hurricane Katrina in the southern United States; 2016 marks the tenth anniversary of Hurricane Amy around the planet. Both were about stormy weather; one was physical and geographic and the other creative and musical. But both will be easily remembered whenever we reach for a superlative to describe something both unique and unforgettable.

One prime indicator of the impact of Hurricane Amy on producer Mark Ronson was his customarily humble response to being nominated for and winning the 2015 MTV Best Male Video for his song "Uptown Funk" (with Bruno Mars). In a rare display of self-deprecation—rare at least for the music industry—he tried to express his amazement at his good fortune since encountering that Winehouse weather front, well aware that before doing so he was all but ready to pack it in and call it a near career. As he himself put it, "I used to just be a DJ, just playing records at the MTV after-party and playing the music during the TV commercial breaks, and now suddenly I'm making my *own* records, and sitting in the front row at MTV's gala event with Bruno Mars. It just doesn't get any better than this." Truer words were never spoken.

Playwright Marsha Norman once remarked, "Success is always something you have to recover from." Equally true, if you're lucky enough to do so. I suspect that the subtext message behind Mark Ronson's self-effacing comment was his awareness that if he had never encountered that unruly Winehouse weather front, he may never have ended up in that front row seat with Bruno Mars.

The message I hope the reader of this narrative takes away in response is twofold: first, an astonished appreciation for Amy Winehouse's innate musical skills, abilities that were so instinctual that they couldn't ever be learned and barely even be practiced; and second, a deep sense of loss over the fact that even her towering creativity couldn't save her from herself. Evidently nothing was enough to enable her to make more music, the thing she loved to do more than anything else in life. Not even life itself was enough to heal her.

For my part, what I most personally regret, and even almost resent, is the sad fact that there won't be any more Winehouse records of the breathtaking caliber of *Back to Black* to keep us company in the dark night of the soul. While this is admittedly selfish on my part, I feel I almost have to paraphrase that consummate survivor, Iggy Pop, when he barked, "I want more!" I too want more music by this gifted creature; I'm not going to get any, and that just isn't fair.

I looked around for consolation, and luckily (in addition to the sad *Lioness* release) a second posthumous album emerged from the vault in her absence. Titled *Live at the BBC* and released November 19, 2012, it contains further *Back to Black* song material of interest for the way in which it reinterprets her original themes.

This very worthwhile album includes a version of "Rehab" performed on the BBC Radio 2 show hosted by Pete Mitchell in 2006; "You Know I'm No Good" and "Tears Dry on Their Own" performed for the Jo Whiley Live Lounge show in 2007; Winehouse's theme song, "Love Is a Losing Game," performed during a late appearance on Jools Holland's show in 2009; and "Just Friends," given a full orchestral format for *The Big Band Special* show in 2009, returning Amy to a kind of 1940s big-band jazz-style splendor that actually suited her talents so remarkably well.

Considering that you'll never likely hear another sound coming out of her, these may be a soothing balm for the Winehouse lover who just can't get enough. Yet perhaps it's that very sense of unfairness that prompts some listeners to make an effort to enjoy the posthumous releases that inevitably emerge in the wake of losing any truly talented artist. Who can blame them really? In Amy Winehouse's case, these releases offer a revealing combination of older pieces and alternative versions of *Black* pieces as well as those literal fragments of songs which were intended for the post-*Black* phase of her career. As such, they do still comprise a curious kind of archaeology of this great album as an artifact, from the multiple perspectives of past, present, and future. Maybe this really is as good as it gets.

9

THE LEGACY OF LADY NIGHT

Too Soon to Be a Legend?

"There is a downside to having one of the biggest selling albums ever."
—Carole King, *Natural Woman*

Ernest Hemingway was a specialist in breakage. In *A Farewell to Arms* he declared, "The world breaks everyone and afterward many are strong in the broken places. But those that will not break it kills. It kills the very good and the very gentle and the very brave impartially. If you are none of these you can be sure it will kill you too but there will be no special hurry."

No special hurry indeed. But Winehouse's oblique and bluesy narrative would seem to suggest otherwise. My, my, how time flies when you're dead. Ten years later, *Back to Black* is still a curious anomaly, an unusually seductive documentary movie for your ears that opens with a deceptively bouncy upper, a refusal to seek help, and closes with that mournful "He Can Only Hold Her," a lament that openly declares no one is home but the lights are still on. In between though, we're exposed to what feels like a personal and intimate journal of human feeling with few equals.

This album is also that rare mix of white soul, hip hop, and maximum rhythm and blues that has similarities, not in style but in spirit, to the jazz-folk fusion accomplished by Joni Mitchell with *Hissing of Summer Lawns* in 1975. A perfect fusion doesn't come along every day—not even every year or decade—and that's exactly why it deserves to be celebrated for its musical achievement, above and beyond the tawdry drama that inspired it, accompanied it, and followed in its glistening platinum wake.

Now, ten years later, when we return to the brief tsunami that was Amy Winehouse, the true artistic power and pop stature of the *Back to Black* album can hopefully come to the foreground, as can the magical way it transmuted the torch song tradition from one era to another so seamlessly. That tradition has always been founded on the simplest of emotional ingredients without any excessive theatricality. The torch song doesn't need any special effects, elaborate sets or wild costume changes, simply because its only stage set is the broken human heart and the only props required are its emotional pleas. Strangely enough, her pleas pleased us, and that inexplicable fact is now a big part of her paradoxical legacy.

What we discover through repeated listening is that it's her old-fashioned storytelling motif that captivates us every time. All great torch songs are a means of transmitting vital data into the future like an emotional story virus that touches whoever hears them. The stronger the virus, the longer the song lasts. Lady Day's "Autumn in New York" has lasted this long because its viral content is so powerful, and for the same reason "Wake Up Alone" will also last. In fact, I suspect that another of Lady Night's songs, "Love Is a Losing Game" may well prove to be her own personal "Strange Fruit," the song that burned itself into the legacy of Billie Holiday with the strength of a corrosive but gorgeous acid.

It's not that I'm trying to elevate Winehouse's songs to a prominent classical status they don't deserve. I'm merely pointing out what they do deserve: to be taken seriously. Pop music itself needs to be taken more seriously as a genre because it's a mirror of the time in which it takes place. The power of that mirror is mostly the result of creative mutation fueled by fortunate combinations of social and economic conditions. In some rare cases, such as this one, pop music can even evolve into an actual work of pop art.

Many are strong in the broken places, even world-famous pop stars, and surely that's the essence of what all great blues and soul music is really about. Hers was great, but how do we know we're not over reacting when it comes to the lasting value of bright short-lived comets as such the Winehouse passing through our popular culture skies?

Here's one last use of the Rashomon effect metaphor as it might apply to the late Amy Winehouse. Depending on your angle of sight and vantage point, your perspective on what happened in that musical clearing in the forest she burned down will vary drastically. The events are not fixed but very mutable, and each report on her overall career arc will reveal something highly relative to the position of the observer. It now appears that she was one of the following things, depending on who you might ask or care to believe:

She was an exemplary singer/songwriter in the torch-song tradition who was lucky enough to be in the right place at the right time and make it big by defiantly giving people what they wanted.

Or she was a self-absorbed musical prodigy who transcended her doubts to become a performing artist who happened to meet a great producer and great band who helped transform her brokenhearted poetry into shimmering pop music.

Or she was a shy young savant with a vocal gift for mimicking great singers from the past at a time when our postmodern culture craved nostalgia but had forgotten most of its own history.

Or she was a psychologically wounded, emotionally scarred young lady with a father complex who got into bad company and became a drug addict and alcoholic who took her lucky break and broke it in two.

Or she was a great but anxious storyteller who became

a demonic diva and borrowed or channeled the original sounds and styles of jazz/blues/soul goddesses from the golden age of pop.

Or she was a bulimic, self-harming young girl no one would or could help save from herself who was still visionary enough to inaugurate a second British invasion of the music industry and usher in a new golden age of pop.

Life is complicated. By now we also know it's totally relative. She actually seems to have been all these things at the same time. Her family, friends, lovers, agents, managers, label executives, producers, fellow musicians, audiences, and the general public all saw one facet of what they believed to be the whole true story. Every version of her story is therefore equally true, and every earwitness to her phenomenon passage is totally accurate. Just like it was in the Rashomon movie.

Before long, the brilliant album she released in October 2006 will almost have lived longer that she herself did. *Back to Black* was then and still is now a rather singular achievement with few sonic peers in the realm of pop music. This is especially ironic because, as we've seen, it was never intended to be a pop record at all and instead merged Wall of Sound '60s girl groups and something else without a name into an amazing witch's brew with many imitators but few equals.

In fact, the popularity of this record, dark and disturbing despite its shiny surfaces, prompts us all to wonder about the central role of pop music in our contemporary culture: what it does for us and to us, and how that perfect pop hook captures our attention but sometimes clouds our judgment. The hook of more hopeful music such the Beatles was one thing but what about the hook of distressingly sorrowful blues music that takes you to the root of a dilemma that even its glistening glamour can't ever really help us solve?

For the first time since the Beatles, Winehouse's was music that kids with ska, rap, and hip-hop credentials could listen to at the same time as parents with jazz, blues, funk, and soul credentials could appreciate its exotic and entertaining vibe. In the end, that's what makes it perfect pop music: it has something for literally everyone, and on a grand scale, whether or not you know about the tragic undertow that eventually defeated her. Often, pop music simplifies everything wonderfully and it also heals almost every heartache. Almost.

Sometimes comparison-shopping can be helpful. Recently, Jared Bland of the *Globe and Mail* made some pertinent observations about the talented Vancouver-born singer/songwriter Grimes (aka Elise Boucher) and her approach to making alternative music which is still firmly lodged in the seductive domain of pop motifs. While he was specifically referencing her excellent 2016 album *Art Angels* and how it subverts our pop expectations at the same time as satisfying them, his insights also helped to situate her in the post-Amy musical environment. He calls her work "professionalized and at once resistant to the sheen of professionalization . . . it's controlled yet unpredictable and somehow sits within the pop paradigm while existing outside of it . . . it's unlike anything else I can think of."

Grimes was born five years after Winehouse, is currently a seemingly steady twenty-seven years old, and continues to deservedly rise in a music industry profoundly impacted by the Amy legacy she inherited in her wake. Though her style is unlike Amy's, her creative approach is all Amy: exceptional, thunderous, exhilarating, terrifying, and yet exquisitely beautiful. She also has a similar arsenal of emotional weapons that she uses to explore some unconventional territory, in her case violence, in a manner reminiscent of the near-operatic Winehouse ethos for self-revelation and self-concealment at the same time.

Most important in his appreciation of Grimes is Bland's assessment of that pop paradigm itself: "Pop music is about extremes, and our attachment to it is based upon our needs for those various extremes. We like a given song because it's sadder than our sadness, or sexier than our sexiness, or happier than our happiness, because it's a more interesting and intense version of what we feel or wish to feel."

My own sense of the Winehouse legacy, and of all the greatest pop music, hinges on that shared impulse. Winehouse was mesmerizing because her deep sadness was sadder than ours; Grimes is alluring because her quirky sexiness is sexier than ours; the Beatles are still pop gods because their happiness is so much greater than ours that it increases ours exponentially. Bland also astutely points out that what we are attracted to in the best pop music is that it often contains a more dangerous and volatile vision of the world we ourselves occupy.

My contention is that Amy Winehouse didn't just push the envelope of pop music: she tore up the envelope altogether and re-addressed it. My sense of her legacy is that just as her own precursors (Billie Holiday, Carole King, Helen Shapiro, and the Ronettes, among many others) gave her permission to fully be herself, Winehouse gave the generation of singer/songwriters who followed her an identical permission.

What Bland declares for Grimes, "Her music becomes a dare: to like it is to admit to liking a particular darkness in ourselves," goes double for Winehouse, an artist who clearly made the Grimes approach at least as accessible as it is today. When it comes to being attracted to the darkness, surely an even larger part of the inherited Amy legacy that nourished Grimes is also contained in the insight that "her genius lies in making that attraction so pleasurable." A similar Amy legacy echo can be felt in the music of Ruby Amanfu, Tia Brazda, and Miya Folick, who all learned from Winehouse the way Amy did from Billie and Ronnie.

In a decade-long retrospect, we can also now observe how paradoxical Amy Winehouse was as a person and a performer:

she possessed an exotic kind of turbulent ambiguity that made her music magisterial, apparently as a result of her uncanny ability to merge such emotional sorrow with such musical joy. She is definitely unlike anything else we can think of. The girl-group gospel and jazz/soul vibration that this young vocalist was seemingly born with, blended with the current hip-hop and pop sensibilities of her almost as young producers, gave her a kind of unexpected maturity far beyond her tender years. Together they all gave *Back to Black* a spooky, timeless quality that remains just as gripping to this day.

No matter how long artists may have been with us, the questions about legacy are always thorny ones, perhaps even more so when a singer/songwriter has a mighty impact but produces a slim body of work. How do we compare them to musical artists who became senior statesmen or women due to their longevity, maturity, and staying power—the very things so sadly missing from the heartbreaking Winehouse saga?

Let's try to address that dilemma of potentially overreacting by talking about the perils of poptimism. It's a great concept, one first dreamed up by music critic Chris Richards in the *Washington Post* last year. I introduce it here and now because I want to make it clear that I'm in no way suggesting that Amy Winehouse was the greatest thing since sliced bread. Only that she offered a whole new way of slicing bread, one that fused every sharp musical knife that came before her.

"In the new world of poptimism," Richards observes, "critics are quick to hail the shallowest sugary CD as a masterpiece on par with the Beatles' *Sgt. Pepper*, or other gems of the rock canon." He explained this compulsion in a simple enough manner: we want to feel as though our irrational universe obeys a hidden logic and that we each belong to something greater than only ourselves alone. Something like great music.

Richards's salient concept of poptimism as a commercial driving force manipulating our tastes helps us to realize that today's music is technically no better or worse than at any other point in our pop history. However, via the magic of poptimism we're seduced by the "flattering hallucination" of perpetual evolution. It's a kind of musical Darwinism: the allure of the new. He goes on to clarify that this hallucination—one shared by listeners who feel a communal bond with the artists they imagine speak on their behalf (the way the Beatles actually used to, for instance)—has to do with the fact that today when a pop star reaches the upper stratosphere of fame, the level up there with Beyoncé, Drake, Taylor Swift, Arcade Fire, or whoever the flavor of the momentary age might be, something "magical" happens. They no longer seem to get bad reviews, Richards points out. Neither did Amy Winehouse, but only because she wasn't around long enough. He reminds us of the uncomfortable fact that average or mediocre pop stars quickly become superstars, and that the natural side effect of this is that music critics become their cheerleaders. As a result, he writes, "the discussion froths into a consensus of uncritical excitement." This is an unfettered rush to acclaim the next big thing, the next Beatles, the next Dylan, the next Fleetwood Mac—bands for whom in actuality there is no *next* and never can be. This, Richards opines, in a much needed splash of cold water in our feverish pop faces, is the collateral damage of *poptimism,* which he identifies as the prevailing ideology of most of today's music critics, especially those laboring for daily newspapers, monthly magazines, and the television and radio shows most incestuously wedded to the music industry itself.

Few people, Richards suggests, would use this word in a party or at a nightclub, but in music-journalism circles unspoken poptimism has become a kind of holy writ, a situation he identifies with the past decade of poptimists flogging what he calls a basic nagging falsehood: that rock songwriters with rough-hewn voices and real instruments are inherently more *legitimate* (that tricky word again) than pop stars with auto-tuned voices and heavily stylized, over-produced, and choreographed music videos. This notion may focus on, say, Neil Young being more *authentic* than James Blunt, though that one may be a little too obvious an actual contrast.

Richards pinpoints the coming of age of poptimism as occurring in 2014, with the rise of the "unlikely figure" of Taylor Swift, a relatively talented and savvy young songstress and performer, but certainly not one as gifted as Amy Winehouse. The *Guardian* newspaper seemed to anoint her as such in December of that year, extolling how "a blossoming industry juggernaut came to be regarded as a cool, authentic, unassailable planet-devouring super-genius."

To Richards, a wide-awake music critic, it's not that poptimists don't mean well, since they do try to broaden the acceptance for multiple musical styles in a less hierarchical manner. It's just that they can end up worshiping fame and celebrity for its own sake, which can create the illusion that megastars are somehow still underdogs. Worse still, poptimism ends up granting critical immunity to a lot of inferior music.

I for one find his take most refreshing—especially since I'm claiming that Amy Winehouse really was an underdog, or even one that, in the words of jazz great Charles Mingus, was beneath the underdog. Richards further hopes that poptimism—the shameless adulation of new untried megastars who are too favorably compared to the giants of the past—should be toppled by now. But of course it never can be.

In short, the hype machine may have cracked the long-sought formula for perpetual motion: fame begets fawning praise, fawning praise begets huge web traffic, massive web traffic perpetuates fame. Indeed, just as certain kinds of musical favoritism misjudges pop as frivolous entertainment and maintains that today's music isn't as good as it once was, poptimism goes overboard by saying that today's music is just as good as it ever was. This is clearly untrue, except perhaps for millennials with a contagious allergy to history.

My position is in accord with Richards to the point where I'll even willingly exaggerate and claim that Amy Winehouse may have been the last of the *real* pop stars, regardless of the fact that she was brilliantly recycling all the pop idioms of the last sixty years. Those who have followed in her wake–a Duffy or an Adele, for instance—are merely the emblems of poptimism run rampant, as gifted as those young ladies may be. Thus such a brand of cultural amnesia encourages an unhealthy consensus that everything is a good as everything else, and in that respect it is somewhat postmodern. But it isn't true. Few were as good as Winehouse.

My take on this *vis-à-vis* Ms. Winehouse is straightforward: she is not being extolled as an emblem of that phenomenon, the flashing comet mistaken for the sun, but rather as a direct conduit to music history through which many old suns are freshly reflected. Due to the brevity of her narrative, she's been exempt from ever disappointing us artistically, since having made one good album and one great one, she didn't have the opportunity to finish a third album that we potentially could have criticized as being beneath her standards. We'll never know. Which is exactly why *Back to Black* remains a high-water mark deserving our attention.

Deprived of what every artist needs and deserves—the chance to fail creatively—she permanently remains a metaphor for failing existentially, which is a shame indeed and one that accidentally makes it sometimes appear that poptimism lifted her up to those heights she achieved. Actually, the reverse was true: she was a healthy and much needed antidote to all this, but one that didn't hang around long enough to prove it. Her music will hang around for a very long time indeed, however, first as a highly successful pop-music achievement that the public embraced, and later as a pop-culture touchstone that influenced several generations of musical artists still to come.

Even if we won't be able to actually see her legacy, we'll most certainly be able to hear it. The very word is a loaded one for sure. Paul McCartney can reflect on his legacy, Bob Dylan can reflect on his, Mick Fleetwood can savor his, the Stones can marvel at theirs; they've all had half a century to think about their legacies, let alone develop and nurture a real one.

Legacy, legend, lesson: perhaps all three words apply equally to Amy Winehouse. Surely there are also both real and imagined legends, especially in the overheated world of pop music. Bessie Smith, Billie Holiday, Dinah Washington, and Anita O'Day, all legends in blues and jazz. And all of these artists created twenty times the number of albums that Winehouse did, and as many more masterpieces. But hers still has a special place in this glittering pantheon of mutation, fusion, and reiteration, of reinterpretation and renovation: it was a living renaissance in style and practically a reincarnation in substance.

Many other stars have hit it big even since her passage across the global stage, but most of them, and they know who they are, are more the products of poptimism at its most feverish. Nothing in the decade since *Back to Black* has quite reached the same levels of personal intimacy or creative intensity. Ten years doesn't seem like a very long time in the history of the world, but in the rarefied, feverish, hyperactive, and super-charged world of pop music, it's almost a lifetime. How she was able to deliver this musical feat so skillfully and swiftly is rather baffling.

Back to Black's power is also still a little puzzling, until we realize a crucial fact about the often sizzling poetry of popular culture: the men and women who produce great works are not always those who live in the most sophisticated or delicate atmospheres, not those whose conversational style is the most intelligent, or whose personal cultural experience is the most extensive, but rather those who have had the ability, even the power, to suddenly cease living only for themselves and to somehow transform their very personalities into a mirror, a shiny surface into which we can all gaze forever.

In other words, a legacy.

■ ■ ■

Looking for legacy is a tricky business. Surely that was one of the motivations in what I call the posthumous album as grave digging. *Lioness: Hidden Treasures (Prequels, Demos, Outtakes, and Sequels)* was released on December 2, 2011, only five months after her demise. This compilation was not the follow-up to *Back to Black* but rather a compilation of unreleased songs and demos spanning from prior to her debut album through the period of her second and on up to 2011 (including two obvious leftover *Black* tracks created supposedly for the third album that never materialized.)

Considering the disparate range of debris accumulated from across the landscape of her brief career, this album is rendered remarkably coherent by the involvement of both her talented producers, who crafted something almost resembling a real record from the leftovers and follow-up raw materials at their disposal. Almost, but not quite.

Still, plundering the tape vault only twenty weeks after her demise must set some kind of world record for commercial necrophilia, any way you look at it. I've attempted in this book to avoid as much as possible practicing necropsy (the examination of a body to determine the reasons for its demise), instead choosing to focus on her *living remains* in the form of her beautiful music.

The songs on *Lioness* are so dismally unfocused that it's not advisable to include that posthumous release as anything like an indicator of legacy. That would be poptimism writ large.

But it's still a road sign on her historic highway nonetheless. There are individual songs on *Lioness* that can be considered real gems, of course, just none that indicate what she may have been doing to achieve a new direction for a third album, and certainly nothing as fresh and new as her Grammy-grabbing second album. Sometimes legacy can be so elusive.

Another posthumous release, but a more welcome and insightful one than *Lioness*, is *Live at the BBC*, a record of beautiful songs that may in fact have been coming out anyway during her lifetime, had she stuck around. Its material sheds light on her early development and adds more to her legacy than the barrel-scraping aura of *Lioness* could ever hope to. It offers us live performances of songs recorded on BBC television specials from 2004 to 2009, during her most productive creative period, and one worth hearing all over again.

Proceeds from the album go to the worthy work of the Amy Winehouse Foundation for addiction assistance, and sales-wise it achieved a moderate degree of success. For reviewer Gary Mulholland, it was a record that offered an alternative approach to the usual "best of" format and was especially valuable because it emphasized her remarkable empathic abilities as a live performing artist.

How about in the posthumous film documentary *Amy*, quite sincerely directed by the worthy Oscar winner Asif Kapadia and released in July 2015: any legacy there? It does cleverly eschew any on-camera interviews or voiceover, using assembled footage instead and letting the content speak for itself. But it also tends to dwell less on her musical roots and more on her personal dilemmas. It's almost all soap opera and very little music. The viewer who doesn't already know the story of her '60s influences, her stylistic inspirations, her producer's techniques, or her band's background, may be left a little puzzled as to what all the hoopla was really about. They will see a beautiful and gifted young girl with the voice of an angel who got mixed up with the wrong crowd but they may be distracted from the very proportions of her gift by a well-intentioned film that ends up doing what all the rest of the media also did with and to her.

Sean Michaels offered a touching take on the film in the *Globe and Mail* in September 2015, suggesting that *Amy* "presents a vivid portrait of the late singer . . . her unguarded, meteoric rise feels almost as tragic as her well-publicized fall, and this revelation is conveyed purely through home movies and archival footage. Yet the viewer's sense of intimacy is also faintly grotesque: here we are, still voyeurs, watching Winehouse through the lenses of the paparazzi. So many people failed Winehouse. Lovers, colleagues, family, and I find myself wondering whether we failed her too, we listeners with ravenous appetites."

From my perspective, as a viewer as well as a music journalist, I just wish it had focused a little less on personal elegy and tragedy and a little more on her musical roots and thus on her legacy. The mere inclusion of some more archival footage of Anita O'Day, the Ronettes, the other Spector goddesses, or even Sharon Jones alone would have accomplished that task quite efficiently.

For me, though it was emotionally compelling, the film didn't come close to delivering a complete enough portrait of her remarkable musicianship, her ultra-flexible ability to mash historical formats together through her stylistic Cuisinart and yet somehow make them work perfectly together. She was a powerful link in that historical continuum. We probably won't see the likes of her brand of alchemy again. If there is any legacy in the film, it might mostly be the legacy of loss—something it accomplishes to a very high degree indeed, which is why I think it probably deserved to be recognized with an Oscar. Perhaps there should be a special category for lamentation.

Perhaps Winehouse's independent label, Lioness Records, might be a place to search for a few scraps of legacy, at least in the way it focuses on Amy Winehouse as a musical mentor and creative producer? Maybe we were hoping it could acknowledge the importance of several key mentors in her own professional life, to pay it forward and hopefully encourage other young artists with big dreams to reach out and grab them. But without her own peculiar taste buds to personally guide it, how would the label, no matter how well intentioned, ever really manage to evoke her sense of style being discovered or nurtured in other young talents?

At least one saving grace in the heated posthumous climate following her passing was the July 2015 news that Universal Records executive David Joseph had admitted to destroying all fourteen existing of the demo tapes ostensibly slated for the mythical third album. "It was a moral thing," he told *Billboard*. "Taking a stem or a vocal is not something that would happen on my watch. It now can't happen on anyone else's, either." This benevolent gesture thus prevents the fiasco that befell other doomed artists such as Elvis, Tupac, Hendrix, and Jackson. Maybe there is a musical God after all?

Further to that slippery notion of legacy, some of Amy's future importance in music history may also be calculated by her creative and stylistic influence on the large group of female artists who could be called the Amy Inheritors: Adele, Duffy, Lady Gaga, Ellie Goulding, Florence Welch, Estelle, V. V. Brown, La Roux, Little Boots, Eliza Doolittle, Rumer, Carly Rae Jepson, and the extremely talented Lana Del Ray, Joanna Newsom, Ryn Weaver, Grimes, and Halsey.

Another key musical inheritor of Winehouse's creative legacy, as well as an ability to exponentially push the envelope of emotional intensity, also continues to thrive. The gritty rapper soul-chick Angel Haze (Raeen Roes Wilson) is fast becoming a new queen of what Stacey Anderson once called "confrontational gusto" and has released her own gripping second album, *Back to the Woods*. Since the stylistic growth spiral of torch songs is recursive, both she and Andra Day (*Cheers to the Fall*), and also Judith Hill (*Back in Time*), have taken confessional songwriting and vintage soul to some gripping new places that often make Winehouse seem like Lucile Ball by comparison.

Legacy-wise, we should also factor in the resurgence of critical interest in great artists such as Sharon Jones and the Dap-Kings as an obvious but unintended part of the post-Winehouse era. If more people now have the opportunity to listen to and appreciate their remarkable musical spirit and more attention comes to such a well-deserving old-school soul-revivalist family, then we also have Amy Winehouse to thank for that accidental blessing. The same goes for the great girl-groups of the Spector era: welcome back ladies.

Another potential place where a legacy might be situated was announced in 2015 by Hollywood, a dream factory ever ready to mine a legend for yet more dramatic spectacle and cash. At the time of writing, a new cinematic biopic is being readied for the big screen featuring Noomi Rapace, the Swedish actress who brought her dark gravitas to *The Girl with the Dragon Tattoo*. She seems a plausible casting choice, though only time will tell. No, the biopic won't be called *The Girl with the Daddy's Girl Tattoo*, instead it will simply let the name of the late singer say it all and be called *Amy Winehouse*. She has obviously now become a recognizable brand in her own right. Many of us just wish she were acknowledged more for her stellar musical skills than for her tragic depths.

■ ■ ■

Even though by any standard Amy Winehouse's music was the creative consequence of a personal contradiction of spectacular proportions (a ferocious appetite for success merged with a dreadful fear of stardom), it was still a transcendent art form that captured the hearts of listeners and viewers to an almost unparalleled degree in recent times. Now, after she became so well known that she remained a mystery to herself, her elevated stature in popular culture is one of the most revealing aspects of our civilization's shared obsession with fame and notoriety. It's also, however, a good reminder that celebrity is a mask that eats into the face.

When asked by MTV News early on in her brief career, in between the releases of *Frank* and *Black*, how big a star she thought she might become, her answer was: "I don't think that way; my music doesn't operate at that scale." And that was one of the key paradoxes of her fame: she made music of harrowing intimacy that fit perfectly in our nightclubs or living rooms but fell apart once it was magnified up to the scale of the Rolling Stones. Even so, her bluesy power still captivates the heart and transforms every attentive listener into an earwitness to the heart's anger.

The kind of blues music that Winehouse embodied so well is best experienced, appreciated, and understood as a specific branch of the torch song tradition: hers is contemporary torch music on an almost operatic scale. In addition to Edith Piaf and Billie Holiday, I would naturally propose both Joni Mitchell and Amy Winehouse as being among the finest contemporary proponents of the postmodern torch song.

In this regard I think Piers Ford, in his *Art of the Torch Singer*, offers a suitably flexible definition of the style: "Torch singing is not limited by the genre of the music. It's more about a sensibility evoked by a combination of the singer, her voice, the melody, the story, her performance and the lyric, that touches the listener in a special way. It's a mood. A particular sound." Clearly, Winehouse touched listeners in just that special way.

Ford also shared with *Cabaret Confidential* his excellent take on this phenomenon in a way that is especially applicable to

Winehouse: "The ability to tell a story in a song, with emotional conviction. Singers like these can hold a room in the palm of their hands, make the audience identify in a single note or word with the experience that they are singing about. It's a very rare gift and not something that comes simply with being a professional singer. Acting comes into it, to an extent, but it's also about using experience to render the lyrics authentic in that particular moment. Perhaps that's why people turn out in droves for a Whitney Houston arena show, or why a low-key Amy Winehouse gig in North London excites such interest." It's all about heart.

Perhaps a little more comparison-shopping? Last year's documentary on Janis Joplin, *Little Girl Blue* directed by Amy Berg, also offers both obvious and revealing parallels and differences between two singer/songwriters who weren't quite equipped to cope with massive fame and celebrity. Their legacies obviously overlap. Stephen Holden's *New York Times* review of the film zeroed in on precisely the right contrasts: "Although Ms. Berg's enthralling film tells a story somewhat similar to *Amy*, Asif Kapadia's recent documentary portrait of Amy Winehouse, the demons that devoured Winehouse came from outside as much as from within. . . . Fame and celebrity in the twenty-first century are far more toxic than in the early 1970s. Some of the most memorable images in *Amy* show Winehouse cringing on the street as she is virtually eaten alive with flashbulbs, and at such moments, it feels like a true-life horror movie."

As we've witnessed, there's been a lot of media examination of Amy Winehouse's torments but not much of an exploration of her musical talent. Her mysterious music and its roots seldom even entered the larger public narrative in any palpable way. Most coverage is drenched in touching and admiring elegy but offers almost no clue as to why the music she made seemed to transcend the historical sources and musical origins of its making. The creative musical genealogy that would have placed her in a clear context is all too often absent and unaccounted for. In other words, what made her truly exceptional as a singer/songwriter and musician faded into the background under the weight of what made her so sad as a person. I hope to have contributed in some small way to a remedy for that inequity.

The source of her indelible mark on pop music, an exotic fusing of vibes funneled through a compositional style that was all her own: that odd miracle often seems to easily get overlooked. Also often under-acknowledged is her huge influence on subsequent singer/songwriters such as Lianne La Havas, Emeli Sande, Paloma Faith, Jessie J., Shingai Shoniwa, Rebecca Ferguson, Caro Emerald, and Laura Mvula. *Spin* magazine's editor Charles Aaron has called Winehouse the official "Nirvana moment" for all such female artists—in other words, their big fame breakthrough threshold.

For some artists who inherited her outsized mantle, Amy can barely even be considered a singer in the conventional sense of the term. In 2011, Laura Mvula stated bluntly to *Rolling Stone*, "I don't talk about Amy Winehouse as a singer. She was a pioneer." Even the occasionally overrated Lady Gaga is not immune to embracing the Winehouse legacy, admitting to the same publication, "Amy is a real artist. There is something about her that is so honest. Of course you always listen to the greats. Amy Winehouse was great. I remember knowing there was hope and feeling not alone because of her. Amy changed pop music forever. Somehow Amy was the flu for pop music. Everybody got a little bit of flu and got over it and fell in love with Amy Winehouse. And now when more flu comes along, it's not so unbearable."

In a somewhat memorial tone, producer Salaam Remi observed in his liner notes to *Lioness*, "It has been hard, but it has also been an amazing thing. Amy was a gifted girl. I believe she has left something behind beyond her years. I'm blessed to be part of that process, to have known that person, and to continue her legacy."

Mark Ronson, meanwhile, was devastated enough by her passing to enter into a kind of self-imposed exile to avoid the swirling press that had already become overwhelming during her difficult last years. He still finds his whole experience with her rather a mystery, and can't quite identify the source of what made their connection so strong, apart from their mutual love for soul sounds, girl groups, and blues. He's often lamented the all-consuming attention her erratic behavior garnered at the expense of her obvious talents. "I think everybody had forgotten the reason everybody loved her in the first place," he told *GQ* in 2015. "It was because of her music, and her voice, and her lyrics."

Perhaps the deepest insight into the young artist's gifts and the loss of her presence in pop culture was offered by the erstwhile vocal master Tony Bennett, a survivor if ever there was one, when he explained simply to *Rolling Stone* that Amy was "a *real* jazz singer." He also expressed his regret for what the ears of the world have lost with the passing of someone too young to have figured out the sheer scale and scope of her own gifts. "Life teaches you really, how to live it, if you can live long enough."

So swiftly now, ten years later, all of us are still blessed by her remarkable creative achievement as the high priestess of melancholy. As a means of reorienting ourselves, perhaps a decade later is an ideal time for a shared remembering of those shimmering torch songs from the broken heart. In the end, perhaps her real legacy is every life that she touched through her music.

That's a lot of lives for one person to live. To me, the ability to live more than only one life is at the heart of what a legacy really means. Even though her whole life may have gone back to black, we still have a deeply touching souvenir of that strangely empathic journey she made. We have the album. Maybe that's more than enough.

In his book *The Shape of Time*, George Kubler writes, "For those who aim beyond narration the question is to find cleavages in history where a cut will separate different types of happenings." For many of us, Winehouse represents just such a sharp cut in music history. There are many artists who came before her and many artists who came after her, but no one quite stands where she once stood.

Perhaps the best epitaph I can imagine for Amy Winehouse and her legacy comes from another poet, Dante Rossetti: "Look in my face, listen to my voice. My name is Might-Have-Been, I am also known as No-More, Too-Late, and Farewell."

AWARDS

One of the pleasures of celebrating the actual artistry of a gifted performer such as Amy Winehouse is to remind us just how universally her rare talents were acclaimed. Here is synopsis of the critical and commercial recognition she received during her brief stay in the public eye.

Awards for the Singer

Ivor Novello Awards, Best Contemporary Song, "Stronger Than Me," 2004
Ivor Novello Awards, Best Contemporary Song, "Rehab," 2007
Elle Style Awards, Best British Music Act, 2007
BRIT Awards, Best Female Solo Artist, 2007
MTV Europe Music Awards, Artist's Choice Award, 2007
Glamour Awards, UK Solo Artist, 2007
Vodafone Live Music Awards, Best Female Artist, 2007
South Bank Show, Best Pop Award, 2007
World Music Awards, Best Selling Pop/Rock Female, 2008
Urban Music Awards, Best Neo-Soul Act, 2008
BRIT Awards, Best British Single, "Valerie" (with Mark Ronson), 2008
Ivor Novello Awards, Best Song, "Love Is a Losing Game," 2008
Grammy Awards, Best New Artist, 2008
Grammy Awards, Best Female Pop Vocal, "Rehab," 2008
World Music Awards, World Best Pop Female Artist, 2008
Meteor Music Awards, Best International Female Artist, 2008
NME Awards, Worst Dressed, 2008 and 2009
Guinness World Records, Most Grammy Awards by a British Female, 2009
Echo Awards, Best International Rock/Pop Female Artist, 2009

Awards for the Album

Mercury Prize, Album of the Year, *Frank*, 2004 (nominated)

Mercury Prize, Album of the Year, *Back to Black*, 2007 (nominated)

MOJO Awards, Best UK Female Artist, 2007

MOJO Awards, Best Album of the Year, 2007

Pop Justice Music Prize, Best Pop Single of the Year, 2007

Q Awards, Best Album, *Back to Black*, 2007

Grammy Awards, Song of the Year, "Rehab," 2008

Grammy Awards, Record of the Year, "Rehab," 2008

Grammy Awards, Best Pop Vocal Album, *Back to Black*, 2008

Echo Awards, Album of the Year, *Back to Black*, 2009

NME ranks *Back to Black* at #27 on List of 100 Greatest Albums of the Decade, 2009

Posthumous Awards

Echo Awards, Hall of Fame, 2012

Grammy Awards, Best Pop Duo/Group Performance, "Body and Soul" (with Tony Bennett), 2012

LIVE PERFORMANCES

Here's the rundown of Amy Winehouse concerts in support of *Back to Black*, up to St Lucia in 2009 (after which the singer took a much needed break from performing until her ill-advised return to the road, leading to her later troubled concert appearances, which are best forgotten by those who enjoy her music).

September 14, 2006, BBC Television Centre, London / Little Noise Sessions, Union Chapel, Islington, England
November 10, 2006, O2 Academy, Liverpool, England
November 11, 2006, the Wardrobe, Leeds, England
November 12, 2006, Oran Mor, Glasgow, Scotland
November 14, 2006, KOKO, London, England
November 19, 2006, the Junction, Cambridge, England
January 22, 2007, Midem, Cannes, France
January 24, 2007, Kalkscheune, Berlin, Germany
February 9, 2007, Paradiso, Amsterdam, Netherlands
February 18, 2007, O2 Guildhall, Southampton, England
February 19, 2007, Astoria, London, England
February 21, 2007, O2 Academy, Birmingham, England
February 25, 2007, Manchester Academy, Manchester, England
February 26, 2007, Northumbria University, Newcastle-upon-Tyne, England
March 1, 2007, Ulster Hall, Belfast, Northern Ireland
March 2, 2007, Ambassador Theatre, Dublin, Ireland
March 3, 2007, Octagon Theatre, Dublin, Ireland
March 6, 2007, Cardiff University, Cardiff, Wales
March 8–9, 2007, O2 Shepherd's Bush Empire, London, England
March 13, 2007, Bowery Ballroom, New York, NY

March 16, 2007, La Zona Rosa, Austin, TX
March 19, 2007, Roxy Theater, West Hollywood, CA
March 20, 2007, the Satellite, Los Angeles, CA
April 19, 2007, Dublin Castle, Camden, England
April 19, 2007, Camden Crawl, London, England
April 26, 2007, 330 Rich, San Francisco, CA
April 27–29, 2007, Coachella, Indio, CA
April 30, 2007, Fox Theatre, Boulder, CO
May 2, 2007, Varsity Theater, Minneapolis, MN
May 3, 2007, Schuba's Tavern, Chicago, IL
May 5, 2007, Electric Factory, Philadelphia, PA
May 6, 2007, Theatre of Living Arts, Philadelphia, PA
May 7, 2007, House of Blues, Boston, MA
May 8, 2007, Highline Ballroom, New York, NY
May 9, 2007, Bowery Ballroom, New York, NY
May 12–13, 2007, Virgin Mobile and Mod Club, Toronto, Canada
May 26, 2007, Megaland, Landgraaf, Netherlands
May 28, 2007, Shepherd's Bush Empire, London, England (filmed)
June 1, 2007, Rock Im Park, Nuremberg, Germany
June 8–10, 2007, Isle of Wight Festival, Newport, England
June 14–16, 2007, Hultsfreds Festivalen, Hultsfred, Sweden
June 15, 2007, Provinssirock, Seinajoki, Finland
June 16, 2007, Parken, Copenhagen, Denmark
June 20–24, 2007, Glastonbury Festival, Pilton, England (filmed)
June 21, 2007, O2 Academy, Bristol, England
June 27, 2007, Hove Festival, Arendal, Norway
June 28, 2007, Rock Werchter, Wechter, Belgium
July 6, 2007, T on the Park, Kincross, Scotland
July 7, 2007, Live Earth, East Rutherford, NJ
July 13, 2007, North Sea Jazz Festival, Rotterdam, Netherlands
July 17, 2007, Eden Project, St Austell, England

July 19, 2007, FIB, Benicassim, Spain
July 20, 2007, Somerset House, London, England
July 25, 2007, Institute Contemporary Arts, London, England
July 28, 2007, Emirates Old Trafford Grounds, Manchester, England
August 3, 2007, Lollapalooza 07 Chicago, IL
August 4, 2007, Virgin Festival, Baltimore, MD
August 7, 2007, Oya Festival, Olso, Norway
August 8, 2007, Skanderborg, Denmark
August 18, 2007, V Festival, Staffordshire, England
September 8, 2007, Osheaga Festival, Montreal, Canada
September 12, 2007, Rumsey Playfield, Central Park, New York, NY
September 13, 2007, Tower Theater, Upper Darby, PA
September 18, 2007, Austin City Limits Festival, Austin, TX
September 19, 2007, the Wiltern, Los Angeles, CA
September 21, 2007, Indigo at the O2, Greenwich, England
September 22, 2007, the Warfield, San Francisco, CA
September 24, 2007, the Orpheum, Vancouver, Canada
September 25, 2007, Paramount Theatre, Seattle, WA
September 29, 2007, Aragon Ballroom, Chicago, IL
October 2, 2007, Aragon Ballroom, Chicago, IL
October 10, 2007, Le Zenith, Paris, France
October 15, 2007, Tempodrom, Berlin, Germany
October 16, 2007, CCH, Hamburg, Germany
October 17, 2007, VEGA, Copenhagen, Denmark
October 24, 2007, Muffathalle, Munich, Germany
October 26, 2007, Rolling Stone, Milan, Italy
October 28, 2007, Palladium, Cologne, Germany
October 30, 2007, Ancienne Belgique, Brussels, Belgium
November 12, 2007, O2 Apollo, Manchester, England
November 14, 2007, Barclaycard Arena, Birmingham, England
November 16, 2007, Barrowland Ballroom, Glasgow, Scotland

November 18, 2007, O2 Academy 2 Newcastle, Newcastle, England
November 20, 2007, Empress Ballroom, Blackpool, England
November 22, 2007, O2 Academy Brixton, London, England
November 24, 2007, Eventim Apollo, London, England
November 26, 2007, Brighton Centre, Brighton, England
November 27, 2007, Bournemouth International Centre, Bournemouth, England
November 28, 2007, Motorpoint Arena, Cardiff, Wales
December 1, 2007, RDS Simonscourt, Dublin, Ireland
December 3, 2007, Waterfront Hall, Belfast, Ireland
December 12, 2007, O2 Apollo, Manchester, England
December 16, 2007, O2 Academy, Brixton, England
May 30, 2008, Rock in Rio, Lisbon, Portugal
June 12, 2008, Garage Gallery, Moscow, Russia
June 25, 2008, Glastonbury Festival, Pilton, England
June 27, 2008, Hyde Park, London, England
July 3, 2008, Rock in Rio Madrid Spain
July 12–13, 2008, Haight-Ashbury Festival, Kincross, Scotland
August 16, 2008, V Festival, Hylands Park, Chelmsford, England
September 5, 2008, Bestival, Newport, England
May 2, 2009 St Lucia Jazz, Festival, St Lucia

Post St Lucia

January 8, 2011, Summer Soul Festival, Florianopolis, Brazil
January 10, 2011, HSBC Arena, Rio de Janeiro, Brazil
January 13, 2011, Summer Soul Festival, Sao Paolo, Brazil
February 10, 2011, Gulf Bike Week, Dubai, UAE
June 18, 2011, Kalemegdan Belgrade, Serbia

SOURCES

Amy Winehouse Discography

Album / Extended Play Releases

Frank, October 20, 2003, Island Records

Sessions@AOL, June 24, 2004, Island Records

Back to Black, October 27, 2006, Island Records

Back to Black, Deluxe Edition, January 1, 2007, Island Records

iTunes Festival London, August 13, 2007, Island Records

Back to Black B-Sides, January 15, 2008, Universal Records

Frank B-Sides, May 13, 2008, Universal Records

Frank / Back to Black (boxed set), November 21, 2008, Island Records

Lioness: Hidden Treasures, December 2, 2011, Island Records/Lioness Records

The Album Collection, September 21, 2012, Island Records

Amy Winehouse Live at the BBC, November 19, 2012, Island Records/Lioness Records

Singles

"Stronger Than Me" / "What It Is," 2003, Island Records

"Take the Box" / "Round Midnight," 2004, Island Records

"In My Bed" / "You Sent Me Flying," 2004, Island Records

"Fuck Me Pumps" / "Help Yourself," 2004, Island Records

"Rehab" / "Do Me No Good," 2006, Island Records

"You Know I'm No Good" / "Monkey Man," 2007, Island Records

"Back to Black" / "Valerie," 2007, Island Records

"Tears Dry on Their Own" / "You're Wondering Now," 2007, Island Records

"Love Is a Losing Game" / "B-Boy Baby," 2007, Island Records

"Body and Soul" / "Our Day Will Come" (with Tony Bennett), 2011, Island Records

As Featured Artist

"Valerie" / "California" (with Mark Ronson), 2007, Columbia/ Island Records

"B Boy Baby" (with Mutya Buena), 2007, 4th and Broadway

"Cherry Wine" (with Nas), 2012, Def Jam

Video Albums

Live at the Orange Lounge, Toronto, 2007

I Told You I Was Trouble: Live in London, 2007

In Concert, Belfort, France, 2007

Documentary

Amy. Directed by Asif Kapadia. Cannes Film Festival, June 2015; general commercial release, July 2015. Krishwerkz Entertainment. Produced by James Gay-Rees and George Pank. Archive Producer: Paul Bell.

Biopic (tentative)

Amy Winehouse, starring Noomi Rapace, directed by Kristen Sheridan, 2016

Books

On the Soap Opera

Barak, Daphne. *Saving Amy*. New Holland Publishing, 2010.

Jonstone, Nick. *Amy Amy Amy*. Omnibus Books, 2011.

Newkey-Burden, Chas. *Amy Winehouse, The Biography*. John Blake Publishing, 2009.

O'Shea, Mick. *Amy Winehouse, A Losing Game*. Plexus Publishing, 2012.

Winehouse, Janis. *Loving Amy: A Mother's Story*. Random House, 2014.

Winehouse, Mitch. *Amy, My Daughter*. Harper Collins, 2012.

On the Music

Irvin, Jim. *The Mojo Collection Music Companion*. Canongate, 2000.

Kureshi, Hanif. *The Faber Book of Pop*. Faber and Faber, 1995.

O'Brien, Lucy. *She-Bop: The Definitive History of Women in Rock, Pop, and Soul*. Penguin, 1995.

O'Dair, Barbara. *Trouble-Girls: Rolling Stone Book of Women in Rock*. Random House, 1997.

Ribowsky, Mark. *He's a Rebel: Phil Spector, Legendary Producer*. Cooper Square Press, 1999.

On Celebrity

Braudy, Leo. *The Frenzy of Renown: Fame and Its History*. Vintage, 1997.

Marcus, Greil. *Dead Elvis: A Chronicle of a Cultural Obsession*. Harvard University Press, 1991.

Marshall, P. David. *Celebrity and Power: Fame in Contemporary Culture*. University of Minnesota Press, 1997.

Rojek, Chris. *Celebrity*. Reaction Books, 2001.

On the Aesthetics and Politics of Pop

Blount, James. *Commodification of Image: Production of a Pop Idol*. Unpublished thesis.

Frith, Simon. *Art Into Pop*. Methuen, 1987.

Frith, Simon. *The Industrialization of Popular Music*. Newbury Park, 1987.

Frith, Simon. *Taking Popular Music Seriously*. Ashgate, 2007.

Seabrook, John. *The Song Machine: Inside the Hit Factory*. WW Norton, 2015.

Torch Song Reference

Ella Fitzgerald: Original Keys for Singers. Hal Leonard, 2003.

Hombach, Jean-Pierre. *Amy Winehouse*. CreateSpace, 2012.
Jazz Standards: Female Voice, Volume 1. Hal Leonard, 2011.
O'Day, Anita, with Fells, George. *High Times, Hard Times*. Limelight, 2004.
Torch Songs in Sultry Keys: 45 Standards in Low Keys for Women Singers. Hal Leonard, 2003.

Other Sources

Anderman, Joan. "Of Course She Should Go to Rehab." *Boston Globe*, December 15, 2007.
Assar, Vijith. "Gabriel Roth." *Tape Op*. May 2007.
Ayers, Michael. "Mark Ronson." *SF Weekly*, July 4, 2007.
Beauchemin, Molly. "Amy Winehouse, Kurt Cobain, and the Gendering of Martyrdom." *Pitchfork*, June 22, 2015.
Beauchemin, Molly. "We Need to Talk." *Pitchfork*, June 22, 2015.
Bonner, Michael. "Amy." *Uncut*, June 3, 2015.
Brown, Helen. "Why The Knives Are Out for Amy Winehouse." *Daily Telegraph*, November 15, 2007.
Calhoun, Dave. "Amy." *Time Out*, June 30, 2015.
Cavolina, Robbie, and McCrudden, Ian (directors). *Anita O'Day: The Life of a Jazz Singer*, AOD Productions/Élan Entertainment, 2007.
Clayton, Richard. "Ronson and Business." *Financial Times*, September 30, 2010.
Cohodas, Nadine. *Queen: The Life and Music of Dinah Washington*. New York: Pantheon, 2004.
Coyle, Jake. "Celebrity Is the Monster." *Vancouver Sun*, July 2, 2015.
Crane, Larry. "Sonic Travels." *Tape Op*, January 2015.
Dalton, Stephen. "NIA Birmingham." *Times*, November 2007.
Davis, Johnny. "Ronson Changes the Record." *Esquire*, April 29, 2015.

Dennis, Jack. "Top Amy Winehouse Songs of All Time." *AXS*, March 31, 2015.
Doyle, Tom. "Mark Ronson, Writer/Producer." *Sound on Sound*, May 2007.
Elliott, Paul. "Amy Winehouse Didn't Show Up." *Q*, December 2007.
Elliott, Paul. "The Soul and Heartache." *Mojo*, January 2008.
Elliott, Paul. "Amy Disguised Her Early Songs as Poems." *Mojo*, May 8, 2015.
Eliscu, Jenny. "The Diva and Her Demons." *Rolling Stone*, June 14, 2007.
Enright, Michael. "Remembering Singer/Songwriter Amy Winehouse." CBC Radio, September 18, 2011.
Everett-Green, Robert. "Disc of the Week." *Globe and Mail*, December 9, 2011.
Fallon, Kevin. "Amy Winehouse." *Daily Beast*, March 7, 2015.
Farberman, Brad. "Behind the 'Scene' with Daptone Records Founder Gabe Roth." *Wax Poetics*, April 6, 2010.
Ford, Piers. "The Art of the Torch Singer." *Cabaret Confidential*, November 29, 2010.
Frere-Jones, Sasha. "Amy's Circus." *New Yorker*, March 3, 2008.
Gill, Andy. "She's a Brave Lass." *Independent*, October 27, 2006.
Gunderson, Edna. "Amy Winehouse's Transformation." *Entertainment Weekly*, January 28, 2008.
Hermes, Will. "Back to Black." *Entertainment Weekly*, March 9, 2007.
Hight, Jewly. "Forget Amy Winehouse, Sharon Jones and the Dap-Kings Choose R+B Over Rehab." *SF Weekly*, November 28, 2007.
Hill, Emily. "Her Own Woman." *Guardian*, July 31, 2008.
Hoskyns, Barney. "Live at Somerset House." *Rock's Backpages*, July 2007.
Hutchinson, Lydia. "Mark Ronson." *Performing Songwriter*, July 27, 2011.

Irvin, Jim. *Mojo Collection*. New York: Canongate Books: New York, 2003.

Kandell, Steve. "Lady Sings the Blues." *Spin*, July 23, 2015.

Kaufman, Gil. "Amy Winehouse Posthumous Album." MTV News, October 31, 2011.

Kent, Nick. "On the Rocks." *Times*, January 2008.

Knafo, Saki. "Soul Reviver." *New York Times*, December 5, 2008.

Landoli, Kathy. "We All Destroyed Amy Winehouse." *Pitchfork*, June 17, 2015.

Lane, Anthony. "Amy, Back from Black." *New Yorker*, July 1, 2015.

Lavin, Polly. "Down to Earth." *Ibiza Voice*, July 31, 2010.

Lawless, Jill. "Documentary Reclaims Singer's Legacy." *Vancouver Sun*, July 2, 2015.

Leigh, Danny. "The *Amy* Documentary." *Financial Times*, June 26, 2015.

Lewis, Pete. "Blues and Soul: Amy Interview." *Blues and Soul*, April 2004.

Linden, Amy. "Slow Blackout." *Village Voice*, January 15, 2008.

Male, Andrew. "Amy's Jukebox." *Mojo*, August 29, 2013.

Mao, Jeff. "Mark Ronson." www.redbullmusicacademy.com, April 2010.

Mapstone, Lucy. "Mark Ronson Working with Amy Winehouse." *Daily Mail*, October 28, 2015.

Mason, Kerri. "Amy Winehouse." *Billboard*, March 11, 2007.

Matos, Michelangelo. "Daptone Records." *Wondering Sound*, April 5, 2010.

McCormick, Neil. "Final Interview." *Telegraph*, July 27, 2011.

McCormick, Neil. "Mark Ronson: When Amy Winehouse Wrote a Song." *Telegraph*, June 24, 2015.

McNeilly, Liam. "Mark Ronson Profiled." *DIY*, November 20, 2014.

Micaleff, Ken. "Mark Ronson Gets Real." *Electronic Musician*, September 1, 2010.

McIntyre, Hugh. "Mark Ronson Deserves Attention." *Forbes* January 13, 2015.

Millman, Joyce. "Chasing Amy." http://joycemillman.wordpress.com, July 28, 2015.

Mlynar, Philip. "Top Hip Hop." *Village Voice*, December 5, 2011.

Molotkow, Alexandra. "Dismantling the Mythology." *Globe and Mail*, April 17, 2015.

Moran, Caitlin. "The Beginning of Her Story." *Billboard*, June 26, 2015.

Mueller, Andrew. "First Album Wasn't a Fluke." *Uncut*, November 2006.

National Public Radio (staff). "Mark Ronson and the Producer as Rock Star." *All Things Considered*, February 8, 2015.

Neville, Morgan (director). *The Songmakers Collection, Hitmakers*. A&E Documentary, 2001.

Nicholson, Stuart. "Back to Black." *Observer*, October 22, 2006.

Papermag Staff. "Pied Piper, Mark Ronson." *Paper*, October 22, 2008.

Pareles, Jon. "In Real Time." *New York Times*, January 24, 2008.

Parish, Stan. "Mark Ronson: Funky White Boy." *GQ*, January 19, 2015.

Pearson, Rick. "Bestival Isle of Wight." *Evening Standard*, September 2008.

Petridis, Alex. "Cover Boy." *Guardian*, October 6, 2007.

Pevere, Geoff. *Sound and Vision: Watching Popular Music*. HotDocs-Bloor Cinema, January 2015.

Porton, Richard. "Exploited Amy." *Daily Beast*, May 18, 2015.

Q-Tip. "Mark Ronson Music." *Interview*, March 31, 2015.

Ramanathan, Lavanya. "The Posthumous Album." *Washington Post*, July 3, 2015.

Rodriguez, Juan. "Love Songs." *Montreal Gazette*, April 21, 2015.

Rogers, Jude. "Mercury Prize." *Guardian*, September 2007.

Rogers, Jude. "Year of the Woman." *New Statesman*, December 2006.

Rosen, Jody. "Dark Star." *Slate*, February 12, 2008.

Ross, Peter. "A Year of Living Dangerously." *Sunday Herald*, November 11, 2007.

Shaw, William. "Lost Girl." *Q*, August 2012.

Scoppa, Ben. "Ronson on 'Rehab.'" *Paste*, June 2007.

Smith, Joan. "There's Nothing Poetic About Amy's Self-Destruction." *Independent*, June 26, 2008.

Spector, Ronnie. "Amy Winehouse Saved Me!" *Mojo*, January 29, 2015.

Sturges, Fiona. "Mark Ronson: I Didn't Make Her Career, She Made Mine." *Independent*, October 22, 2011.

Simpson, Dave. "Carling Academy." *Guardian*, November 2007.

Sullivan, Caroline. "30 Minutes with Ronnie Spector." *Guardian*, April 17, 2014.

Swerdloff, Alex. "Painted Lady." *Paper*, February 21, 2007.

Tingen, Paul. "Secrets of the Mixers." *Sound on Sound*, August 2007.

Unterberger, Andrew. "Ronson Looks Back." *Spin*, January 8, 2015.

Wheeler, Brad. "Producer Cites Pain." *Globe and Mail*, December 27, 2011.

Williams, Mike. "Amy, Inside Her Studio Sessions." *New Musical Express*, November 28, 2011.

Wolfe, Tom. "First Tycoon of Teen." *New York Herald Tribune*, January 3, 1965.

Wolk, Douglas. "Amy's Frank." *Pitchfork*, November 13, 2007.

Wolk, Douglas. "Back to Black." *Blender*, July 13, 2010.

—. "The Influence of Amy Winehouse," www.burrunjor.com, March 22, 2015.

INDEX